"RED HONDA, PULL OVER!"

She sat looking at the total darkness around her. The cop sauntered over, shining a flashlight in her face. He was smiling.

"Your headlight has a crack in it. I think you should get out and take a look."

She did as she was told. "Why don't you come back to my car?" he suggested pleasantly. "I have heat in my car."

She thought it odd but figured, *He's a cop. He knows what he's doing, right?*

She kept quiet and got inside his car.

BADGE OF BETRAYAL

JOE CANTLUPE AND LISA PETRILLO

AVON BOOKS ◆ NEW YORK

BADGE OF BETRAYAL is an original publication of Avon Books. This work has never before appeared in book form.

AVON BOOKS
A division of
The Hearst Corporation
1350 Avenue of the Americas
New York, New York 10019

Copyright © 1991 by Joe Cantlupe and Lisa Petrillo
Cover photograph of Cara Knott courtesy of the Knott family; cover photograph of Craig Peyer courtesy of *San Diego Union*
Published by arrangement with the authors
Library of Congress Catalog Card Number: 91-92066
ISBN: 0-380-76009-6

First Avon Books Printing: December 1991

AVON TRADEMARK REG. U.S. PAT. OFF. AND IN OTHER COUNTRIES, MARCA REGISTRADA, HECHO EN U.S.A.

Printed in the U.S.A.

RA   10 9 8 7 6 5 4 3 2

CONTENTS

I

Memory and...

1

Murder at Mercy Road

CHRISTMAS comes gently to San Diego, bringing with it balmy temperatures and mild breezes off the glittering Pacific.

It is a special time of serenity in a region where politeness is not an exception, where people don't jaywalk, and where nobody dares be sedentary. Even the dead of winter and the holiest of holidays never seem to stop San Diegans from their endless summer, surfing and sailing, hang gliding and marathon running, hiking, biking, kayaking. And when San Diego's citizens aren't playing, they are driving on the maze of slick, wide freeways of fresh new concrete that gleams under the blue sky.

Christmas spirit here is more Beach Boys than Currier and Ives. Living in a land born yesterday by the standards of most cultures, these westerners create their own traditions. One of San Diego's favorites is the annual holiday parade of yachts and sailboats decorated with twinkling lights. The event draws thousands of Southern Californians to line the embarcadero along San Diego Bay and watch the glittering boats glide past the palm trees at twilight.

When the city's many transplanted midwesterners and easterners get hungry for a taste of the white Christmas of their childhoods, they only have to drive an hour east to the Laguna Mountains. But even then they never leave the beach too far behind as they sled down the mountainside in inflatable rafts and inner tubes. And for those parents and kids who didn't feel like getting cold and wet, Sea World, the giant aquatic theme park, would actually make fake snow for its legions of visitors to frolic in while nearby killer whales leaped about in stadium-sized pools.

San Diego was California's first settlement, the site of the first of the Roman Catholic missions that would eventually line the thousand-mile coastline, from here to San Juan Capistrano to Carmel to San Francisco. The flavor of Mexican culture remains rich in this city which shares with Tijuana the world's busiest border crossing.

This is home to the Navy Pacific Fleet and Camp Pendleton, one of the largest marine bases in the country. But don't call San Diego just a military town if you want to make friends here. As the citizenry will proudly explain, San Diego grew out of the military mold long ago, evolving into a metropolis of two million people, second in size only to Los Angeles in the state, and sixth largest in the United States.

Here is where Star Wars scientists develop fantastic weapons for the Strategic Defense Initiative. And where Jonas Salk, the man who helped conquer polio, leads teams of researchers to beat cancer and AIDS.

Here is where Gregory Peck grew up, where Wyatt Earp ran a gambling den, where Dr. Seuss lives and Raymond Chandler died, where McDonald's heiress Joan Kroc lavishes her fast-food millions on the poor and the afflicted, where the legendary Victor Mature plays golf and astronaut Wally Schirra settled down.

Here is where avocados and the world's supply of Christmas poinsettias are grown. Here in this southwesternmost corner of the nation, thirty-seven million tourists flock each year to explore the patch of paradise where the flowers always seem to be blooming. This is a town that calls itself "America's Finest City."

Christmas 1986 was another matter.

Nobody could remember the holiday season weather ever being so cold and rainy. But by Christmas Eve the storm broke and the sun shone across San Diego County, an area bigger than the entire state of Connecticut that stretches from beaches to mountains and to the edge of the Mojave Desert beyond. As the glitzy decorations baked in the sun, it looked like the holiday would have a happy ending after all.

In this genteel spot during this gentle time of year, no one was prepared for the grim discovery made by San Diego police officer Bill Maheu three days after Christmas 1986. A few miles north of downtown San Diego, Maheu found a young woman's bloody and battered body sprawled below a bridge on a desolate dead-end street called Mercy Road.

The call came into San Diego Police Department's northeastern substation from a headquarters dispatcher shortly after seven o'clock Sunday morning, December 28.

A young woman said her sister was missing. She said her family had spent the entire night searching for the girl, and now they had found her car abandoned in a canyon beside Interstate 15. An officer relayed the message to Acting Sergeant Bill Maheu, who was just assembling the morning lineup of cops starting their shifts at the suburban substation. Because it was a Sunday, staff was short, but Maheu decided to send two officers to check out the mysterious call just in case. "It's probably run-of-the-mill, but you and Mary better go talk to this family," Maheu told Officer Jim Spears.

Spears, a seventeen-year veteran, and Officer Mary Cornicelli headed to Mercy Road and introduced themselves to the woman who had called in, Cynthia Knott Weick, her husband, Bill, and her father, Sam Knott, who had just arrived on the scene.

Cynthia Weick filled them in on the horrendous night—the long search that had ended at Mercy Road. Spears excused himself and walked around the abandoned car, a white VW bug.

The officers sensed immediately that this disappearance might not be so routine. Spears went to his car radio and called Maheu back at the station. "This is bigger than just the both of us. You better come by," Spears said.

"I'll be right there," Maheu said.

When Maheu arrived, he and Spears huddled quietly, discussing the Knotts' search. Spears told his boss what he had found at the scene. "We better get some detectives here," Maheu said anxiously. He got back in his patrol car and drove up the freeway to call in some detectives for backup. In the meantime, he called the department's dog unit and helicopter patrol for assistance. After making the call, Maheu decided to drive back to Mercy Road from another direction, the next exit off I-15, Poway Road. He swung his big Ford LTD Crown Victoria across the abandoned road and parked near the bike path that ran along one side. Maheu knew the terrain well. He lived across the hills in the suburb of Poway and often jogged across this same bridge and bike path. He got out of his car and walked north along the hilly bike path at this dead end of Mercy Road, intently scanning the horizon. Something seemed to draw him out onto the old highway bridge. He stopped at the middle of the bridge and peered down into the dry creek bed below. His heart started beating hard. It was the only sound he heard.

On a bed of rocks about sixty-five feet down, he saw the body of a young woman. He could see a great deal of blood even at that distance. Maheu's eyes focused on the woman's white boots. She had to be the Knott girl.

Maheu tensed. He had been a cop for eight years, but no number of years could have adequately prepared him to face a scene such as this. The sergeant stood upright and suddenly felt the urge to run, to move quickly, as if it were not too late to save the fair-haired girl below. Who could do this to such a beautiful girl? He thought of the family standing over there, their nightmare not ending, but just beginning. Maheu bit his lip. He wanted to think carefully about the possible events of last night, but he just didn't have time. He had a crime scene to preserve.

Maheu got back in his car and drove slowly toward Spears, who waited on the edge of the dirt path. Maheu gingerly opened the door and stepped out. He knew now that the entire crime scene covered hundreds of square yards, and every move his men made might obscure a crucial piece of evidence.

"I just came down from the upper end and I stopped at the bridge to look around," Maheu told Spears. "There's a body under the bridge. I think it's her." Maheu looked across the canyon at the family huddled by their cars. He turned to

Spears and whispered, "Just casually walk with me and we'll get a closer look."

San Diego police officers were still arriving at the Mercy Road exit off Interstate 15. Patrol officers, unaware of Maheu's discovery, were encouraging the family to be hopeful. A patrolwoman told the family she would return to the Chevron station where the missing girl was last seen and check for leads there. Another officer told them that a police helicopter and a dog unit were on their way to help.

Sam Knott leaned against his car watching police officers circle and talk, while more police cars rolled onto the road. The seconds dragged on. An image of Sleeping Beauty ran through his head. His mind flashed back to the Disney movie his family had been watching at home the night before when Cara called. It was the last time he had heard her voice. Sam remembered watching the fairy tale princess and hearing his daughter's sweet voice at the same time on the other end of the line. She promised him she'd be home soon.

This was no fairy tale he was watching now. He watched two police officers walk over to the trunk of their patrol car and pull on rubber surgical gloves. Were they avoiding him?

Indeed, Maheu, Spears, and a member of the K-9 unit, John Haustetter, wanted to steer clear of the Knotts until they were absolutely sure of what they had found. They walked down the trail together toward the battered body of Cara Knott. As Maheu and Haustetter stood back, Spears moved closer.

The way her left arm was draped over her chest, Spears thought she looked like she could have been asleep. He leaned over and touched her. She was so cold he knew there could be no pulse, but he checked the carotid artery in her neck anyway. Nothing.

Cara Knott wore a necklace of thin red abrasions; three across her slender neck. She had been strangled; that was obvious. Blood darkened her light-colored hair. Her right hand was extended and her nails were neatly manicured. A small ring decorated her index finger, but the stone was smashed. Blood drenched the right side of her white sweatshirt, which was hiked up to expose her flat, honey-tan stomach. Her purple sweatpants were still tucked neatly inside her white leather half boots. Spears could clearly see a drop of blood on the left boot.

"Who should tell the family?" Spears asked. "Do you want to do it, or should I?"

"Jesus," Maheu replied.

Spears, who had more years on the force than Maheu, decided he would tell Sam Knott. For a moment, Maheu felt relief.

When they returned to the waiting cars, they found Sam. Both officers looked into the older man's eyes, which were consumed with every parent's worst fear. Spears tried to speak.

"Your daughter," Spears began, his voice quavering as he struggled to fight back tears. "She's dead."

"So this is it," Sam said quietly.

The shocked father and the officers instinctively reached for each other's arms. "If you had only known her," Sam told them. "My daughter was an angel."

2

Not a Day for a Wedding

THAT Sunday, Homicide Lieutenant Phil Jarvis woke up early, anticipating a day of eating and drinking at the wedding of Charlie Grimm, his buddy for the last twenty years on the San Diego police force. Jarvis was going to be best man. Now that he was in his fifties, Jarvis didn't get many chances to be a best man. Then the phone rang.

It was one of his homicide sergeants. The body of a twenty-year-old San Diego State University student had been found at the bottom of a creek bed, probably strangled. The girl had been a good, cautious kid. Oh hell, there goes the wedding, Jarvis thought. Instead of putting on his tuxedo, he was reaching for his gun.

Within twenty minutes, Lieutenant Jarvis, head of the homicide squad for a city of one million people, was taking the long walk down from Mercy Road to the spot in the creek bed where Cara Knott lay.

He thought she looked like she'd been thrown from the bridge. Her ribs appeared to be broken and her torso was bruised. Jarvis could see the beauty in her face despite the fact that she'd obviously been beaten. The lieutenant had seen enough corpses in his line of work to tell that this young woman had taken care of herself. Her nails were long and well groomed; her hair was pulled back in a prim ponytail; her tan was even.

"What kind of madman would do this to such a nice kid?" he almost shouted at Maheu, who stood silently beside him.

Jarvis knew Cara Knott hadn't simply died. She had been murdered. "Call the evidence detail," Jarvis ordered.

The police investigators set about the business of finding out why she was killed—and by whom. Within the hour, police evidence technician Barbara Beck was combing the canyon, photographing everything: the embankment, the creek bed, Cara's body. Veteran detective Gene Back thought he saw a car's skidmarks on the road to the bridge and he measured them. He also took measurements of the footprints on the bridge and the fresh tire tracks.

The investigators worked methodically, exchanging few words. From the other side of the canyon Sam Knott strained to watch their every move. "She never did drugs," Sam told the officers who were pumping him with questions. "She had no enemies. Everyone loved Cara."

Sam told them how Cara still dated her one and only boyfriend, Wayne Bautista. The two of them had no problems that Sam knew of. "They were going to be married," he explained. There was no way a stranger could get near enough to Cara to do this, he told the police over and over again. She had taken self-defense classes and would never stop for a hitchhiker. Never.

"Do you have any idea how she could have gotten to this place?" one of the officers asked Knott.

"No, I never knew it existed," Sam Knott said. "We live at the other end of the county."

"Well, this dead end has a reputation. It's sort of a lover's lane. A lot of junkies hang out here, and there are a lot of rapes. A lot."

Maheu and Jarvis walked back to the bridge across grass, now beaten down because of all the police traffic. Maheu turned to the homicide lieutenant. "Hey, look at this!" On the edge of a concrete rail the homicide chief spied a glint of gold; it was a blonde hair clinging to the upper outside of the rail.

Jarvis instinctively grabbed it. He knew it wasn't the most scientific way to collect evidence, but damn if he would let the whims of Mother Nature ruin his crime scene.

He looked at the victim's body. Who had inflicted those deep bruises over Cara Knott's right eye and near her mouth? Whoever did it, Jarvis figured, clobbered Cara with something very hard. Somebody had to be standing or hovering over her, Jarvis thought.

Jarvis turned away and walked resolutely to his car. He felt sick. This victim wasn't just anybody. This wasn't some dope dealer caught in a drive-by shooting. This wasn't a thug or prostitute. This could have been my girl, Jarvis thought. His own daughter was also a San Diego State University student and blonde, tan, and athletic.

So much police activity attracted the curiosity of the press. News teams were arriving. When Jarvis walked to the police lines they swarmed around him like gnats. Everyone at the scene recognized Jarvis, the one from the department who usually gave statements about homicides for television reporters. They knew Jarvis was the man who was supposed to have the answers. But this time, he didn't want to talk.

"Why are you so upset with this one? What's the problem?" one asked.

Jarvis usually joked around with the press corps. But he ignored the question. The reporter tried again. "What's the big deal about this one?" The homicide chief just stared back at the newswoman. "Yeah, I love looking at people getting killed. What the hell? I love this job." With that Jarvis walked off toward his car, and immediately felt like kicking himself. He had lost it; he was unraveling and wasn't sure why.

3

A Call to the Soul

THE darkness in the Knotts' living room on Saturday evening was broken only by the flickering lights of the Christmas tree and the image of Sleeping Beauty on the television screen. Sam Knott watched the classic Disney cartoon movie from his favorite easy chair while his family sat transfixed—his wife, Joyce, and their oldest daughter, Cynthia, with her husband, Bill; the middle daughter, Cheryl; and the youngest, John.

It was two nights after Christmas and a relaxing conclusion to the perfect holiday, the kind of celebration that Sam loved the most because the whole family took part. Looking back on that night, he would think of it as the last time he was truly happy.

Sam was a big man, with a face that reddened easily when he laughed, which was often. Now in his fifties, Sam's commanding stature made it easy for people to see him as the star college rugby player he once was. But when his blue eyes saddened, they betrayed a teddy-bear soul.

Protecting his family was paramount to Sam. He encouraged Joyce and the girls to take self-defense courses and insisted that Cara, his youngest girl, call him whenever she was leaving to come home, at whatever time, from wherever she happened to be—a shopping mall or class or her boyfriend's house. If anybody ever got in her way or tried to stop her as she drove her old Volkswagen beetle, Sam advised Cara, she should run him down.

Tonight Sam had eaten too much leftover turkey and was feeling groggy as Joyce fed the *Sleeping Beauty* tape into the video cassette recorder. As they did most holidays, the family had gathered in the living room instead of the recreation room downstairs in their rambling split-level country house, built on the rolling hills two dozen miles east of downtown San Diego. Sam dragged the TV in from the kitchen and everyone had to step over the extension cord. They turned out the lights and spread pillows on the lawn green carpet to be near the fire burning merrily behind the gold-framed glass fireplace screen. Joyce brought out bowls of popcorn. Beauty was still in slumberland and the prince had yet to make his move when the phone rang. It was Cara.

"Hi. It's me. What are you guys doing?"

Sam smiled when he heard his daughter's voice on the phone.

"We're having a great Saturday night," he answered. "We're all here watching *Sleeping Beauty.*"

"Again?" Cara teased. She loved calling him a "Disney dad." "I think I'm going to come home tonight," she said. "Wayne's feeling better, but we couldn't go to the wild animal park. He's going to sleep, and I miss you guys."

Wayne Bautista, Cara's boyfriend of three years, was confined to bed with a 104-degree fever. How like Cara, Sam thought, to devote part of her Christmas vacation to caring for him. Sam checked his watch. It was a little after eight o'clock.

"It's getting late," he told her. "Why don't you stay up there another night and come back in the morning?"

But Cara wanted to come home.

"Be careful," Sam cautioned her automatically, and hung up.

Soon the prince woke Sleeping Beauty, they rode off to live happily ever after, and the lights came back on. Joyce brought out a jigsaw puzzle and they gathered around the dining room table at the end of the long living room and put the pieces together as they talked, as families so often do, about nothing in particular. After a while, Joyce wandered into the kitchen for something to drink and glanced at the clock. It was 10:30 P.M., more than two hours after the phone call. "Cara should have been home by now," she said to herself.

A chill went through Sam. He jumped out of his chair, startling Bill who was seated in the chair next to him. Later, Sam would describe this moment as a call to his soul.

"I've got to go find Cara," Sam announced. "Let's go." He snatched up the keys to his blue Cutlass parked in the driveway.

Bill watched Sam head for the door. He wondered if Sam was being overprotective. True, it was only a forty-five-minute drive from Wayne's house in Escondido to the Knotts' home in El Cajon. True, if Cara had left when she said she was, she should have been home more than an hour ago. Thousands of young women across the country came home late all the time and their parents didn't think twice about it. But those parents weren't Sam and Joyce Knott.

Another father might have had suspicions that his adorable daughter was snuggled up with a secret boyfriend or hitting the town with old pals, especially when her steady date was home in bed with the flu. But that wasn't Cara. She was an open book, more like a Disney movie than a mystery novel; she was Sleeping Beauty come to life.

Joyce followed her husband toward the car and then stopped abruptly. Maybe we're overreacting, she thought; Cara can take care of herself. "Let me call Wayne before we head off," she suggested. But Sam seemed to know what the answer was going to be and was already out the door. It was cold out, so he went out to warm up the car; he didn't want to waste another second.

Wayne's sister Monica answered the phone. "Hello, Monica? This is Joyce Knott. Is Cara there?"

"No," the teenager said. "She left about eight-thirty."

Joyce lowered her head and put the receiver closer to her ear. "Can I speak to Wayne?"

"Wayne's asleep. I'll get him."

Joyce barely noticed how scratchy and groggy Wayne sounded when he picked up the phone. "Cara's not home yet," she announced. Wayne woke up in a hurry. He told

Joyce he had given Cara twelve dollars for some gas, and that was the only stop she planned to make. He felt weak, but he told Joyce reassuringly, "Let me get some clothes on, and I'll go look. I'll find her. Her car must've just broken down."

Wayne grabbed a sweater, stuffed tissues in his pocket, and ran out to his car. He drove down Alamo Lane from his mother's house in the hills of the northeastern city of Escondido, down to Bear Valley Parkway that led into the main drag of Via Rancho Parkway, past the immense North County Fair shopping mall, past the Chevron station at the edge of the freeway where Cara usually bought gas. No Cara. He then headed south on Interstate 15, checking every exit off the freeway including the tract housing developments that lined the inland highway and the strip shopping centers near the off ramps. The canyons beyond the freeway were black against the dark night except for dots of light from a few new neighborhoods and the occasional country house.

Meanwhile, at the other end of the county, Joyce and Sam Knott had begun their search. Sam drove slowly along the interstate that led him west to the I-15 freeway, which linked Mexico and San Diego's inland valley up to Riverside County and the Mojave Desert beyond. He and his wife stared out the windows of the Cutlass, keeping their thoughts to themselves.

They rode north toward Wayne's house seeing no sign of Cara along the freeway shoulders, and then turned around and headed back down the southbound side. Sam spotted two California Highway Patrol officers sitting in their black-and-white cruiser on the side of the freeway and he brought his Cutlass to a squealing halt behind them. He jumped out of the car and waved his arms.

The officers stayed in their car and eyed him suspiciously. Sam leaned into the window and said as calmly as he could, "Excuse me, I was wondering if you could help me. My daughter was supposed to be home two hours ago and she hasn't arrived. It's unlike her. I'm afraid something happened to her on the freeway."

The patrolmen flashed an amused look at each other. "How old is your daughter, sir?" one of them asked.

"Twenty," Sam answered. "She's blonde and she's driving a white VW beetle. She always comes home on time. Always. Something is definitely wrong. Here, I'll give you her license plate number. WW1437.''

''Well, sir, we can't put out an APB on someone until they've been missing for twenty-four hours,'' the other patrolman drawled. APB was something Sam heard all the time on cop shows, an all points bulletin, alerting all police departments within scanner range of some major event. He never thought he would ever need one in his life.

Sam kept trying to get the California Highway Patrol to listen to what he was saying. ''She's been missing for two hours and that's long enough for me to be worried,'' Sam said. He struggled to remain calm so he didn't give the impression that he was drunk or some kind of lunatic. He was so calm he surprised himself. Joyce stayed in the car, watching out the window.

''Well, I'm sorry, sir, there's nothing we can do now,'' the officer said. ''Maybe if you call the station in the morning.''

Sam was undeterred. ''You can at least take down the information and keep an eye out for her, can't you?'' Sam insisted. ''Tomorrow morning may be too late!''

Sam carefully looked them both in the eye, then whirled around and stalked back to the car. Joyce couldn't bring herself to say anything. She just looked at Sam.

''They won't put an APB out on her. They won't help. Can you believe that?'' Sam said. ''Let's go.'' He put his foot to the accelerator and took off. It was almost midnight.

Meanwhile, Wayne had been up and down the freeway for hours without finding any sign of Cara or her car. He called the Knotts' house to see if she might have called. The answer was no. Tired and out of ideas, Wayne headed to the Knotts' to regroup. He got there at 2 A.M. and found Sam, Cheryl, Cynthia, and Bill plotting their next move. The kids looked pale and scared but listened to Sam's every order.

''All right,'' Sam told his family. ''This will be the command post. Cheryl, you start calling everyone; all Cara's friends; call Aunt Julia. Call the hospitals and every police station. Bill, you take Cynthia and check the southbound exits. Everyone must check in here every half hour.''

Taking deep breaths to keep from getting hysterical, Cheryl

decided it was time to call the 911 emergency line. In what she hoped was a rational-sounding tone, she began, "Hello, I want to report a missing person—"

The dispatcher interrupted her, "Is this an emergency?"

"I think so," Cheryl answered.

"Who's missing?" the dispatcher said.

"My sister Cara Knott. She's six hours late and we've searched the entire freeway for her—" The dispatcher interrupted asking for information and Cheryl gave their address in El Cajon.

"Have you called the El Cajon police?" the dispatcher inquired.

She admitted she hadn't.

So Cheryl called their hometown police department. They referred her to the police in Escondido, where Wayne lived, since that was where Cara was last seen. "I can't believe this," Cheryl told her mother. "Nobody will help. Now they want me to call in the morning!" She slammed down the phone.

As the hours ticked by, Sam and his family made many desperate calls to the California Highway Patrol, the sheriff's department, the San Diego Police Department, the Escondido and the El Cajon police departments. Each time they were told to call back in the morning, or that the police had to wait twenty-four hours before they would start looking.

One cynical dispatcher told the Knotts, "If I had a nickel for every call we get about a missing person, I'd be rich."

Sam went back on the freeway alone and for the next four hours he searched, his face red and his throat sore, his body cold and tired. Deep into the morning, Sam flagged down a deputy sheriff's car. The officers wouldn't roll down their windows beyond a crack but Sam wearily repeated his plea through the glass. Again, he insisted they write a missing person's report, but to no avail. He must have been quite a sight, this distraught middle-aged, middle-class man, demanding a massive search for this daughter who, to hear him tell it, was the all-American girl.

The cops weren't sure he wasn't a little tipsy from holiday revelry even though not a trace of drink mixed in the steam of Sam Knott's breath on this cold night. He could feel the chill creeping into his bones. He couldn't remember the last time he had felt this cold. San Diego nights even in December were never as bitter as this night was.

Sam couldn't get anyone to understand that something was out of kilter. Cara was gone and there had to be a reason. Why couldn't they understand? Sam poked around side streets, and then hit the off ramps again. When he couldn't find her in the well-lit areas, he started searching the dark desolate spots. He drove by parks, by abandoned truck lots, by a reservoir.

Of the dozens of off ramps from the inland Interstate 15 freeway, Mercy Road was the only exit not illuminated with street lights. Just south was the exit leading to the newly built suburban haven of young families, Rancho Penasquitos. To the north sat the exit leading to the tract house and country-style bedroom community of Poway.

But Mercy Road remained untouched by development along its canyons and creeks and mesquite scrub brush. It was an exit to nowhere. There was an off ramp, but the road it led to hadn't been finished. The old highway that the new I-15 freeway replaced had been abandoned and turned into a bike path. It was an isolated getaway spot for joggers and off-road motorbikers by day and for lovers to rendezvous and poor migrant farmworkers to camp by night. Police kept a continual eye out for rapists and crooks they believed infested the underbrush and canyons of Mercy Road.

Wayne and Sam each had scoured the dozen exits along Cara's route home, but they'd stopped only briefly at Mercy Road. They found it desolate and forbidding, just rubble and scrub brush, a dust-covered abandoned car, two sets of barricades and signs that said, ROAD CLOSED. "Cara would never stop here," Sam said to himself as he turned his car around at the barricades and headed back onto the interstate. He was still searching for Cara when the sun rose through a gray blanket of mist over San Diego.

At dawn, Cynthia and Bill took their first look at the Mercy Road exit. When Bill saw the sign saying the bike path was closed to vehicles he ignored it and slipped his little blue VW beetle past the bright orange barriers.

"Don't, Bill," Cynthia pressed.

But something made him keep going. ''Well, we've looked everywhere else.''

They drove down a hill and into a canyon, and there at the end of the road sat Cara's white VW shining like moonlight through the early morning haze.

Bill and Cynthia were frozen with relief—and fear. They drove toward Cara's car, and Cynthia jumped out while they were still moving and ran to the passenger door. Bill was so excited he leaped out as well without thinking. When his car kept rolling he realized he had forgotten to set the brake, so he had to jump back in to stop it.

Cynthia tugged on the passenger door of Cara's car. It was locked. She looked inside, but the dew-coated windshield blocked her view. She ran around to the driver's door and saw the window was rolled down part of the way. She pulled on the door. This one opened.

Frantic, Cynthia worked quickly. She pulled down the front seat and checked for Cara in the back, thinking her sister might have been tied and gagged. But there was no Cara; only her white purse, her makeup bag, and a Nordstrom's shopping bag on the rear seat. She saw the keys in the ignition. On the passenger's seat was the credit card receipt showing that Cara had stopped for gas after she'd left Wayne's house. A cheap black Casio watch with a broken band was on the floor.

Cynthia rifled through the Nordstrom's shopping bag and found Cara's white wallet. She checked inside, found twelve dollars and Cara's driver's license tucked safely inside its plastic window. Behind the floor board of the driver's seat was a broken tail pipe baffle wrapped in a dirty washcloth. That was the piece of pipe Bill had spent hours trying and failing to pry loose from the tail pipe for Cara only a few days before. Cynthia turned to Bill. ''Cara's not there.''

''What do you mean she's not there?'' Bill asked, almost angry at his wife for her inability to produce her sister now that they had tracked down her car. They held each other's eyes for a moment, then took off, running into the brush like frightened children. ''Cara! Cara!'' they shouted. For ten minutes they yelled, but the only responses were echoes and the hum of cars sounding like ocean waves on the freeway beyond. Their throats as well as their hearts ached.

Cynthia ran back to Cara's car and gathered up the shopping bag and her sister's purse to put in their car for safekeeping. She and Bill knew what they had to do. The couple drove back up Mercy Road, the little car chugging over rubble and potholes, passing the barriers. They got back onto I-15 and drove to the next exit, where they found a pay phone at a gas station.

The San Diego police kept Cynthia on hold for fifteen minutes. Finally, the duty lieutenant got on the line and Cynthia spilled her story. Her sister was missing but they'd found her car. . . . This time the police listened. Bill and Cynthia headed back to Mercy Road to wait for the law. They waited forty minutes.

It was 7 A.M. when Officer Jim Spears was ready to make his routine rounds from the San Diego Police Department's northeastern patrol station. Sergeant Bill Maheu briefed him on the Knotts' search, and sent him and his partner, Mary Cornicelli, to Mercy Road to check it out.

Spears and Cornicelli talked to Cynthia and Bill briefly and then turned to the VW. Spears pulled on some rubber gloves, opened the driver's door, and got inside. The key was in the ignition and Spears turned it. The car started up right away, with that familiar groan of a high-powered lawn mower. The arrow on the gas tank shot way past full.

Spears turned to Cynthia and gently asked her, "Now, was there anything in the car?"

"Her purse and her bags. We were afraid they would be stolen so we took them," Cynthia said.

To a cop like Spears, a crime scene is sacred and never to be touched. But he patiently asked Cynthia, "Why don't you put everything back exactly as you found it. Do you think you can remember how it was?"

Cynthia nodded and went to fetch the bags.

Then Spears saw something on the door. It was a smudge—blood. He straightened up. As casually as he could, he motioned to Officer Cornicelli and headed toward his cruiser and got on the radio. He got Maheu back at the northeastern substation. "We've got something here. I need backup," Spears said. "This is bigger than the both of us."

On the other side of the freeway, Sam was following Wayne up I-15 to the Via Rancho Parkway exit leading to Escondido. He waved good-bye as his daughter's boyfriend headed home. Sam started driving down the parkway when he spotted a San Diego police cruiser speeding down the parkway.

Maybe now that it's daylight, the police will listen to me, Sam thought. He honked his horn and flashed his high beams, but the cop ignored him. Sam wasn't going to let this one get away. He ran a red light and drove right up behind the cop's bumper, but the policeman still didn't notice.

Sam didn't care if the cops pulled him over and threw him in jail as long as they found his daughter. Damn, if the cop would just stop, he thought. The policeman kept speeding down Interstate 15. How bizarre, Sam thought. Now I'm chasing the cops.

The officer made a U-turn and screeched down the Mercy Road off ramp. Sam followed him, ignoring the barricades that he had heeded before. He could barely see through the cloud of dirt sprayed up on the dusty road. Then he was able to make out Bill and Cynthia waving at him. And Cara's white Volkswagen.

4

The Precious One

STANDING in the dust at the heart of this desolate canyon, Sam Knott felt surely that this must be hell on earth.

He leaned against his car and watched with bleary eyes every move the investigators made, as if he could will them to find every possible clue. How could there be any clues in this wasteland? he wondered. Everywhere he looked was scrub and dirt littered with broken bottles and scraps of paper. There was nothing more for him here.

What time was it when he finally left Mercy Road? Was it ten o'clock or noon? He remembered thinking he should feel more tired, but all he felt was numb.

He drove down the interstate as if on autopilot, barely thinking about the road before him while his head composed the words he needed to tell his wife that their daughter was dead, murdered. The weird thing was that the sun was shining. It just didn't seem possible the sun could be shining, he thought. He steered his Cutlass off I-15 to eastbound Interstate 8 and then through the tree-lined hills to his country haven, his refuge.

Joyce was there on the living room couch, her eyes fixed on the fireplace. Sam sat down and hugged her, and all his rehearsed words evaporated from his head. "Our baby's gone," he said simply.

After twenty-seven years of marriage Sam and Joyce didn't always need words to communicate. She understood instantly and nodded through her tears. "Cara always comes home on time," she said.

Sam didn't want to overwhelm her with the awful details of the murder scene he had just left behind, but he sketched out what he saw there for her in the godforsaken pocket of wilderness beside the freeway. "They told me that's the number-one crime area up there," Sam said angrily. "It's a hangout for druggies and rapists."

He shook his head sadly and stared at the fireplace. "Could we have saved her?" There was no answer before him, only the ashes of their Christmas wrappings.

Sam looked up around him as if for the first time and saw that the house had filled with people bustling about, neighbors and family and friends, all awkwardly trying to help in the search for Cara. Sam found it ironic that there were more people here now than there had been at Christmas.

The grieving father acknowledged the gestures of sympathy, but all he saw was Cara—her sneakers, her drawings, her magazines, her hairbrush, the corner of the couch she always sat on. The anger and sorrow inside him started growing into something solid, a decision, a conviction. He must save his family.

"Something good must come of this," Sam declared later to his family when the visitors had left. "We can't have police officers turning their backs on people when they want help. We are going to change the system, so maybe this will never happen again."

Sam knew this was supposed to have been their last Christmas together, but not like this. Never like this. The Knott kids were grown and ready to leave the nest. Cheryl was going off to school again, this time to San Francisco for her graduate studies in archaeology. The oldest, Cynthia, had just married and although she was still living at home with her husband, Bill Weick, they too would be heading north to the other end of California soon to start graduate school and their life together. John, the baby of the family, was just starting college at University of California. And Cara, the youngest girl, had her life all planned: she would stay at home for her last year of college, then get a job teaching elementary school and marry her boyfriend, Wayne Bautista, and they would have four children just like her mom and dad had done.

For Sam and Joyce Knott, this last Christmas together was to have been a celebration for the great job they had done in raising such wonderful kids—kids who had become strong and independent adults.

This was to have been the first Christmas that Santa Claus didn't come to the Knott homestead. Joyce and Sam finally had to accept the fact that their children were too old to get presents from "Santa." Besides, since when did Santa give computers?

Christmas Eve was always an occasion for the Knotts. Cara's grandparents, both sets, would come over and spend the night so they could all share the big moments together the next morning.

When she was a little girl, Cara jumped out of bed early on Christmas morning, eager to see her presents. But she never touched them until it was time. All the Knott kids were exceptionally well-behaved in that regard. Sure, they got antsy when Grandma Knott took forever to get ready, but they never broke the Knott family code by plunging into the pile of gifts without Grandma. The Knotts did everything as a family.

Back when the children were little in the sixties. Sam had moved around the living room at holidays like Cecil B. deMille, setting up the klieg lights for his super-eight movie camera. He'd wanted to capture the magic moment when his kids peeked around the corner of the living room and their eyes widened at the wonder of the Christmas bounty. As the years went on and the children grew, their smiles never changed. This was not a jaded family. The holiday brought magic to all the Knotts.

This year, Christmas 1986, the movie camera was less clunky, Grandma still took forever to get ready, and everyone grew restless for the big surprises waiting for them in the living room. Everybody got computers except Cara, who was due to receive a bigger and better surprise from her parents— a new compact Hyundai Excel—for her twenty-first birthday, which was coming up right before Valentine's Day. It was hard for Sam and Joyce to keep the secret to themselves, but Cara hardly seemed disappointed by her smaller gifts.

"Ooh, Mom, these are so cool, where did you get them?" Cara was so excited her voice squeaked as she unwrapped the big box and saw her flat-heeled, ankle-high white leather boots.

Everybody stopped tearing through their own gifts to laugh at Cara's childlike enthusiasm, and Cheryl started teasing Cara by trying to mimic her squeal, "Ooh, Mom." Cheryl laughed, collapsing in a heap of torn wrapping paper and ribbons. All eyes were on Cara as she kicked off her slippers and carefully pulled on the soft leather boots that folded at her calves. She modeled them for her admiring family.

Cara couldn't believe an even larger package than the one that held the boots had her name on it. She slowly unwrapped it and lifted the lid to see yet another gift she had secretly coveted, a soft white leather jacket. Her high voice cracked with more squeals of excitement, "Oh, Grandma! Thank you! You're so wonderful," setting everybody off again in a chain of giggles.

Nobody could read Cara better than her mother. Joyce could tell her daughter was a little disappointed with the jacket's less-than-hip style. So she drew Cara into the kitchen later and whispered, "Grandma tried, but seventy-year-old ladies don't know much about leather jackets. We'll get you the right kind tomorrow."

Cara threw her arms around her petite mother appreciatively. "Oh, Mom, you don't miss anything, do you?"

For Christmas dinner, Joyce served the traditional turkey and her special creamed-corn casserole with bread crumbs that she could never make enough of. It was a recipe handed down from her Nebraska farm family for years. She had made batches and batches of cookies, but she still had to smack Sam's hands away when he tried to take too many at once.

"How about whipping up some pumpkin pie? It's a crime to have Christmas without pie," Sam said, trying not to grin. He already knew what his wife was thinking; Joyce was a professional nutritionist by training who had to close her eyes when she poured the called-for pounds of butter into her Christmas cookies.

"Oh, Sam, come on, it's for your own good. I'll buy you a pumpkin if you want, but no pie," his wife said. "Have an apple instead."

As Joyce and the girls cleared away the wrapping paper and stuffed it all into the fireplace, Cheryl called out to Joyce in the kitchen, "What are we having for supper, ribs?" Cheryl winked at her dad, who took up the family joke.

"Yeah, Joyce, what are you experimenting with this year? Quiche?" For posterity, Cheryl retold the story of the Christmas that Joyce Knott tempted fate by breaking family tradition and actually serving prime rib instead of tried-and-true roast turkey.

"You guys, will you ever let me forget that?" Joyce laughed. "Boy, you are all so boring. What am I going to do with you?"

Joyce headed into the kitchen to start dinner with Cynthia at her heels, who insisted that she take over for her mother. "I'll do that. You go relax, Mom." Joyce just stared at her daughter. She thought about telling her what a monumental task preparing the holiday meals could be, but she stopped herself. The Knotts never tried to stop their children from learning, and Joyce figured, If anyone can survive a crash course in cooking for twenty, Cynthia can.

Joyce couldn't abandon the kitchen so easily though. She watched from a stool at the breakfast bar as her tall, thin daughter tied on her apron and started pulling food from the refrigerator. After all, Joyce mused, she's married now, I guess she wants to learn the family traditions to carry on in her own home.

Joyce looked into the living room and smiled. Cheryl was sitting on the couch talking a mile a minute. At least Cheryl hasn't changed, she thought. If there was a choice between washing dirty dishes and debating world politics, Joyce knew exactly where Cheryl stood.

Cara wandered away from the action and into the kitchen. "Anything you need me to do, Cyn?" she asked. Joyce thought, That's pure Cara, the one trying to please everyone.

Joyce was content to sit on the sidelines, watching her children, obviously so at ease with one another and the world around them. Bill was talking with Cynthia; John was trying to be polite and pay attention but was distracted by his new computer. Cara's boyfriend, Wayne, was trying hard to get in the spirit of things, Joyce noticed, but he was feeling sick and was half asleep in his chair. "You love all your children, but they're all different," Joyce would tell her friends. "But Cara was my little buddy. She had the best qualities of each."

The Knotts lived out in the country in the rural town of El Cajon where Joyce had grown up. Their home stood on a hillside between the Laguna Mountains to the east and the city of San Diego and the ocean to the west. This was dusty pickup-truck country, but Sam had staked his own ground. The son of a doctor, Sam preferred books to boots.

Rugged individualism was in Sam's blood. His grandfather, John Knott, joined a socialist utopian community comprised of New Yorkers who settled near the Sierra Madre mountains in the Mexican state of Sinola. But like many utopians, their individual ambitions broke up the perfect society, and John Knott drifted into the sugar business, which led him to the Caribbean.

Sam was born in St. Croix in the Virgin Islands, where his father, a doctor like his father before him, was a physician for the sugar company. Sam's father took his family all over, from the Virgin Islands to New Guinea, until the Knotts finally settled in San Diego. That allowed Sam to finish high school in the States and then do as his father wanted—become the fourth generation Knott to practice medicine. But Sam's heart wasn't in medicine.

Still, Sam listened to his father and dropped his first love, history, to study business. He pursued a career, not as a doctor, but as a hospital administrator.

Sam started dating a cheerleader named Joyce Smith in high school and they kept going together while they both attended San Diego State University. They married after graduation and moved to the San Francisco Bay area where Joyce attended Mills College for her advanced degree in nutrition. Sam, at loose ends, decided to fulfill his military obligation with a six-month stint in the army reserves.

Stationed in Fort Ord nearby on the lovely rugged central California coast near Monterey, Sam learned to loathe every moment in the military world—they could drill his body all they wanted but not his soul. He found solace and escape in poetry, his own poetry; he wrote reams and reams of it. He enjoyed pouring many thoughts into just a few words. To him, those few lines of poetry said more than three hundred pages of a book.

Sam finally won his honorable discharge. He and his young bride moved to Ventura where he worked as a hospital administrator. But his interest still wandered from medicine and after their two oldest girls were born a year apart, Sam became involved in planning an archaeological tour of Egypt, a place in which he had a passionate interest.

Joyce decided to skip the trip because she was pregnant, although she eventually miscarried the child. Within the year, Joyce was pregnant again with the child they would call Cara, a Portuguese word that means "precious."

Sam soon tired of the politics inherent in running a hospital. He moved his family back home to San Diego to a big house in the country. Professionally, Sam ventured out on his own as a stockbroker and a financial consultant. He planned to give his family the stability he had never known, and also the intellectual stimulation he'd grown up with—the best of both worlds.

When the children were small, Sam built a tree house for them in the huge tree-filled backyard where the kids let their imaginations run wild. Golden-haired Cynthia and Cheryl would have tea parties in the days when Cara was still too young to play along. But she eased into the game by being their pet puppy. They played, patting her occasionally, and that kept everybody happy.

All the Knott children loved to read. Sam made sure of that by showering them with books and telling them that the words inside were like the best ice cream they could ever eat, the best food for their minds.

The books were to be consumed, Sam said. They shouldn't be decorations to be admired on the shelf. He taught the children not to be intimidated by what writers said, but to actually think about what they read. Don't be afraid to write in the margins, Sam would tell them; ask questions and underline what interests you. His kids took Sam's teachings to heart. John would curl up in bed with encyclopedias instead of toys.

Sam practiced what he preached. He absorbed volumes of history and philosophy and anthropology, arguing with the world's greatest minds in the margins of their books. If a particular passage insulted his interpretation of the facts, Sam would write in beside it, *Wrong!*

In conversation, Sam peppered his remarks with seemingly obscure references to ancient kings and quirks of history. "If only John Wilkes Booth hadn't failed in the oil business . . . ," he would say.

Joyce teased him, "Sam Knott, what good are you? You know when the Magna Carta was signed but you can't remember your own mother's birthday."

"Yeah, well, when they put my mother's birthday in a history book, I'll never forget it," Sam joked in his own defense.

As he had about everything else, Sam Knott had his own ideas about child rearing. "You put little drops of knowledge in each one. And like a seed, you watch it grow," he would say.

Not all the lessons were so cerebral. Many of his teachings had to do with the nuts and bolts of daily living that Sam believed too often were taken for granted. There is random evil out there, he told his children time and again. Stay away from strangers, he told them, because you never know what lurks behind their smiles.

Sam also told the children that they should learn to take responsibility for themselves. He warned them that smoking and drinking could not only destroy their bodies, but also their minds. Even their grandmother's addiction to cigarettes—and the cartons she stashed in her garden so she would never be far from a smoke—became an example of how strong a hold drugs could have on lives.

So it wasn't surprising that Cara, who didn't date much in high school, routinely left teenage parties before they were over. "Why are you home early?" her mother would ask.

And Cara would just shrug. "You know, drugs."

Cara hated watching people get messed up on drugs and too much beer. "It's so gross," she would tell her mom.

"Why do they have to do that?" She considered it a weakness, and Cara wanted nothing to do with weakness. The Knott children were clearheaded about such matters. Their closeness was a strength, and so were their differences.

As Cara grew, she intuitively realized her sister Cheryl was the brain and the philosopher. Cynthia, studious and scientific, also excelled and earned straight As. Cara herself was no stranger to good grades, but she was searching for something she could claim as her own. Always the more outdoor-oriented of the kids, she naturally turned to athletics. Her mother had been a cheerleader, but Cara wanted another kind of athletic challenge, and tried out for the track team.

She had a talent for running even as a kid, but she never thought much of it. As a little girl she always won the races on the school playground. Sam became accustomed to seeing teachers lavish praise on his older girls' academic skills, but he was surprised when he opened Cara's second grade report card and all it said was "fast runner."

"What does this mean, 'fast runner'?" Sam asked Joyce. She just shook her head. She had never noticed Cara running around anywhere. Cara was the one who always wanted to wear dresses.

Their youngest daughter had never bothered to tell them she won the races; she didn't think it important. Her family downplayed athletics; Sam never watched football on Sunday afternoons. He read instead. Whenever his daughters joked about his sedentary ways, Sam would reply, "Yeah, but I talk a good game from this chair."

Actually, Sam had done more than just talk a good game. He had had the chance to play professional baseball but had opted for college instead of a career as a first baseman. Even with his talent and love for baseball as a young man, he had already conquered that sport and he'd wanted a new challenge. So he'd founded the rugby club at San Diego State University in the fifties. The anarchy of jumping all over opponents and the purity of a sport without cumbersome padding and equipment had appealed to him. Best of all, Sam had liked the verbal jousting with opponents after games, a rugby tradition.

Out of that environment Cara grew to become the athletic

star of the Knott family. Her years of ballet had given her long legs and a lithe body. But she didn't stick with dance like her sister Cheryl. Instead, she chose track and field. Being untrained, at first she was awkward and didn't show much promise. The coach didn't even have a uniform for her, so her mother had to alter a leftover boy's jersey for her to wear.

Now the problem was choosing an event. Cara loved running the four-hundred-meter dash, but she was overshadowed by a friend at a nearby high school who happened to be state champion and was destined for world-class competition. As always, Cara turned to her mother to talk about her problems.

"Try another event," Joyce advised. "The hurdles look good. If I were running track, I think I would try them."

Cara, who thought her mom was superwoman, misunderstood the advice. So she went back to the track and attacked those hurdles with a vengeance, trying not to be afraid as every step brought her closer to the obstacles and made them look larger and more ominous. But she cleared them. She came home that night and asked, "Mom, when you ran hurdles, did you do the three-step or the five-step approach?"

Joyce stared back at her daughter in disbelief. "Where did you get the idea that I ran track?" she managed to say between hoots of laughter. "Can you imagine me, all of five foot two, trying to jump over hurdles?"

Cara looked at her diminutive mother and, realizing her mistake, she laughed too, even though the joke was on her.

"It was pretty funny," Cara said. "The only thing that got me over those hurdles was that I kept thinking if Mom could do it, so could I."

Cara persisted in the hurdles and finally licked the event. She won her varsity letter in track for Valhalla High, a school named for the Nordic mythological heaven where the souls of slain heroes were celebrated.

Cara won races right up to the league championship. Her track coach started paying attention to her and even went out and bought her a sort of uniform—flowered shorts and a white jersey that actually fit.

Sam never saw Cara run until that final race at the league championships. He hurried over from work with only enough money in his pocket to pay for parking; he couldn't even buy a program.

The proud father watched Cara on the outside track leave the other runners behind. She cleared hurdle after hurdle with the grace of a deer. On the final hurdle, she caught her toe. Cara stumbled, but sheer determination kept her on her feet, and she forced herself forward, wobbling all the way, until she fell flat on her face. She was over the finish line. Cara won the race and the championship for Valhalla.

Sam went wild with jubilation. "That's my daughter! That's my daughter!" he screamed. He ran up and down the stands clutching the program someone had given him as though he were bearing the Olympic torch.

It was on the track team that Cara met Wayne Bautista, a handsome football player who ran track to keep in shape. It took Wayne months to work up the nerve to ask her out, and when he did it was for keeps. Wayne became her first and only boyfriend.

Although Cara and Wayne were constant companions, Cara still had special time for her big sister Cheryl when she came home from college. The girls would put on their bikinis and go boy watching at the premier surfing beach in posh La Jolla, about forty minutes from their house.

Cara didn't spend her summers just perfecting her tan like so many southern California girls. She worked; first, as one of the wholesome salesclerks at Hickory Farms cheese shops in the local shopping mall, then at a health food store run by her boyfriend's father, and one summer at a gift shop in the world-famous San Diego Zoo. Cheryl visited her at the zoo, and smiled to herself as she watched Cara bowling over the tourists. "She always had this sweet smile on her face and she'd be saying, 'Can I get another size for you? Oh, oh that looks great on you,' " Cheryl recalled.

On Cara's work breaks the two sisters took off around the zoo, trying to stop tourists from feeding the animals. "They'd think it was funny," fumed Cheryl, the eternal activist. "It's so bad for the animals." Cheryl would tell off anybody she caught feeding them, and Cara was right behind her.

Cynthia was the oldest, a year ahead of Cheryl in school and just as beautiful, but she was shy and didn't make as big a splash. The oldest girl started dating an artistic young man named Bill Weick her sophomore year, and they stayed together all the way through college until they married nine years later.

But it was Cheryl who carried on her father's eclectic interests, traveling by herself across the world while still in high school, first as an exchange student in Mexico, then in Sweden. She spoke several languages, had lots of interests, lots of boyfriends. As Cara came up through school behind them, she was known as Cheryl Knott's sister.

Cheryl knew she was shaping her baby sister into a firebrand like herself, even from the distant reaches of northern California where she was going to college at University of California in Davis, outside Sacramento, the state capital. She marched to keep the United States out of Nicaragua, protested against the whites-only apartheid policy of South Africa, collected bottles for recycling, spoke out on abortion at prochoice rallies. She wrote Cara letters about all of it, and they exchanged newspaper clippings with key phrases underlined. Cheryl loved to arouse her sister's righteous indignation.

Cheryl laughed when Cara told her how she had stood up to her high school humanities teacher who had been provoking his class with talk about women being inferior to men. Cara hadn't jumped up and challenged him as her older sister would have. Her style was to speak up with a more tactful approach—"Well, what about this, sir?"

Cara missed her big sister so much. "I'll write to you every day," she'd promised Cheryl each fall when it was time for her to go back north to college. The older girl was touched; even though she knew Cara wouldn't keep her promise, at least she wanted to. When Cara did write, her letters were long, detailed accounts of every move she made. But Cara was focused not just on herself; she worried about her sister up there in the foggy cold northern California valley. Cara drew funny little pictures to keep Cheryl from taking life too seriously. In one letter she drew a cartoon of the sun. "If it's not a sunny day, then pretend it is." Cara's sun wore dark glasses and was so hot beads of sweat dripped from its forehead. Cheryl saved the sun and all the other letters Cara sent in a bundle she tied with a pink ribbon.

Above her desk Cheryl kept an old Polaroid snapshot of the two of them as little girls, sitting on their front porch one Halloween with carved pumpkins, and Cheryl dressed as a witch. The camera caught them giving each other their special grins. Looking at the snapshot Cheryl said later, "I keep this because it shows how much I love her."

As Cara got older she needed no more molding. She started on her own causes: animal rights, the environment, recycling, women's rights. She even traveled through Europe after high school with a group of friends. The next summer, she and Cheryl planned to travel through Europe unchaperoned with backpacks and Eurorail passes, as sisters and as equals.

The younger girl set out to be as independent as her sister. Cara spent her first year of college at the University of California campus in Santa Barbara, a picturesque beach city and home of Ronald Reagan, five hours up the California coast. But Cara missed her mother, and her mother missed her.

And Cara missed Wayne most of all. She was ahead of him in school because of all the college prep work she had done, so he stayed behind to catch up at a local community college, with the aim of joining her at the university the next year. By the end of her freshman year, Cara decided she wanted to be an elementary school teacher. And since San Diego State University had a strong education program and was only ten minutes from her parents' house, it was a good excuse to transfer to the less prestigious college. Wayne could get in State easily and they could both go there. She returned and everything seemed to be falling into place.

For Joyce, it really hit home how great her family was when she joined some of her old high school classmates for their annual reunion dinner right before Christmas 1986. All the friends she had grown up with were there talking about divorce, kids with drug problems, hating their jobs, having money troubles. Joyce just sat there thinking to herself, I have nothing to contribute to this conversation. She knew she'd better keep her mouth shut because she doubted they would want to hear how wonderful things were in the Knott household.

A couple of weeks after her reunion dinner, the whole family decided to go out together on the Saturday night before Christmas. Sisters, brothers, mothers, grandmothers, fathers, boyfriends all filed into the local triplex theater to see one of their favorite movies of all time, the Disney classic *Song of the South*.

They giggled at how odd they must have looked to the people around them, these fifteen grown-ups hogging two rows, surrounded by little kids and their bored parents. But the Knotts were not embarrassed. They adored Disney pictures. Joyce and the girls used to joke that they had to preview all movies for Sam since he hated anything racier than a PG-rated film. One dirty word, and Sam was out the door. "I have no use for profanity," he'd say.

Afterward, they went out for pizza, and it seemed like they laughed all night long. Nobody could remember when they had had so much fun. "It was a magical time," Sam said later.

The magic continued all the way through Christmas.

For Cara, the only flaw in an otherwise perfect holiday was Wayne. It was the first Christmas he had spent with the Knotts and she felt bad that his flu kept him from some of the fun. While everyone ran around the house full of Christmas cheer, Wayne slipped into a back room and slept the day away. He left before dinner and spent the night alone, since his family was in San Francisco visiting relatives.

The next morning was a Friday and nobody in the Knott household had to work. Wayne called Cara and asked her if she would come up and take care of him after he finished work at the farm, because his family was gone and he really felt awful.

"Of course I'll come up, you poor thing," Cara assured him. They planned to have him call before he left work at eight o'clock that night.

That left the whole day ahead of her. Cara was sitting in the kitchen eating turkey sandwiches with her mom and sister, when she piped up, "Let's go shopping. I have to get a new comb, I lost mine."

Joyce laughed, "A comb? That sounds like as good an excuse as any to go to Horton Plaza."

So Cara, Cheryl, and their mother took off for the fanciest mall in the city in downtown San Diego. It is the Disneyland of malls, a pastel pink, green, and blue structure with a whimsical design, always full of blooming flowers and sunshine. They hit Nordstrom's first, even though one of San Diego's most exclusive department stores doesn't specialize in such mundane items as combs.

Cara had no trouble picking out a more hip leather jacket, one with feminine tailoring, gathered shoulders, and silver studs. "Are you sure it's okay, Mom? It's so expensive," she said, admiring the to-die-for jacket in the mirror.

"Well, I don't know, Cara, are you worth it?" Joyce teased. "It's a beautiful jacket. You deserve it, honey."

Cara also picked up a new white oversized purse to match, a deal at ten dollars. She was not the kind of girl to go wild with her parents' credit cards even at an after-Christmas sale. But she was in such a great mood.

Cheryl picked up a purse as well, though she spent hours considering the selection and it was Cara's gentle nudging that settled her. And then it was time to go. They gathered up their shopping bags and headed to the parking garage, with the strains of Christmas carols floating over their heads from the mall speakers.

They headed home and Cara rushed in and took a quick shower, something she got used to sharing a bathroom with two older sisters and a brother. She put on her purple sweatpants, threw some clothes into her shopping bag, loaded her contact lens case into her makeup bag, and tossed them inside her expandable mesh bag she had bought in Mexico.

She pulled on her new white leather boots, cut the tags off her new jacket, and then laid it carefully across the backseat of her white VW bug. Joyce followed her out to the car.

"I guess we'll see you late Saturday or Sunday? Take care, sweetie." And she gave her daughter a hug.

Cara pulled out of the driveway and waved good-bye.

It was dark by the time Cara pulled up to Wayne's house on Alamo Drive. He was only a few minutes behind her in his pickup, exhausted by flu and a day of work at the mushroom farm he helped run.

She quickly made him some soup, and put him to bed. Always a big reader, she reached into her mesh bag for her paperback copy of *Sophie's Choice* and settled into the rocking chair by Wayne's bed and read while he slept. Every time Wayne woke up, he saw her sitting there, watching over him.

The next morning, Wayne had to get up and go to work at the mushroom farm in the rural town of Bonsall a dozen miles east of his house. It was work he usually loved—examining cultures, setting the temperatures, and tending to the complex raising of the mushrooms. He was studying microbiology at State and this was going to be his life's work, but on this day after Christmas the flu was torturing him. He couldn't remember being this sick in his entire life. He was back home in two hours and his fever seemed worse.

His whole body ached and he felt terrible for letting Cara down, for they had planned to take a picnic the next day to the wild animal park nearby and wander around the green hills filled with exotic game. But Cara didn't mind. By late afternoon, Wayne felt even hotter, and Cara was worried.

"I can't believe there's no thermometer in this house. How could you survive without one? I'm going to the store to get one."

When she returned, Cara took Wayne's temperature and was astonished to see it registered 104 degrees.

She gently closed Wayne's door and went into the kitchen to call her mom for help. That high a fever scared her.

"Mom, hi, it's me. Listen, Wayne is really sick. He has a one hundred and four temperature. What should I do? Should I take him to the hospital or something?"

"First, why don't you try to cool down his fever, bring his temperature down. Give him a bath," Joyce advised. "Make it tepid."

"Tepid? Is that cold?" Cara asked.

She told Wayne what her mother advised but he protested weakly, "There's no way I'm going to get into a cold bathtub."

"Oh, Wayne, it'll be all right," she said.

She started working on the bath and decided to add some bubble bath hoping the cheery suds would take his mind off the coolness of the water.

Then Wayne's sisters arrived early from San Francisco and one of the girls, sixteen-year-old Monica, poked her head in to say hi to Cara, one of her favorite people, the one older person who always had time for her.

Monica couldn't believe her eyes. "Cara? What in the world are you doing?" she exclaimed.

Bubbles were exploding all over the bathroom. Cara had filled the bathtub with bubble bath and then turned on the Jacuzzi jets in the tub, which were whipping up the suds. It looked like a waterfall with Cara frantically trying to beat back the froth. Monica started laughing uncontrollably.

Cara started to think things were funny too. She didn't embarrass easily, especially with silly things like a bubble bath out of control. It was almost like she expected life's little jokes on her. Even Wayne, as bad as he felt, thought the bubble bath was pretty funny. It was one of the goofy things he loved about her. He remembered the time she wanted him to teach her how to surf, so he put her on a board in the backyard swimming pool, and the slick fiberglass board kept shooting out from underneath her when she tried to stand. It smacked into the wall and broke the nose. The board was never the same.

She spent a long time scrubbing the tub trying to get the bubbles out. Finally, Cara drew a hot bath for her feverish boyfriend, who slipped in gratefully.

"Ready?" she asked.

"I can handle it," Wayne agreed.

She quickly yanked the plug on the tub and started running cold water as Wayne tried not to watch or think about it. Finally, the temperature was about right and Wayne just soaked there for about twenty minutes.

She helped him out of the tub and he immediately felt better. "It worked!" he told her. "I feel one hundred percent better." He truly felt like he had that punishing flu licked.

She took such good care of him. Sometimes he spent the night at her house in a room the Knotts had set up for him, so he wouldn't have to commute all the way north to Escondido and come back again the next morning for college classes. He imagined what it would be like to be married to Cara, and knew it would be heaven. She always got up first and made him breakfast before she went in to wake him. It was always their special time.

Wayne remembered how they met at Valhalla High and all the months he'd spent talking to Cara, building up the courage to ask her out. It had taken him close to half a year to do it. He'd been mortified when one of his best friends had told him that he had a crush on Cara too. But it had been Wayne who'd finally stepped forward and asked her out to a sunset barbecue at the beach on a balmy evening in late winter. He remembered how carefully he'd lit the hibachi, trying to make everything perfect, and how he'd sat on the blanket and come right to the point. "Do you want to be my girlfriend?" he'd asked. And she had said yes. He couldn't believe his wish was coming true. "Do you want to go to the prom with me?" he'd asked so nervous he could barely breathe. And she'd said yes again.

They'd been so busy with each other they had forgotten their hamburgers on the grill and it had only been the smell of the burned meat that had brought them back to reality. Their dinner had been burned to a crisp. "We didn't eat that night," Wayne recalled later, smiling at the memory.

Then came the senior prom at the Hotel del Coronado, a romantic century-old seaside hotel where local legend had it that Edward, the Prince of Wales, met Wallis Simpson, the divorcée he fell in love with and left his throne to marry. It was here that Marilyn Monroe wooed Tony Curtis in the classic film, *Some Like It Hot*.

Cara Knott walked up the steps of the Hotel del wearing an off-the-shoulder satin gown in deep green. For the occasion she had talked Wayne into renting tails and a top hat. They ate dinner in the immense ballroom and danced under a vaulted ceiling. Afterwards there was a party at a friend's house, but Wayne and Cara never showed up. "It was a magic night," Wayne recalled.

The next morning the couple joined the entire senior class and boarded a bus for Los Angeles that would take them to the ferry to Santa Catalina Island. The teenagers roamed the picturesque island until the final ferry left that night.

Now after three years together Cara felt proud that she could take care of Wayne. She was glad her nursing was beginning to work, but it was almost Saturday night and she thought about heading home to her family.

As always, they discussed their plans first. Through all the years they'd been together they rarely fought because they talked about everything first. Now that Wayne's sisters were back, they could look after him. He only had to work two hours the next morning at the farm and then the day was free. Wayne and Cara decided she should go home, and that he would drive down to her house the next day and they would do something, maybe go on a picnic as they had planned.

Cara called her parents to tell them she was on her way home. It was 8:09 P.M. She picked up her bags and loaded them into the car.

"Oh, Wayne," she called, "do you have any cash? I may need gas, and all I have is my dad's credit card, and the Chevron may be closed for Christmas."

Wayne was in the kitchen eating some toast she had made him. He gave her twelve dollars and a hug and started to thank her again when the telephone rang.

"It's my dad. He wants to wish you merry Christmas," Wayne called out and Cara took the receiver.

Wayne's parents had separated when he was only four years old, so he had had to adjust to having a stepfather and a stepsister, as well as a sister. Although he was happy with his families, it was pretty strange to Cara, whose own family was rock solid. Ever since he started going out with Cara in high school, he loved becoming part of the Knott family circle. Though he and Cara were not formally engaged to be married, he knew his destiny was with Cara and her family. Their plan was that he would finish his degree in microbiology and run the mushroom farm, she would teach elementary school, and they would have a big family and live by the beach. They had it all planned.

Cara was a little let down about not getting to go to the wild animal park, which was a couple of miles from Wayne's house. Sometimes she thought she loved animals as much as people. But she wanted to be cheerful for Wayne's sake. She skipped out of the house, her ponytail swaying and her new white leather jacket tucked under her arm.

Wayne watched her walk away, admiring her beauty. He

smiled a little looking at the new white boots, thinking that she may have bought them to please him. He had been telling her for years how good she would look in them, and he always loved wearing his cowboy boots when he worked on the farm. Then there was the leather jacket. He had no idea she had even wanted one. But he had to admit she looked absolutely spectacular in it.

"I love you," he told her as she left and gave her a kiss on the cheek, careful to protect her from his flu.

"I love you, too." She smiled at him and headed out into the night.

5

The Outrage

"WHAT's up?" asked reporter Jim Okerblom as he walked into the newsroom of the *San Diego Union*, the county's major newspaper, on Sunday, December 28.

"Well, today, it being the holiday season of peace on earth, goodwill to men, we've got murder, lots of murder," editor Joe Schneider informed Okerblom as the reporter sat down at his desk. Schneider had covered wars in the Third World earlier in his career and had developed a defensive way of joking away the uglier side of life.

"We've got a murdered college girl up in some lover's lane in north county—no suspects. We've got a quadruple homicide over in east San Diego," Schneider said. "Take your pick. Don't say I never gave you anything."

Police scanners squawked beside Okerblom, and the television murmured above. It looked like it was going to be one of those days. He fortified himself with a big gulp of coffee. Okerblom wasn't interested in the mass killings; it looked like another sad episode in the drug wars, and there wasn't much mystery in that. It was the other story that looked interesting.

"This girl, who was she?" Okerblom asked.

Schneider shrugged. "The cops haven't said a thing. Check it out."

Okerblom headed north to the Mercy Road murder scene. Yellow police tape marked off the canyon, so he climbed the hill near the freeway overpass to get to a vantage point. From there he watched a cluster of officers huddled over a body. He could see it was a young woman. Okerblom shivered, though it was afternoon now and the sun was beating down. He headed over to homicide chief Phil Jarvis for the details, and then pumped the other detectives milling about for the more bits of information.

All the reporter could get from the cops were the basics—who, when, where—but not the why. Why was this young woman dead at the bottom of a canyon during the Christmas holidays?

Okerblom headed back to the newsroom and tracked the victim's family to their home on Vernette Drive in El Cajon. He headed east on the freeway toward their house and worries started to creep into his mind about how the family would react to him. Would they yell at him for bothering them or start crying as they spilled out the girl's life story? Talking to a victim's family was the worst part of the reporter's job. He turned up the sound of the car radio to drown out his nervousness.

Twenty minutes later, Okerblom stood on the Knotts' front doorstep. The man who answered the door had tragedy etched on his face. Okerblom took a look at the man's swollen eyes and his unshaven jowls and knew he must be the father. The man looks like a ghost, Okerblom thought.

As soon as the door opened Okerblom started talking. "I'm sorry to disturb you, I know this must be a terrible time for you, but I just want to get some information about Cara Knott. Was she your daughter? I want to tell her story in the newspaper so people can understand what a loss her death has been. . . ." Okerblom took it as a good sign that the door hadn't been slammed in his face so he raced on. "What kind of girl was she?"

Sam Knott nodded suddenly and pushed the door open all the way. He looked like he had decided something. Sam would later say that fate had brought to his doorstep a tool to help him flush out the monster who had killed his baby girl, and he was going to seize it.

"She was the sweetest girl you ever saw. . . ." Sam began, as Okerblom yanked his notepad out of his back pocket and started writing. "And smart. She got As at San Diego State. She was going to be a teacher. My Cara was not naive; she knew about crime; she knew how to take care of herself," Sam continued, watching the reporter write down his every word. He emphasized the next part, "She would never, never stop for anyone, except me, her family, her boyfriend, or someone she trusted.

"Remember those rapes over at the State campus?" Sam asked Okerblom, who nodded emphatically; the reporter had covered the stories on a gang rape in a fraternity house and rapes in classrooms on the massive campus of thirty thousand students. Well, Sam told him, instead of being overwhelmed by the sexual assaults, Cara refused to let herself be taken off guard. "She and my wife took a self-defense course together," he explained, and related the lessons they had learned from their self-defense teacher, a former San Diego police sergeant named Sandy Strong.

Strong told them to never trust a crook, Sam explained. Cara had filled him in on the ex-cop's strategy that it was useless to try to negotiate with a rapist, or even to try to talk your way out of trouble. The only way was to fight back, quickly, Strong had told them. Fighting back, Sam figured, must have been what Cara did. When someone threatens you, you should explode and run. Strong had told his pupils to make noise, scratch faces, reach for eyes. "Do not go gently . . ." seemed to be the motto.

Sam talked about Cara's goals and her activities. But the essence of his daughter, how could he put that in words? "She was precious," Sam said simply.

Back in the newsroom, Okerblom sat writing his story, thinking how different this family was from the seemingly hundreds of other victims' families he had interviewed in his fifteen years in the news business.

"Here they were, with all this grief, and they had the presence of mind to try to change things. They were pretty amazing. I wouldn't have been that rational," Okerblom said later. His first story on Cara Knott conveyed her family's determination that this case wouldn't end until they found Cara's killer and changed the system that had failed to help them rescue her.

On Monday, Sam was up before dawn smoothing the *San Diego Union* out on the breakfast bar and reading Okerblom's story carefully. It was a strange feeling to see his words before him in black and white, to see the cold hard details of death and grief. Did I really say that? Did all this really happen? The black newsprint came off on his fingers, but there was no erasing the fact that Cara was dead.

For a second Sam wondered if he had done right by Cara, dragging her private life out in public this way. This two-dimensional account of her life and death now sat on 275,000 doorsteps across the county. But Sam worried only for a second. It was right, he knew, that the world understand how precious she was and feel the outrage he felt. He wanted a community up in arms in search of the monster who had done this.

Over his morning coffee Monday at his San Diego house, television news editor Mike Workman read the *Union*'s account of the Knott murder and decided the story was strong enough to lead that night's broadcast. He had done this kind of story a thousand times before: Nice Kid Gets Killed, Family Grieves, Film at 11.

There was the follow on the quadruple homicide down in another part of town, he knew, but those victims were drifters, unknowns, maybe drug pushers, the kind of people that even if you could get information on them, nobody wants to hear about it. The more cynical cops have a name for the almost-daily slayings of low lifes, drug pushers, and pimps: NHI, they say, no humans involved. Workman's instincts told him that even four people killed execution-style was nothing compared to the Knott case.

When Workman walked into the newsroom of the local CBS affiliate, KFMB-Channel 8, he found waiting on his desk a phone message from one Terri Green. "Wants to talk about the Knott murder," the message read.

Workman called right away. He reached her at Von's supermarket where she worked. "I know this is odd," Green told him, "but I was pulled over at that same place, that Mercy Road exit, on November 23. I drive a Volkswagen bug too. Just like that girl who was killed this weekend."

"Yeah?" Workman said.

"Yeah," Green repeated. "There was this cop who told me to go down to this really dark freeway exit and then he told me one of my headlights was dim. I mean—dim headlights! Come on. I had to tell *him* my license was expired, he didn't even notice it. He was too busy talking."

Workman sent a cameraman and one of his more seasoned newsmen out to talk to Green, and leaped into the heap of work on his desk. An hour later the newsman came back skeptical. "Here's a woman pulled over by a cop. He's polite to her so she's suspicious. Makes no sense," he told the editor.

"So nothing, huh?" Workman asked.

"That's right, just another hysterical female," the reporter said.

Workman started to throw Green's note into the trash can, but something stopped him. He decided to pass the tip on to the California Highway Patrol, but they didn't seem too interested. They thanked him, and then referred him to the San Diego Police. So he called the homicide department in San Diego. They connected him to a detective he had never worked with before, and the cop was polite, but Workman sensed his tip was going to the bottom of the heap.

It was the vulnerability-of-women angle that television station channel 39, the local NBC affiliate, pursued that first weekday after Cara's body was found.

Reporter Rory Devine knew a lot of women felt the same reaction she did to the killing, first of all sympathy for the girl but in the back of her mind fear that the same thing could have happened to her. Was there a homicidal nut roaming loose preying on isolated women? How many nights had she driven alone and been vulnerable to some maniac? Devine set out to do a story about how women might develop better self-defense. The kind of self-defense Cara Knott needed.

Keeping the highways safe was the job of the California Highway Patrol and Devine called the CHP brass to put her in touch with someone she could interview on patrol. The CHP was a formal agency and every civilian request went through a militaristic evaluation. Devine and all the reporters knew that no member of the public was allowed to ride in a CHP car without the approval of the top officials.

Patrol supervisors picked one of their best spokesmen, Officer Craig Peyer. Peyer knew the Mercy Road area near Interstate 15 like the back of his hand because it was on his beat. The highway patrol always sent him to civic groups to lecture on highway safety. He always looked neat and professional as he stood at the podium warning his audience that southern California's sleek labyrinth of freeways was fast and clean, but could also be deadly if you weren't careful. People listened attentively, knowing all too well about the outbreak of shootings on the freeway over traffic disputes and the brazen crimes against motorists whose cars had broken down on the road.

Peyer believed in the highway patrol. Known as one of the most gung-ho cops in the barracks, he loved being tagged ''hot pencil'' by his colleagues. His nickname came from his zealousness. He routinely wrote twice as many tickets as most CHP officers, sometimes up to three hundred citations a month. He demanded an orderly world out there on the highways. Headlight out of alignment, that's a ticket. License plate light bulb out, that's another ticket. ''There are two people you don't piss off in this world: God and a highway patrolman,'' Peyer liked to say, ''and not necessarily in that order.''

He was as straight an arrow off duty as he was on. Peyer wasn't the kind of cop who spent his spare time in the police watering holes, shooting the bull and some pool. Oh, maybe he would stop in for a beer, but he reminded his friends that he was a family man. He was even a hero—however briefly—after his dramatic capture of a car thief. Peyer had joined a freeway chase and when the crook had jumped out of his car and run down the street, Peyer had run after him and made a flying tackle that had brought the bad guy down. His Hollywood-style heroics had made all the papers and TV news, too.

The other patrolmen may have thought of him as a by-the-book kind of guy, but they looked up to Peyer, because of his thirteen years on the force and his professionalism—

nobody ever saw a sloppy uniform on him or a messy car on his shift. He was very proud of that.

Monday afternoon, the day after the body was found, Officer Peyer and Devine, a young petite brunette, rode around in his CHP cruiser for two hours. The patrolman calmly and professionally explained how people could protect themselves from attack.

"Don't get into anyone else's car, because you're at their mercy," Peyer told the attentive reporter. "You could be raped if you're a woman—if you're a man, robbed—all the way down to where you could be killed. People are safe with law enforcement officers," the CHP officer assured Devine's viewers.

"But," Devine asked him, "how are people supposed to know for sure if it really is a cop who is stopping them?"

"Make sure they are in a black-and-white and have a badge on," Peyer told her simply. The world of law and order is as easy as black and white.

Rory Devine's interview with Officer Peyer and his reassuring advice to the motoring public ran on the evening news. The CHP brass was pleased with the image their spokesman projected. He was informative, authoritative, and sincere, a professional lawman through and through.

That night Sam Knott's tears over his daughter's death led the six o'clock news. The evening *San Diego Tribune* splashed the Cara Knott murder story across the front page. EIGHT HOURS OF HELL, screamed the banner headline that topped the story and Cara's portrait. The chilling news reached hundreds of thousands of people returning home from work.

6

She Could Have Been My Daughter

HOMICIDE Lieutenant Phil Jarvis arrived at work the Monday after the murder, his mind spinning with troubling possibilities.

"Is there a wacko loose on the streets?" Jarvis asked no one in particular as he assembled his homicide unit in the cramped conference room at police headquarters. His detectives were used to such outbursts from Jarvis because he was a cop who wanted real answers and wanted them yesterday. Usually he just fumed for a few minutes and then apologized and became the loudest cheerleader on the squad, patting everybody on the back for the great job they were doing.

But this time, Jarvis stayed angry. "We don't have squat on this Knott homicide," he kept saying over and over. The homicide cops shuffled in their chairs, accepting for the moment their boss's frustration. The detectives listened to Jarvis as he complained about what little they had to go on. There were some blood on the girl's boot, but whether it was hers or her killer's was still to be determined by the lab. Then they had that little bit of hair and some fibers from the bridge railing, making it look like she might have been pushed over its edge.

The preliminary coroner's report found Cara had been strangled before she was thrown from the bridge. This was somehow small comfort to the detectives to know she hadn't

47

felt the pain of that sixty-five-foot drop. The official cause of death was ligature strangulation. Whatever ligature the killer had used—a rope, a necktie, a scarf—it had kept slipping, because her wounds showed she must have been squirming to escape.

Jarvis had already called the detectives down in the sex crimes unit and asked them to review their recent cases to look for rapists who might have been released from prison recently, or rape suspects who were still on the loose. But the coroner's report said there was no sign of any sexual assault, and although they couldn't rule out rape as a possible motive, it looked like it might become another dead end.

The team of detectives went over the tire tracks they had found in the dirt path near the bridge the day before. The tracks were about thirteen feet from the bridge, near the spot from which Cara's body must have been dropped. The tire marks were about eight to ten feet long, with the left tire track slightly shorter than the right one, as if someone was tearing around in a hurry. The distance between the marks was fifty-three inches, indicating an unusually large or heavy car. The evidence technician had felt the dew in the tracks and could tell the marks were fresh, maybe even just a few hours old. There were so many acres of crime scene to scrutinize that the evidence technician didn't make casts of the tracks but moved on to hunt for other clues. He planned to go back to those tracks in the next few days.

Right under the bridge within a few feet of where Cara lay, detectives found three half-full cans of Budweiser beer, the beer still cold. The beer could mean that someone had been there the night of the murder. It could have even been the murderer or murderers themselves, but detectives thought it was more likely that the beer was left there by homeless people or Mexican farm workers camping out in the canyon—the kind of people who weren't the most reliable witnesses. And they had more important clues to chase than flat Budweiser beer.

It was a depressing list of evidence for the homicide crew to review that morning. Twenty-four of the first forty-eight crucial hours of a homicide investigation had passed, and the police lacked their most important element in solving a crime:

the motive. Veteran detective Paul Olsen understood why Jarvis was frustrated and angry. That was the way Jarvis operated, like a drill sergeant who inspired his crew to march through fire with him. Like his boss, Olsen also wanted to see the Knott case finished quickly. That day Olsen asked to delay his transfer out of homicide until the case was solved.

The fact that his friend Olsen was staying was about the only good thing about the case in the view of Detective Bill Nulton.

"Maybe," Nulton suggested, "the killer saw her at the gas station and followed her down the road." Nulton pointed out that the service station attendant had confirmed that the young woman had been there, and Cara's credit card slip proved that. The credit card slip had a complete computerized record of when she had stopped and exactly how much gas she'd pumped. It was one of the few solid clues they had.

Nulton's theory seemed plausible to the room full of police investigators. "Except," Nulton added, "nobody saw anyone go off after her from the gas station. She drove off alone."

Nulton and Olsen had just worked fourteen hours the day before on the case. They were more than tired. Investigating homicides was like fitting together a puzzle. The pieces fit into a logical order and created a nice, neat picture—at least at the end. But this Knott case had nothing that fit. At first, when he'd received the call Sunday morning that a young woman's body had been found near the remote stretch of freeway, Nulton had thought she might have been the latest victim of a serial killer.

Every cop on the force was painfully aware that for the last two years, San Diego County, one of America's vacation spots, had been haunted by an unknown killer or killers who stalked prostitutes and dumped them in remote areas. The speculation among the cops was that the killer might have moved to southern California from the Green River area in Washington state, where the rash of call-girl slayings had begun. By December 1986, the San Diego tally had reached thirty unsolved deaths. The bodies had all turned up in remote areas like Mercy Road. But absolutely nothing else about the Cara Knott case fit the profile of these other homicides. Cara was a college student who was in love with her one and only boyfriend. The other victims were prostitutes, transients, and drug abusers. So what did that mean? Nulton wondered. This girl was either killed by someone else—or the serial killer was tiring of seeking out hookers and was starting to attack any woman in his path. He shook the idea from his head and brought himself back to the facts at hand.

Nulton filled in the other homicide detectives on what he and Olsen had learned when they had visited the Knotts the night before. All the way out to the house they'd thought their killer was probably the boyfriend, Wayne Bautista. But after checking him out Nulton told the group that it seemed pretty solid that the kids were in love, and besides, the boy had been sick as a dog the night of the murder.

Then they'd started to get excited about another clue. At the murder scene the detectives had noticed some yellow paint on the fender of Cara's VW, indicating the possibility that the killer had driven a yellow car and scraped against Cara's beetle to force her down the dead end. Then, when Nulton had walked up the Knotts' driveway the night before he'd been surprised to see a yellow car with white paint scrapes on it. It was sister Cheryl's car. Everybody's a suspect, and nobody's a suspect. That's what Bill Nulton had been thinking as he'd walked through the door.

Sam Knott, his eyes reddened, had solemnly greeted the two officers and had managed a weak smile. "My wife's in the bedroom," he'd said, hoping that explanation would be enough to spare Joyce from police questioning at least one day.

"I understand," Nulton had said. The family had been gathered solemnly in the living room and Nulton had begun. "What about those paint chips on your daughter Cheryl's car?" The question had brought a smile to Sam's tired face. Cara bumped into Cheryl's car all the time in the driveway, he had explained. She never could seem to be able to back up the car straight. Another possible lead came to a dead end.

For the next hour, the officers had sat on the flowered couch and drunk coffee as they'd asked about Cara and her boyfriend. "Were there any peculiar habits that she had— anything out of the ordinary?" Nulton had asked Sam.

"No, not at all." He'd kept repeating that he was sure his daughter would never stop for a stranger. Of course, the detective had realized, the family could be lying. Nulton was changing his theories as quickly as if he were switching channels on a television set. By the end of the visit he had decided that somebody who knew Cara Knott had to be responsible. As Sam had walked the detectives to the door, Nulton had felt a sudden need to comfort the older man.

"Don't worry, you have the best homicide team in the city on this case," Nulton had assured him. "We'll find the guy."

Nulton and Olsen had been quiet as they'd left the house. "You know, they don't realize how close they were to the body," Nulton had said. "Cynthia and Bill drove down that ramp, and they were no more than thirty yards away."

The trip to the Knotts' house was going through Nulton's mind as he sat in the conference room and briefed the homicide squad about what the family had to say. This family was getting under his skin.

Jarvis dismissed his crew and they filed out the door. He reached into his pocket and pulled out a small photograph of Cara that Sam had given him. It was her high school portrait, and she was smiling with all the fearlessness of youth. Her blonde hair curled gently around her flawless face and her blue eyes were sparkling. Jarvis propped open the frame stand and put it on his desk. He stared at this smiling and happy face and wondered if it would ever give her family peace of mind if they found her killer.

At first Jarvis had followed procedure and assigned a single homicide team to the case, a veteran four-member unit headed by Sergeant Ted Armijo. Armijo had handled more than three hundred homicide cases in his twenty years on the force, more cases than anybody else in the department, including Jarvis. But because of the kind of attention the Knott case was receiving in the press and the kind of victim she was—the all-American girl—Jarvis took the unusual step of assigning two homicide units to track down the unknown killer. Such all-out assaults were usually reserved for cop killers. After Jarvis announced that he was assigning a second homicide team to the Knott murder, Armijo became upset.

"We could do it alone," Armijo told his boss. "We're the best team on the force."

"It's too high profile," Jarvis said. "I want everybody on this case. This one has to be solved. I don't want her to die in vain. That kid could have been my daughter."

No two personalities could be more different than these two cops. Phil Jarvis was a good old boy from San Diego, while Armijo was of Mexican descent from New Mexico, an outsider who had to fight his way up the ranks. Jarvis was outspoken, while his sergeant was quiet and determined. Jarvis was a big man with blonde hair and a blustery manner. In contrast, Armijo was a small man with ink black eyes that enveloped his face with a kind of sadness.

Armijo was a witness at the scene of one of America's worst mass murders in 1984. Unemployed forty-one-year-old security guard James Oliver Huberty had opened fire on a crowd of people at a McDonald's in San Ysidro, the small border community in San Diego. Huberty had told his wife he was heading out to "hunt humans." That he did—he slaughtered twenty-one people, nine of them children. A police sharpshooter's bullet had finally ended the killer's rampage.

Armijo took one case at a time. None was more important than the other. They all were important to him, whether it involved a striking, all-American girl from the suburbs or a migrant worker from a poor border town. Armijo thought that Jarvis might be taking this case too much to heart. He didn't like the idea of his boss keeping a photo of Cara Knott on his desk. Somehow that didn't seem very professional.

From the outset, Sam Knott made it clear to Nulton, Olsen, and the rest of the officers that he didn't want to interfere in their investigation. "You guys are doing your job," Knott said. "I'm confident you'll get the monster who killed my daughter." Sam had his own job to do. While the cops were trying to find his daughter's killer, he wanted to make sure nobody else experienced the same jarring nightmare of having to search alone for a missing child without the assistance of law enforcement.

Sam called his family together after the TV crews left and

the household chaos settled a bit. "There is no reason in the world someone should have to go through something like this," Sam said. "There's got to be a way for police to kick off a search when someone is missing before twenty-four hours are up. They should look for an abandoned car, a lost car, but not one with a person in it."

Cheryl, near tears, sat on the living room couch and said, "If only I had called sooner, or if I had been more emotional, maybe they would have listened to me."

"When you make a call, you don't yell and scream and rant and rave, it's a mercy call," Sam assured his daughter. "You know, there are these myths and perceptions—you think you're doing the right thing. We think, well, you call the police, and that's it—not that you're dealing with a bunch of different bureaucracies."

"There would have been a better response," Cheryl said, "if they called the fire department and reported a false alarm."

Fortified by the news coverage that showed his daughter's death had become the talk of the town, Sam started making rounds of calls asking to see the city leaders. He called Mayor Maureen O'Connor, Police Chief Bill Kolender, and City Manager John Lockwood.

Sam drove to a meeting with Kolender right after the murder, armed with a list of problems he wanted solved. Kolender smiled and brought Sam and Cheryl into his giant conference room on the seventh floor at police headquarters looking out on the city.

"I can't tell you how sorry I am," Kolender said. "We are doing everything we can to apprehend whoever did this to your daughter, and I can guarantee you we'll catch him. We have the best people on it."

Sam looked into the police chief's eyes, bracing himself for Kolender to react defensively. Sam just plowed ahead, there was no turning back. Victims are lost out there because police don't act fast enough, Sam said. Here he'd been searching for his daughter, a good kid, and they'd been just turned away by every police officer. It doesn't look like there was much they could have done, but what about the chance that they could have stopped the killer?

"We didn't know what agency to call at times," Sam said. "You'd think it was San Diego Police or the sheriff's [office], or there was some communication between the two. No, these dispatchers—some of whom were very rude—just told us to call other departments."

"What if it wasn't too late to find her?" Cheryl piped in.

Kolender said he understood, but he defended the 911 emergency system. It was linked to all the county law enforcement professionals. It wasn't perfect, but it worked as well as it could.

"Okay, to trash nine-one-one isn't fair—but it's a violation of trust," Knott said. He felt that the citizenry had been taught they could always count on the police to "protect and serve." Therefore, the procedures should be expanded to fit everyone's needs. Otherwise, the system fails.

"I know what you're feeling," Kolender told them. He said his wife had lost her son, who was slain following a party. "There is no worse feeling in the world. You have my word that we're going to change these policies, one way or another."

Buoyed by their meeting with the police chief, Sam and Cheryl made their rounds through the various offices, telling everyone who would listen what they thought was wrong with the system. It was a fulfillment of those early lessons Sam had given his kids: just because it was printed in a book doesn't make it so. And now the Knotts were out to prove that just because it was policy didn't make it functional. They went about their crusade in as businesslike a manner as they could muster, and the civic leaders didn't know what to make of them. Most families of murder victims were wrapped in their own sorrow and didn't want to be disturbed any further.

Sam had met with everyone he could think of, so he thought. Two weeks later, when he was driving home from work, listening to his favorite classical music station on the radio, a news reporter cut in and Sam found himself hearing the coroner's report detailing the torture suffered by his daughter. Nobody had told him Cara's skull had been fractured. That her ribs had been snapped and her face smashed in. He had no idea how badly she had been hurt. Sam burst into tears behind the wheel and quickly pulled over to the shoulder of the road to regain his composure.

When he got home he didn't dwell on the cold facts of an autopsy but immediately wrote to the chairman of the county supervisors, asking for a meeting. He pleaded with the county leaders to be more considerate when they released documents like autopsy reports. "Let a family know before you tell the press, that's all we are asking. The point is: let's not victimize the family again," Sam wrote.

Chief Kolender, meanwhile, had taken Sam Knott's words to heart and had Lieutenant Jarvis meet with the missing person unit. The homicide chief railed into them for their lack of courtesy in dealing with an anguished family like the Knotts.

"When you get a call from a guy like Sam Knott who's lost a daughter who's a good, decent girl, you don't walk away. I know you can't look [out] for everybody and immediately drop what you're doing. But goddamn it, we don't have to be rude about it!" Jarvis shouted.

Everybody listened when the lieutenant barked. They didn't know it was said more in frustration than in anger. There was a killer out there and none of them was sure he was going to be found.

7

Highway Games

KATHY Deir was driving home to San Diego along a deserted and undeveloped stretch of I-15, when she noticed a police car following her. She tensed and automatically let up on the accelerator, but the cruiser stayed behind her little white Ford Escort for a couple of miles, and finally the cop flashed his red lights to pull her over. It was cold and dark, about eight o'clock on a Thursday night, two weeks before Christmas 1986. The officer got on his loudspeaker and ordered her to drive off the freeway down the next exit, Mercy Road.

At least she didn't have to back up on the freeway to reach the Mercy exit, like the cop had made some of the other women do. But Kathy had no way of knowing that.

The officer led her down the ramp to a place so eerily dark that she had trouble making anything out. When her eyes adjusted, she saw that there was virtually nothing to see—no lights, no houses, nothing but some construction-site leftovers and scattered sagebrush. The cop approached her and Kathy, a slender twenty-nine-year-old real estate professional, cautiously rolled down her window a little.

"What's the problem, officer?"

"Your headlights are out of alignment," he told her.

Headlights? She thought, You brought me down here for my stupid headlights? She knew better than to tell the officer what she was thinking and instead she told him, "Yeah, I

56

know. I put them in myself and I knew that one was a little too low.''

The cop looked about thirty-five years old, medium height, on the husky side. He had a badge on his chest that looked like the real thing, and he seemed friendly.

''Can you step out, please?'' he asked politely. ''I'll show you how to fix the lights.''

She obeyed and walked around the front of the Escort as he opened the hood. ''Where are you from?'' he inquired, poking his head near the engine block.

''Tucson,'' she replied.

''Yeah? I was stationed there, at Davis-Mothan Air Force Base.'' They chatted about Arizona for a while, then the talk turned to southern California's infamous, frenzied freeway system. The officer told her that the area they stood on now beside the mammoth new freeway had once been the two-lane highway that stretched from the U.S.-Mexico border just below San Diego all the way to the east side of the Sierra Nevada mountain range and through the desert up to Nevada. Kathy nodded, trying to look impressed.

The cop offered to show her where the old 395 highway passed. It was right near where they were. Kathy looked at him; he seemed like a nice enough guy. In some ways, he seemed like the policemen back home. She knew a lot of them because she volunteered for the local crime victims' programs.

''Sure,'' she said.

They got in his patrol car, and he drove her around some barricades and then onto a dirt road that appeared to have no end. ''We kept going straight all the way down, down, down, down, down, down,'' she said later.

The cop drove her over to the bridge, which was just a two-lane span with plain concrete ledges. By now, she felt they were miles from the current I-15 freeway, and she could barely hear the hum of traffic behind. They were on the old highway bridge, he told her, but the area was so dark Kathy couldn't even tell it was a bridge. They sat for half a minute and she felt a need to say something to break the silence.

''Can you check my new driver's license number in the computer?'' Kathy asked him. ''The numbers are odd, and people have been giving me a rough time when I try to use the license as identification in cashing checks." The patrolman picked up his radio microphone and called in Kathy's license, eager to be helpful.

"You're right," he told her. "You don't exist. It's not in there."

An hour and a half had slipped by. It was pushing ten o'clock. "I have to get going," she told him. To her he seemed like he was in no hurry, but he drove Kathy back to her car. He hadn't asked her, like he had the other blonde he pulled down to Mercy Road a while back, if she had called her boyfriend to let him know what time to expect her home.

The two-way police radio was on, unlike the time he switched it off to talk with another woman down there in the dark. But nothing seemed amiss to Kathy when she climbed back into her Escort, started the engine, steered toward the lights of the freeway, and headed home.

The officer had said nothing out of line to her, not like he had to the girl he had pulled down there and remarked, as he wrote her a moving violation ticket, "You have beautiful eyes." Or the woman he had discussed real estate with down there at the Mercy Road off ramp, and whom he had told that his girlfriend lived nearby.

Nobody knew about them, or about the girl he had pulled down to Mercy Road and lectured about the importance of good brakes, showing her what he meant by jumping into the front seat and yanking her parking brake up and down, up and down.

On the same south side of I-15, two weeks after Kathy got her fix-it ticket, Shelly Sacks was driving home south on I-15 in her sporty red Honda CRX. It was a Friday night, December 26, and Shelly was just cruising along listening to her car stereo when she heard a voice behind her boom from a loudspeaker. "Red Honda, pull over!" The command came so loudly and suddenly it gave her a jolt, but she automatically pulled over to the freeway shoulder and slowed to a stop. But the voice coming out of the black-and-white police car behind her kept calling, "Keep going, keep going, keep going."

Shelly thought pulling off the freeway was odd, but she figured, He's a cop; he knows what he's doing.

The cop guided her off the freeway down an off ramp she had never taken before, Mercy Road. She stopped the car and sat looking at the total darkness around her. She turned down her radio as the cop sauntered over, shining a big black flashlight in her face. He was smiling.

"Your headlight is out," the cop proclaimed.

"Oh," she replied. What was there to say? "I just wanted to get it over with and get out of there," she said later.

"You know your headlight has a crack in it. I think you should get out and take a look at it," the cop advised.

Just last week, he had stopped a blonde in a white Volkswagen for having bouncing headlights. Then there'd been that other woman, the one he'd stopped because she had flickering taillights on her little car. All Shelly knew, however, was that the man standing over her was a beefy guy, medium height, dark hair slicked down, with kind of a cute little cleft in his chin. He seemed genuine, so she got out of her car as she was told and walked around to look at her headlights, not something she did often. But, she figured, a patrolman asked her to, right?

The cop started walking back to his cruiser and said pleasantly, "Why don't you come back to my car while I write out the citation for you? It's just a warning."

"Your car?" she asked skeptically.

"Yeah, I have heat in my car," he said.

Shelly started thinking, Well I have heat in my car, too, buddy. But she kept quiet and got inside the patrol car, beside the shotgun bolted to the floor near the passenger's seat and all the radios squawking.

Something about the scene bothered her so she left the car door open. The patrolman said nothing about it.

"What do you do for a living?" the cop asked. He then started taking down all her vital statistics, age, weight, address. She told him she was an announcer for an FM disco-funk music radio station, and they chatted about that for a while. At least her profession allowed more innocuous conversation than the department store security guard the cop had brought down to the dead end over the Thanksgiving holiday. He had asked that young woman if she watched the dressing rooms while people took off their clothes.

Even though Shelly knew none of this, her intuition was sounding alarm bells. She did not like those little side glances the cop kept giving her. It occurred to her that nobody could see them parked under the freeway underpass.

"How was your Christmas?" he asked her.

"Oh my Christmas was really bad. I broke up with my boyfriend," she blurted out. Inside her head she was yelling at herself, Why are you telling him this? But she kept the conversation going. "So it was kind of lonely. It was a lonely Christmas," she told him.

The officer smiled at her and said, "I find that hard to believe."

She was silent, not knowing how to respond. She leaned over as casually as she could to check out his name tag and badge. Badge 8611, she saw. If this little episode got any more bizarre, she thought, she might want to write his name down on something, she wasn't sure what. Something, anyway. Shelly really wanted to get back on the road and put an end to this. Changing the subject seemed like a really good idea.

"Um, do you know if Highway 163 hooks up with Friars Road?" she asked abruptly.

He told her it did, explaining that if she just stayed on I-15 south a few more miles it would merge into Highway 163 and then to the road she wanted. The cop handed her a pink ticket and watched as she got into her Honda. In the darkness he could not see it, but as she put her hands on the steering wheel and drove off, Shelly was shaking.

8

Dead Ends

BONITA is a bucolic section of the county with horse ranches and orange groves southeast of San Diego, an oasis amid a larger area of tract houses, mobile home parks, and industrial sprawl. *Bonita* is Spanish for beautiful, and indeed, this pastoral land has not changed much since the old west pioneers like Kit Carson and Wyatt Earp came to make their fortunes a century ago.

Cara Knott was buried on a grassy hill there early on New Year's eve following a memorial in her honor at the Little Chapel of the Roses in Glen Abbey Memorial Park cemetery in Bonita. Three hundred and fifty people showed up for the funeral of a twenty-year-old woman. In death, Cara Knott became the number one topic in town. Even the homeless people living on the streets of San Diego knew who she was.

Joyce Knott looked out at the crowd and wanted to cry. All of these people loved Cara, so many of them. Then she gasped, and Sam froze when he followed her gaze to the door. Trudging into the chapel were television camera crews carrying enormous black tripods and cameras the size of desks, the crew dressed like ragamuffins.

"Tell them to get out of here," Joyce whispered to Sam through her teeth. Sam agreed with her and ushered the TV crews outside. Up until now, Joyce had kept her distance from the media and the police, but she took a stand now. She refused to let the sanctity of Cara's funeral be invaded.

Her daughters, Cheryl and Cynthia, and her son-in-law, Bill, had organized the funeral, with the help of their uncle Phil Smith and Aunt Jean Faro. They hung Cara's paintings of sea otters in the chapel, along with photographs of Cara with her family and friends, Cara dressed up as a beach bum for Halloween, Cara dressed for the prom, Cara in her blue bridesmaid's dress at Cynthia's wedding last month. It made Sam want to cry every time he looked at the photo, she looked so vibrant and beautiful.

Two of Cara's friends played guitars and sang, "Blowin' in the Wind." Her boyfriend, Wayne Bautista, spoke in a voice thick with emotion, his face ashen with grief. "All of you knew that she was sunshine. To me, Cara was my inspiration and my joy. She should be an inspiration to you."

Her brother and sisters stood before the mourners and wrapped their arms around one another, too deep in grief to feel embarrassed at such emotional displays. They each spoke in turn.

"No matter how busy she was," Cheryl said, "she always had time for everyone. She was my little sister, and she was my friend."

Cheryl was running on pure adrenaline, looking out at the sea of faces without recognition. She tried not to think about the dread she felt walking into Cara's room the day before to perform the terrible chore of picking an outfit for her sister to be buried in. She and her mom had picked out a fuchsia sundress that was Cara's favorite, but Aunt Jean had said gently, "It's so pretty, but we really need something that's going to cover her neck."

Cara's neck. Cynthia tried not to think about it, about the rope burns gashing her sister's skin. She concentrated on what Bill was saying beside her and the arms of the family holding her up at the altar of the chapel.

Bill was speaking proudly of Cara and his voice resounded in the chapel. "Cara was so many things: she was an idealist, an eternal optimist. She was able to find good in every situation. She was always fighting for that underdog. She was a fantastic motivator—an independent thinker. She had many causes, she was a doer and not a talker. She was the best."

The sisters taped bouquets of pink and white balloons over

Cara's grave, which sat on a grassy hill next to the grave of her grandfather, Dr. John Knott, beside an oak tree.

Wayne's father, Jaime Bautista, cried throughout the ceremony. Long after the services ended, he stood alone near the graveside, his hands folded in prayer, and head bowed. The funeral had been pretty routine until the very end for the police detectives who had come looking for clues. They lingered behind, watching Mr. Bautista closely. The police were more than curious. They knew he was the last person to speak to Cara on the phone before she left Wayne's house. And now this unusual display of emotion. They had to think of almost everybody as a suspect, but that still wasn't a large group.

The detectives knew that the previous summer Cara had worked for Jaime Bautista at his health food store in Alpine. The two had become very close, family members had told the investigators. Bautista reportedly loved Cara's sparkling personality and couldn't wait for her to be his daughter-in-law.

The police were pulling together a file on Bautista, and some of the mid-level officers were convinced that he was their man. Jarvis strongly suspected the murderer was someone close to Cara, and Jaime Bautista could not be ignored.

They became increasingly suspicious about Bautista when a district attorney's investigator reported seeing a gold Cadillac in an area not far from Mercy Road the night of the murder. The passenger was a blonde-haired woman who appeared bent over the front seat. Bautista drove a gold Cadillac.

Bautista's neighbors interviewed by police said he had an eye for women and seemed unusually depressed over the death of Cara Knott. Soon after the funeral, detectives Paul Olsen and Bill Nulton talked to Wayne Bautista about his father.

"Oh yes, he loved Cara, he really did," Wayne said.

But he wouldn't hurt her, would he? the detectives wanted to know. "He's not a violent man, he has problems like everybody else, but he's not a violent man," Wayne told the detectives. Still, Olsen and Nulton weren't sure what to make of Jaime Bautista.

The investigation was stalling so the detectives had no

choice but to keep retracing Cara's steps. On one of their numerous visits back through the crime scene, they'd seen Jaime Bautista walking alone on the edge of the busy parkway nearby, seemingly lost in thought.

The cops had pulled over alongside Bautista, and Nulton had yelled out the window, "Hey, Jaime, where are you going? Do you need a ride?"

"Oh, that's all right. I'm just kind of out of it. I'll be all right," Bautista had said.

The encounter only heightened the detectives' growing suspicion about the boyfriend's father. A few days later, detectives received what they considered a disturbing call. "You better come up here, and talk to Jaime," a neighbor told police. "He says he wants to talk to you. He's got a lot on his mind."

"Well, this is it," Sergeant Armijo told Olsen and Nulton. "You better go get him, and bring him down." Bautista came into the station and talked with Armijo for more than an hour. The sergeant got right to the point.

"You did it, you killed Cara, didn't you?" Armijo said.

Bautista bowed his head and wept for a moment and then he shouted, "You've got to be kidding!"

"No, we're dead serious," Armijo told him.

Bautista got up from his chair and started pacing the room. He gasped for air. Olsen, Nulton, and the other cops looked at each other. They grilled him for a while, but Jaime Bautista kept insisting that he was innocent. He said he didn't kill Cara Knott. The police, still not completely convinced, had nothing to hold him on. They let him go.

The clincher came within a few days. Phone records verified his alibi. He had been talking to his son on the telephone when Cara left. He lived twenty miles away, which put him more than a half hour away from the murder scene. There was no way he could have made it, unless he could fly. Jaime Bautista was officially cleared as a suspect.

With the family, the boyfriend, and now the boyfriend's father ruled out as suspects, the detectives turned their attention to reports of a mysterious hitchhiker who had been seen waving money and lunging at cars near the freeway on ramp that Cara Knott would have passed to get on the road home.

At least six people reported having seen the bizarre hitch-hiker. Eventually police found a bus driver who told them he had driven a strange guy in his fifties to the freeway ramp.

"The guy wanted to go to San Diego, but he just didn't have the money," the bus driver told police. "I told him he had to get off at Via Rancho Parkway and try to find a ride. I didn't like doing it, but we just couldn't take him any further."

Other witnesses said the guy had been trying to flag down a ride about eight o'clock that night at the entrance to Interstate 15. Cara Knott might have passed him to get on the freeway that night. The hitchhiker could have been a suspect as well as the numerous transients who frequented the area and routinely camped near the Mercy Road off ramp. They, too, could have done it. The question was why?

Armijo was frustrated. Not only didn't he have a killer, but also an important piece of evidence was missing—Cara Knott's white leather jacket, the Christmas present her boyfriend said she carried with her to the car when she left his house. The police needed to see the jacket to track it down. The sergeant and his officers, guns strapped to their shoulders, must have looked a bit unusual strolling through Nordstrom's, San Diego's fanciest department store, looking for the same style leather jacket Cara had worn the night she was killed.

On New Year's eve, many hours after Cara Knott's funeral, Armijo and some of the other detectives left work late. They tried to celebrate the end of the year, even though they didn't have much good news to cheer them. Armijo bought a round of drinks for everybody.

"Let's hope nineteen eighty-seven is a great one," Armijo said. "We have plenty of work to do, that's for sure."

"I can't believe this case," Olsen said, sipping a beer.

"We're going to get a break anytime soon," Armijo said, sounding like he was having a tough time convincing himself. The cops couldn't help talking about the case even while trying to enjoy some holiday cheer. They rehashed the statements made by several witnesses who said they had spotted transients living in a car near Poway Road, not far from the murder scene. Armijo thought one of those people could be a suspect.

At about five minutes to midnight all the cops' pagers started beeping like a chorus of slot machines hitting the jackpot. Armijo ran to the phone.

"Ted," Lieutenant Jarvis told him when he called in, "those guys you were after; we've got them."

Armijo practically floated back to the table. "Hey, it looks like we got us some suspects in custody. Happy New Year!"

They all rushed back to headquarters and spent the next few hours questioning the suspects and reviewing reports. But the new year had barely dawned when the detectives realized they were saddled with the same old frustrations.

"These guys don't know anything about it. There's nothing there on them," Armijo said. "Back to square one."

As the days wore on, Nulton and Olsen were meeting nearly every night at a Lakeside diner to drink coffee and pore over the case. One night, the two drove down Mercy Road and stood at the dead end, listening to the roar of the traffic on the nearby freeway. Nulton and Olsen walked closer to the bridge.

"I can't believe how dark it is here. It's eerie," Nulton said. "How did she and the car get up here? How the heck did she get off the freeway and why?"

Olsen listened in silence. The detectives kept walking around for several minutes, just soaking in the darkness, and then climbed back into their car. There was a lot more work to do. They were both hoping that the public would begin coming forward with helpful information since a reward had been offered.

One of the San Diego Police Department's major public information-gathering tools was "Crimestoppers," a televised reenactment of the crime and plea for witnesses to come forward. The usual reward was upped to twenty thousand dollars.

Detective Grant Raybould tried to make sure he was there during the filming of "Crimestoppers" in case the reenactment of the crime reminded him of something he had overlooked. But the reenactments always gave him the jitters. This time was no different as he watched the film crew take over the grassy area near the dry creek bed where Cara Knott was killed only a few days before.

The cameras focused on a young actress who resembled Cara Knott and wore her blond hair pulled back into a ponytail, as Cara had that night. The actress wore the white leather jacket the police had just bought and drove a white Volkswagen. The camera followed the VW as it slowly made its way down the Mercy Road off ramp from I-15. Raybould hung around for several hours as the filming took place, hoping to find something, any more clues to the killing.

A voice shook him out of his reverie. "Hey, what's going on?" he heard behind him. Raybould turned around and saw a California highway patrolman walking toward him.

"Hi, my name's Craig Peyer. I'm with the highway patrol," the husky officer said amiably, extending his hand. "This is my beat. I guess this is about that killing."

"Yeah, we'll be here all day," Raybould said.

Are you making any headway in the investigation? Peyer wanted to know.

"Oh, we're doing all right. We've got a lot of tips." Raybould didn't feel like talking.

Peyer was eager to know more about what the police knew. He pumped Raybould for as many details as the detective would give him. Did Raybould have any suspicions of his own? the highway patrolman asked. Raybould was annoyed by the questioning, especially when he had no answers to give. The police had virtually nothing on the homicide, and Raybould had too much pride to concede that to another branch of law enforcement.

The highway patrolman talked about the terrain as if he was pretty familiar with the area there. He pointed out that it was pretty quiet but a lot of people who seemed to be homeless or transients camped out. He himself hadn't been in the area that night, Peyer told the detective.

"Well, we've got some work to do. I'll see you around," Raybould said, walking away.

The highway patrolman wished the homicide detective good luck, and went off.

9

The Hat in the Trunk

CARA Knott's death bothered California Highway Patrol Sergeant John McDonald.

The day after Cara's body was found, McDonald made special note of the homicide as he gave his routine briefing to the afternoon squad at CHP headquarters on Pacific Highway near the waterfront. He asked all the CHP officers who had seen anything at all suspicious the night before to report it, and to watch for unusual activity in the area. As he spoke in front of the room full of officers in khaki and black leather boots, something clicked in McDonald's memory.

He remembered another holiday time when the highway patrol was just as busy as it was now. It must have been about Thanksgiving. An angry mother called about one of his patrolmen and mentioned something about Mercy Road. Back then it seemed like no big deal. She had complained about Patrolman Craig Peyer, and McDonald knew Peyer was a top-notch highway patrolman.

The woman had been upset that her twenty-three-year-old daughter had been flagged down by a CHP officer and taken off the I-15 freeway to a dark, deserted, remote road. McDonald had listened and politely pointed out to the woman that, by the officer's actions, her daughter had been escorted to an area safely away from high-speed freeway traffic.

When McDonald had mentioned the call to Peyer soon afterward, he had commended his patrolman. "Excellent tactics'' was the phrase he had used. McDonald thought he had straightened everything out. Now a month later, the sergeant wondered; was it just coincidence that the other girl had been taken down to Mercy Road?

The veteran sergeant quietly pulled Peyer's daily logs and activity reports to check on his star patrolman's whereabouts the night the young woman was slain. It seemed to McDonald, as always, that Peyer acted by the book. Peyer's movements were all accounted for. He was either writing tickets, helping a disabled vehicle, or clearing the I-15 of boxes, which every good highway patrolman knows are potentially dangerous road hazards.

McDonald also found an injury report Peyer filed over the same weekend. Abrasions on his face, right arm, trauma to his left shoulder and right foot. According to the report, Peyer blamed himself for his injuries. He said he had slipped on some spilled fuel outside the CHP gas pumps in the back lot.

Next the sergeant pulled the thirteen tickets Peyer had written that night. Something caught his eye.

A few miles from the CHP offices, San Diego police detectives Nulton and Olsen found their wishes coming true. The public was responding to the police department's plea for help. Hundreds of calls were tying up special hot lines that San Diego police had devoted to information about the Cara Knott slaying.

For a week, on a detective's desk sat a phone tip about a young woman who had reported having a weird encounter near Mercy Road a while back when she had been stopped by a highway patrolman. And now another tip came in to another detective from a second young woman who had had a similar bad experience in the same remote area where Knott's body had been found.

When he heard about the latest tip, something clicked in Jarvis's memory. Wasn't there another tip like this? He asked Sergeant Armijo if he'd learned anything from the highway patrol about the first woman's complaint. The sergeant told his boss he hadn't had the chance to check on it. The tip was buried under numerous other leads that Armijo pushed his detectives to pursue that looked more important, like the people camping in a car near Mercy Road and the possibility that the father of Cara's boyfriend might be a suspect.

"Ted, we've got to get on this," Jarvis pressed. "We've got to call the Highway Patrol if you didn't do it already."

That morning, Armijo quickly arranged a meeting with CHP officials over coffee and scrambled eggs at Bob's Big Boy, a restaurant in Kearny Mesa. Armijo didn't want to go anyplace that was a hangout for either highway patrolmen or cops. This place seemed to be good, neutral territory and Armijo tried to get the awkward business about the CHP patrolman out of the way quickly.

"This officer's name came up, and we'd like to talk to you. Okay, it's probably nothing," Armijo told his fellow lawmen. "It's just routine that we are going to look into this officer."

Noticing the apprehensive looks of the highway patrol officers, another San Diego detective assured them, "This isn't a witch-hunt." The CHP officers agreed to check it out and the meeting broke up quickly, their breakfasts barely touched.

Four hours later, Armijo picked up his phone and heard very excited Highway Patrol Sergeant Joe Ortiz on the other end.

"Ted, I have to meet you now," Ortiz said. "It's about the patrolman, Craig Peyer."

"Could we possibly make it tomorrow morning?" Armijo said, looking at a stack of paperwork and unanswered phone messages on his desk.

"No, it's got to be now," the CHP sergeant insisted. "I need to meet with you right now. It's important."

"What's the problem?" Armijo asked.

"The problem is this," the sergeant said, his voice tight. *"Peyer had scratches on his face that night."*

Armijo was too experienced an investigator to jump to any conclusions. "Those scratches could have come from anything. The guy could have cut himself shaving," he pointed out.

Two hours later, the California Highway Patrol top brass were huddled at San Diego Police headquarters. The CHP officials briefed the police about the scratches on Peyer's face, and his story that he got them falling on a fence. They also reviewed the thirteen tickets the patrolman issued the night of Cara Knott's slaying, and found that the thirteenth appeared to have been tampered with—the time of issuance was crossed out and back timed an hour. That meant, the highway patrol officials said, they could not account for about ninety minutes of Peyer's time on the road.

Jarvis told them that the tire tracks police discovered at the Mercy Road site were left by a heavy car with extrawide wheel base like the ones highway patrol officers drive. But he also assured them that the investigation was not over, not by a long shot. What they had against Peyer was purely circumstantial.

"We're not sure he's the guy. But we're going to take an in-depth look at Peyer," Jarvis told the solemn CHP officials.

They agreed that they had to find a way to check Peyer's car. The officers were concerned, however, that they might tip their hands about the investigation if they abruptly pulled Peyer's car out of service. The CHP officials had an idea. They would tell Peyer that since he always kept his car looking so professional and spotless, they would use the unit for a highway patrol public relations video.

The ploy worked.

Shortly before midnight on January 7, agents of the California Highway Patrol and the police department gathered in a garage in CHP southern division headquarters and took apart Craig Peyer's state-issue Dodge Diplomat.

Working in the early morning hours under giant spotlights that highlighted everything including lint, these cops, all wearing gloves, might have looked like professional thieves. Investigators drowned the police car seats with a special dye, Luminol, that would illuminate any bloodstains inside the patrol car. They snapped off the lights to make sure they didn't miss even the faintest blue glow that would show when the dye picked up blood. The car remained pitch-black. No glow. The dye had picked up no blood residue.

They searched the glove compartment. Nothing again. They opened the trunk. The flares were there, the first aid kit, the jumper cables, the rope to snare animals, the other leg-restraint rope to tie up human suspects who resisted arrest. Everything looked neat and tidy. Until they lifted up the spare tire. Stuffed underneath was a small length of yellow braided plastic rope.

Armijo called over to CHP Captain Lee Denno and pointed to the dirty piece of rope, "Hey, Denno, what do you make of this?"

The highway patrol captain shook his head. The rope was definitely not standard CHP issue. There was silence in the garage. Investigators all remembered the autopsy photos of Cara Knott's neck and the gashes that looked like they could have easily been made by a rope.

"We're going to have to talk to this guy," Armijo said.

Over at CHP headquarters, Craig Peyer was getting fidgety. He told his wife he was doing some desk duty, and he didn't like it very much. He didn't tell her how much he hated being out of his car. He didn't mention that this latest assignment to do the motorcycle feasibility report was also puzzling, since he had just completed the same kind of report only a few months ago.

Some of his friends stuck their heads into the office to see what was going on. "Hey, I hear your car is over at division headquarters," someone said.

"That can't be," Peyer replied. "It's supposed to be used for a PR taping."

"I hear it has something to do with the Knott homicide," another CHP officer told him.

"No way. I don't know anything about it," Peyer said. "I guess I'll go talk to Captain Denno."

Peyer insisted to Denno that something was wrong. He didn't like this feeling he was getting. And he wanted to keep track of his car; he was, after all, one of the few lucky officers who had a car permanently assigned to him. The captain reassured him that he should not worry about his car.

"What about my cap? It's in the trunk," Peyer asked the captain. Someone over at division headquarters might swipe the uniform hat, he said, and losing a hat would look bad on his spotless work record.

"Don't worry about it," Denno said.

Peyer was still suspicious. "What is going on here?" he asked his boss point-blank.

"There's nothing to worry about. It's routine."

"Look, captain, with all due respect, people have been telling me some stories."

"What kind of stories?"

"Well, I've been hearing through the grapevine that they're up at headquarters looking at the car, about this Knott slaying. That's wild stuff. C'mon," he said pleadingly.

"Okay, Craig, they just want to ask you a few questions. You know, it happened on your beat, and all that." Peyer's eyes popped open and he nearly jumped out of his chair. "I wouldn't worry about it. They just want to clear some things up. So will you go to police headquarters and talk to them?" The patrolman regained his composure.

"Sure," he told his captain. "No problem. I'll cooperate in any way."

By afternoon Peyer was called upon to fulfill that promise. He and Denno drove from the CHP office to San Diego Police headquarters downtown at Fourteenth and Broadway. It was shortly after four o'clock, January 8, twelve days after the murder.

Peyer was ready to meet with them, but the homicide detectives weren't sure they wanted to meet with him—nor were they ready. But the word was out that the police were looking at Peyer as a possible suspect, and it was impossible to keep a secret in the tight-knit world of law enforcement professionals. Peyer might change his mind, or worse, the press might get hold of the story before they knew what they had.

Jarvis hastily threw together a new interview team to perform the delicate art of extracting the truth from their new murder suspect. Detective Paul Olsen was usually teamed with Nulton, but since they had such similar low-key interviewing styles, Jarvis asked the veteran Grant Raybould to step in, because he wanted an experienced and aggressive interrogator on this sensitive meeting. The homicide chief knew it might be hard on the detectives to figure out how best to work together, but they were under the gun.

Grant Raybould had interviewed at least one thousand suspects during his twenty years on the force. He was a different sort of cop. He wasn't one of those who yearned to investigate murders because he thought there wasn't enough action in the other departments. He preferred the robbery detail, what he called real cops and robbers stuff. At forty-two, Raybould was thin, almost fragile, with gray hair that made him seem far older. His clear blue eyes gave him the gentle demeanor of an academician. Denno introduced Peyer to Olsen and Raybould, who took him to be photographed for his mug shot, side view, front view. Peyer was calm throughout.

Raybould led him into the homicide unit's tiny interview room, and Olsen took the good-cop role and tried to put the patrolman at ease. "Do you want any coffee?" Olsen asked.

"Sure," Peyer said, looking around the bare room. He sat across from them at a long table. Raybould grabbed a yellow legal pad and placed a tape recorder on the table.

"Tell us about yourself, Craig," Olsen said amiably.

Peyer gave his life story, speaking in a confident, flat midwestern drawl, starting with his birth in Minnesota thirty-six years before. He told them that his parents moved to southern California when he was a year old, and that his dad worked for various defense contractors. He told about his Vietnam War experience, his determination to make something of himself, and his work for the CHP for the past thirteen years.

"I've been a damn good officer, a good one," Peyer boasted as he fidgeted in his chair. He looked directly at Raybould.

"Let's get to the point, Craig," said Raybould.

The Cara Knott slaying had generated plenty of phone calls, the officers told Peyer.

"I'm glad of that," the patrolman replied.

Raybould ignored him. "There have been a lot of calls from young attractive women, some of them who drive Volkswagens. They were all stopped by you. There were some pretty long conversations, Craig," the detective said. "There was one that lasted more than an hour. And what you talked about—well, it wasn't exactly just about the motor vehicle code."

"Why did you bring those young honeys down there?" Olsen cut in. "It seems like you were after something."

Raybould kept up the pressure. "I don't know what your home life is like, if there are problems with your wife or you're getting a divorce, but you're leading to something, Craig. There's a pattern here.''

Peyer protested. Yes, he talked to women at night at the freeway off ramp, but he brought men down there too. He did it for their safety. There were no lights on I-15 and it was too dangerous just standing on the freeway shoulder like a sitting duck. Never once did he stop a woman all the way down by the road where Cara Knott's car was found.

"I'm a bullshitter," he said. "I never turned off my lights during those contacts and they all took place on the ramp.''

"What about Cheryl Johnson?" Raybould asked, referring to one of the motorists Peyer had stopped on his beat and pulled down to Mercy Road. "Do you remember her? She's a nurse who claims she was questioned by you for 1½ hours. That's a pretty long time.''

"No way," Peyer said. "Forty-five minutes tops.''

"There's something else she said. She said you stopped her for speeding, but wrote her a citation for a bald tire, which wasn't true. There was no bald tire. Why'd you do that?''

"I've got this personal policy," Peyer explained. "I try to cut public servants a break. I don't give tickets to doctors, nurses, cops, or firemen. If that's wrong, well, I can live with that.'' Raybould was tired of playing the nice guy. He wanted to shake this patrolman up a little. They weren't getting anywhere.

"What about those scratches, Craig?" he asked.

Peyer told them what he had told the CHP, that he'd slipped on spilled gasoline outside the gas pumps at patrol headquarters and fallen into a chain link fence. The talk went around and around for hours, ending nowhere but at the end of Grant Raybould's patience. He took a stab.

"Maybe there are some victims who seem to deserve to die," the detective said bluntly, looking straight at Peyer, cop to cop. "Maybe some of them were involved with guns or drugs. But not this girl.''

Peyer sat absolutely still. Raybould hoped he had hit a nerve. Peyer had already said how he kept up on the news about Cara Knott's background.

"There was no dirt on this girl," Raybould said, leaning

across the table only a few inches from Peyer's face. "She was a good college kid. We found nothing in her past, nothing. She was not a floozy; she was not a prostitute. She wasn't on drugs. She was one of the cleanest we've ever seen. And now she's . . . dead.''

Olsen interrupted. "Cara Knott was the type of woman who would not stop for anybody. That's why we're looking at you, do you understand, Craig?''

"And that points the finger at you," Raybould said.

Peyer said nothing.

Olsen broke into the silence. "Craig Peyer, you have the right to remain silent. . . . '' As the policeman read him his legal rights, Peyer shifted uneasily.

"Wow! Am I under arrest?'' he asked incredulously.

Olsen didn't look at the patrolman as he finished reciting the Miranda warning explaining his right as a criminal suspect to contact a lawyer before talking to police. Peyer dropped his bravado and started talking fast.

"I know there seems to be circumstantial evidence. But I have nothing to hide. I didn't kill anybody!''

"Craig, you are not under arrest. You are free to leave at any time,'' Raybould said. Peyer sat still, his eyes skimming the table. When Peyer didn't move, the detectives pressed on, the tape recorder still whirring.

"What about the ropes, Craig?''

"Those are the only two ropes, I don't know about any other rope.''

The cops looked at each other: bingo! Nobody ever told Peyer they'd found three ropes in the car. The detectives waited eagerly for what the suspect might let slip about the possible murder weapon.

"I'm a little scared,'' Peyer said plaintively. "It's not every day that somebody points the finger at you and accuses you of murder. I'd like to talk to Captain Denno. Would that be all right? I need to talk to him,'' the patrolman looked as if he were about to break into tears.

"Sure, go ahead. We'll take a break,'' Olsen said. Peyer met with Denno in a small anteroom near the homicide bureau.

"I'm worried about what's going to happen to me,'' the

patrolman told his captain. Denno agreed to talk to him, but to be cautious he turned on the tape recorder.

"Human being to human being, highway patrolman to highway patrolman, I didn't do anything. I didn't murder anybody," Peyer insisted. "I wasn't raised that way. I have never killed a human being or ever will kill a human being; I never even used my gun as a highway patrol officer."

Denno nodded.

"I'm a talker. I like to talk. Maybe I open my mouth too much. If that's conduct unbecoming an officer, than I'll take my lumps for it," Peyer said. Denno murmured something comforting.

"They can search my house from the shingles to the floor, and they can tear it up and they won't find anything," Peyer said, his voice thick as his brown eyes welled up with tears. The patrolman had had enough. He was tired and he wanted to go home. Denno turned him over to Olsen.

"We'd like you to come back tomorrow. Okay?" Olsen asked Peyer and looked over at Denno for confirmation.

"Okay," Peyer agreed. He and his captain headed out to the parking lot. Lieutenant Phil Jarvis, the man in charge of finding Cara Knott's killer, watched Peyer walk out of the police station. Peyer looked back and saw the homicide chief in the doorway.

"Lieutenant Jarvis!" Peyer said. "How the hell are you? My God, I see you on TV all the time. You guys do a great job."

Jarvis was stunned that the guy could bounce back like that. His detectives had just grilled the man for hours and informed him officially that he was a suspect in a murder.

After Peyer went out the door, the cops trudged back to the interview room and rehashed the interview. Their initial elation about the rope comment died when they realized they didn't have anything else to incriminate Peyer even after a two-hour grilling.

Jarvis, who had been listening from an adjacent room, told the detectives they better bring Peyer back again. Left alone, Grant Raybould stared at his notes, and a slew of questions rattled around in his brain: Why would a good cop with a clean record murder an innocent young woman?

Raybould had seen a lot of killers in his day and he had to admit, Craig Peyer wasn't one he recognized.

Early the next day, Peyer returned to police headquarters looking tired and nervous.

"Are you okay right now, Craig?" It was Bill Nulton who was teamed now with Raybould and taking the good-cop role.

"Yeah, considering what I'm going through. I haven't eaten in two days. I ate breakfast yesterday. I didn't get lunch and I didn't eat today. It upset me. You're talking about a major, major crime."

"Craig, we have a real problem," Raybould began. "Personally you don't seem like a bad person. You are not the kind of person just to go out and brutally murder someone or do something vicious without prompting."

"Craig, did you undress this girl?"

"No, I didn't touch her, I didn't come near her. I didn't even see her. I didn't even stop her."

"Are the scratches on your hand from her?"

"No."

"You are lying."

"As God is my witness, I did not."

"As God is my witness, the reason I think you dumped her over the bridge, I think you wanted us to think it was a suicide."

"Why would I be thinking that, if she was strangled, if there were marks on her neck? I didn't do anything! I'm going to tell you that until you catch the guy who did it."

"You're the guy who did it."

"No!"

"The guy who is sitting here is going to end up going to jail."

"If you're innocent there's got to be something," Nulton said.

Peyer nodded. "If I stopped her, why isn't there people driving by that saw me do this? You know it's pretty obvious a black-and-white California Highway Patrol car with overhead lights. It sticks out like a sore thumb. Being a police officer I wouldn't do this—being a human being, being just me, Craig Peyer, I wouldn't do something this grotesque . . .

of taking a human life . . . just no way I would do it." He raised his voice. "I couldn't bring myself to do it. I can't even stand to see animals killed. I wouldn't do anything like this."

Raybould reminded him that evidence was found at the scene of the murder, which police were checking against his own fingerprints, palm prints, blood samples, and hair samples. "I won't tell you what the results are," the detective said ominously.

"All I can say is . . . I can stand on my word I didn't do anything," Peyer said. "You can check my record. I have all my tickets all the way back to nineteen-seventy-eight in my locker."

Raybould was impatient. "Craig, you didn't have this sort of problem in nineteen-seventy-eight; you didn't have this problem each and every night."

"I never had a problem, that's the problem," Peyer insisted. "I take my job dead seriously."

"The problem is that the time you did that you were desperate. You were very desperate to cover where you had been."

"Why, I'd been patrolling," Peyer insisted. "I didn't do anything that night. I drove two hundred forty-six miles and I wrote thirteen tickets. How would I have a chance to do anything else with two hundred forty-six miles on the unit? Ninety percent of the guys in San Diego don't drive more than one hundred miles on their units."

"I talked to you two nights after this happened. You had not really become a suspect." The detective reminded him of the night the police video team filmed the reenactment of the Knott murder and Peyer had come down to the murder scene to watch.

"You were trying to talk to me, but you know what you were trying to talk about? The murder. You came on so strong, it really threw me, Craig," Raybould said.

"There was no reason for it, just curiosity, what I do in my job," Peyer said. It was, after all, his beat, and he felt he should know what was going on since he was, unofficially at least, one of the patrol's public relations men.

"I think there was a reason for it," Raybould replied.

"Oh, man." Peyer was exasperated. "Well, you can take anything and everything I do and say and probably turn it around where it seems like I'm that way."

"I'm not trying to do that."

"I'm just saying what I did. My facts. What I did that night."

"What about the rope, Craig?" Raybould tried a new tack.

Peyer started talking about the CHP-issue ropes all officers keep in their trunks. "There's a piece of rope. It's standard, like we have it in all our patrol cars, every one of them. Um, white rope; usually in a plastic bag. It's used to tie people's feet if they are combative. I've never used it; I hardly make any arrests."

"What about the other piece of rope?"

Peyer went on to explain the animal snare in the trunk. "You don't want to get your hands all bloody or the animal is injured you don't want the animal to bite you, you snare the animal. That's the only rope I know in my vehicle."

Peyer went on to describe the intricacies inside his trunk: flare box, traffic cones, lug wrench, and jumper cables. He seemed to gain confidence as he went over the familiar ground. "I had my hat in there, but they took my hat out because a cap piece has got to be replaced."

He explained that he had polished the CHP emblem on his cap so often, the gold turned to silver, a testament to his dedication to the badge.

"Did you tell your wife about this?" Nulton asked.

"I just told her I'd been interviewed last night about what happened on Interstate fifteen, the murder of the young girl. I didn't go into too much detail because I didn't want to upset her."

"Craig, there's a chance we'll have to put you in jail today," Raybould said.

"You're kidding?"

"I'm dead serious."

"Why?"

"For murder."

"Oh my God! I didn't do anything."

But the look on the patrolman's face didn't seem shocked

enough to Raybould. "Craig," the detective said, "this is not a joking matter."

"I know it isn't."

"It's nothing to treat lightly."

"Oh, shit." Peyer groaned.

"Craig, something very wrong happened and there's a logical explanation. I don't think you're the type of person you read about that goes around and does something like this half crazed with no rhyme or reason. There's a very good chance you are going to go to jail today for murder. Craig. That's not my decision."

"I didn't do anything. I didn't murder anybody," Peyer said, twisting in his chair. "Oh, man. I'm not deceiving anybody. I didn't murder anybody. I didn't murder a soul. I didn't murder the girl on Fifteen. I haven't murdered anybody in my whole life. I haven't hurt anybody in my whole life."

They talked about all the tickets, the thirteen he wrote the night of the murder, and the hundreds he wrote each month. Investigators were reviewing all the citations.

"I'm glad they are," Peyer said.

"Craig, you write all the same kind of people. You do write a lot of tickets, but you write all the same kind of people—young girls."

"They are not all young girls," Peyer said. "Oh, man, have they taken all my tickets for the last year?"

"We've looked at six months. Many of them are taken to Mercy Road."

"I work that area. It's my favorite spot. Everybody has a favorite spot."

"You stop a lot of people for speeding and then don't write them up for speeding."

"I would write them depending on the circumstances," he said. "You know the speed is rampant; all we want to do is make sure people go from point A to point B as safely as they can. That's all I've ever done in my whole career. A car is a car—I can't tell who is driving without running up behind them. I don't know who I'm stopping until I walk up to the car. Sometimes I go out and talk—I'm a talker. They put me as an assistant public information officer because I talk. I relate to people well. I just talk bullshit. It's no big thing. I didn't think it was a big thing. I didn't mean anything by it. It was just conversation.''

Raybould didn't like the expression on the patrolman's face. It looked like he was smiling. ''This is no joking matter,'' Raybould said.

''I know this is not a game. Don't you think I know this?''

Raybould lit into Peyer. ''If you consider yourself any kind of man at all, don't just sit there and lie.''

''I'm telling you the truth,'' Peyer insisted. ''We're talking about a human being, a girl; I didn't kill a human being,'' Peyer said.

''I don't believe you,'' Raybould said coldly.

Peyer too turned cold. ''Then we're back to a stalemate.''

Raybould ignored the response. ''Do you have any idea what you are facing?''

''I'm a police officer. I know what the punishment is when everything goes down. Of course I know what I'm facing. I'm an adult. That's why I'm upset. You figure I'm going to say 'I did it' when your finger is pointed at me that I killed somebody. Hell, I know what I'm facing in prison. And prison to a cop—give me a break—I'll last a day in cotton pickin' jail. Even though I'm a highway patrolman; a cop is a cop. You think I'm going to go out and kill somebody and put my life on the line for that?''

Raybould quietly reminded Peyer that police officers weren't housed with the general population.

''That's a great comfort,'' Peyer said. ''I don't want to go to jail. Oh, man, I'm scared. Scared shitless.''

''What did happen? Did she fall down and hit her head by herself?'' Raybould pushed on relentlessly.

''I have no idea what happened. I worked that area that day and did my normal highway patrol duties. I wrote tickets, helped disabled drivers, and removed traffic hazards—that's all I did.''

''You can tell us the truth.''

''I'm telling you the truth.''

''I feel righteously sorry for you. I would hate to be in your position,'' Raybould said. ''You are putting your family in a real ugly spot.''

''I didn't do anything. Grant, I didn't do a goddamn thing.

I made a mistake," he shouted. "I fell down at the office. God, I didn't try to hide anything. I went right back in the office and told the office. I made out an injury report. I never hid anything in my whole life—what I've done in school, my jobs, the air force, anything. I've never hid anything. It's always been an open book. My life is an open book."

"Craig, you are very confident of yourself. You're very exact. Those injuries—" Raybould pressed him.

Peyer was practically shouting back at him. "My face hurt that night from hitting the fence, my shoulder, my foot was hurt, my leg, supposed to be nonskid soles.

"I didn't do anything. I'll say that till my grave that I'm innocent. And if you have to take me downtown, and if my family has to go through it, then my family has to go through it."

"Let me get one thing straight. You are going to go through this." Raybould spat out the words slowly and deliberately.

Silence filled the room. Peyer was the one who broke it. "I didn't do anything. I don't know what I can say to make you believe me. I realize I don't have to be talking to you. I realize I don't have to let you search my locker, search my house, search my vehicle. If I had anything to hide, don't you think I would go out and get a lawyer?"

"Exactly. That's why you're doing what you're doing. You want us to think that you have nothing to hide."

"I didn't murder anybody. I've never been in a fight in my life, not even with a guy, not with my wives or anything."

"We know for a fact that this girl fought back to some degree. She broke a nail, her hands were scraped back. Whoever was there was going to have injuries consistent with that and your injuries."

"I have a scratch [from the moment] when I hit the fence. Nobody was out there watching me do my clown act and run into the fence," Peyer said. "I don't have anybody to substantiate that, not at all. . . .

"Did you check the fence? There's got to be skin on it. Why don't you check that? I ran into the fence down at the office. My life is open to you. You can look, you can probe. Above all, I am a law enforcement officer and I know I am straight as I can be. I don't lie. I never lie.'' His voice rose in anguish.

"Why are you so upset?" Raybould said.

"That's the only thing I ever did in that area," Peyer said.

Raybould's heart was pounding. He wrote it down on his yellow legal pad: "That's the only thing I ever did in that area."

The words were still hanging in the police interview room when suddenly everything went black. The overhead lights snapped off, and the tape recorder clicked off. It was pitch-dark.

"I'm not going anywhere," Peyer said excitedly, clearly afraid what the police might do to him.

"Don't worry, Craig. We're going to find out what's wrong," Raybould told him. They put him in another room where the emergency generator kept the lights on and they headed back to the interview room.

When the lights flashed back on, Raybould jumped at the tape recorder and rewound it. They played back the tape, they heard Peyer's voice, but the words that Raybould thought were definitely a confession—"That's the only thing I ever did in that area"—were not there. Apparently it had been accidentally erased.

Raybould sank down in his chair. Six hours of interviewing a fellow law enforcement officer suspected of murder had done him in.

"That's it for today," Raybould told Peyer. "We'll drive you home."

Only minutes after the patrolman begged detectives to believe him, Peyer bounced back to his old chatty self. As they pulled away from downtown headquarters, Peyer started complimenting the police on how nice their gas facilities were.

Nulton turned and looked the patrolman in the eye. "You've got to take this seriously, Craig. We're coming after you."

"You've got a job to do. I understand that," Peyer said.

They drove thirty minutes up Interstate 15 to Peyer's home in Poway, one exit past Mercy Road. The cops looked into the impeccably neat garage, where files were stacked in order, boxes of tools lined up from the smallest to the largest.

Nulton thought of his own chaotic garage and of all the messy garages he had seen in his years. This one was the neatest he had ever laid eyes on. What was it with this guy?

The officers asked Peyer if he kept rope in his garage.

"Oh sure," Peyer said.

The officers looked over the workbench and opened the tool chest drawers where they found a variety of rope and twine, all shapes and sizes, tightly wrapped and neatly organized by size. Peyer showed them his motorcycle and his perfectly clean and waxed maroon-and-silver Chevy pickup truck, as if they were friends over for a visit. The cops weren't feeling very gracious.

"Look, we're going to be back. You are going to be held accountable," Raybould said.

"I've got to go through what I've got to go through," Peyer replied.

Just then Karen Peyer pulled up the driveway.

"Hello," she said briefly and rushed inside.

"She knows that you are asking questions," Peyer explained.

Soon the strains of piano music drifted outside from the house.

"That's beautiful," Nulton said. "Does your wife play the piano?"

"Yeah, but only when something is troubling her."

10

The Guy Next Door

THE Christmas season of 1986 had been good to Craig Alan Peyer. He had everything a man could want in life. His new wife, Karen, was the kind of woman who always tried to make him feel special. She always smiled when he made a joke, and waited up for him whenever he was out late. His barrel chest virtually swelled with pride at the sight of his three children—their baby Kacey, Karen's two-year-old son, Jason, and Peyer's ten-year-old daughter, Michelle. Just as Craig took pride in his own orderliness, his children were expected to be neat. And they were. They didn't leave their toys lying around the house or in the front yard like the other kids in the neighborhood. And just as he expected everyone to respect authority, his children were no exception. They were well behaved.

Craig believed good things came to him because he was so devoted to his work as a California highway patrolman, guardian of the roadways. He possessed the sharpest uniform, the cleanest patrol car, the most used ticket book, and the shiniest black leather boots in the whole San Diego sector. That gold badge was his life.

After thirteen years with the highway patrol he often wondered if he should try moving up the ranks and taking the sergeant's examination. It would mean more money, more prestige, a chance for advancement. But he never did. "I didn't want to sit behind a desk," he explained of his decision. "I'd rather be out on the road helping the public."

Karen reveled in her role as Mrs. Craig Peyer, too. She enjoyed domesticity, running the perfect house and cooking the best meals she could for her family. Finally, Karen had the time and the money to do that. Sure, being a policeman's wife gave life an edge. There was danger in Craig's work, but Karen was proud that he served the public. The days weren't always easy, but they definitely weren't boring.

Karen must have felt blessed. Here she was, barely thirty years old, married only a year and already she had everything most women ever wanted—a baby and two other sweet children, a fabulous new $176,000 house with a backyard swimming pool in one of the better neighborhoods in Poway, a suburb near the foothills northeast of San Diego. To show how wonderful it all was, Karen announced it to the world with a sign on the license plate holder of the little Plymouth she drove: GOD'S GIFT TO US, OUR FATHER.

Craig was as fine a protector of his family as he was a provider. Karen brought in extra money working as a substitute gym teacher and sometimes she stayed late to referee volleyball games over at Poway High School. Craig insisted she call him before leaving for home. Karen was touched by the way he worried about her safety.

Another endearing quality about Craig was his ability to talk to anyone about anything. Everybody who knew Craig liked him. He knew how to fix almost everything from swing sets to cars to swimming pool heaters, and he took the time to do so when friends needed a helping hand. He was generous, too, loaning his big pickup and his motorcycle to his fellow officers when they asked.

Craig had grown up in San Diego when it was still a small town. He was the kind of quiet guy people don't notice in a crowd. His yearbook from Kearny High class of sixty-eight features his picture with nothing printed underneath—no activities, no ambitions, just a clean-cut guy surrounded by long-haired classmates.

After graduation Craig tried a few courses in a local community college, but those were the days when America was taking a beating in Vietnam after the Tet Offensive. He enlisted in the air force, but the military pegged him not as a fighter, but a fixer, and sent him into mechanic's training at the Chanute Technical Training School in unexotic Urbana, Illinois.

Then they stationed him in Thailand for two years during the most intense period of the Vietnam War. He worked there with the Tactical Air Command, repairing the Cobra and Huey helicopters heading to the front. He told friends that he had ridden behind enemy lines on missions with the Special Forces.

His buddy at the highway patrol, Craig Muehleisen, thought of Peyer as a little brother who looked up to him. Muehleisen was tall, thin, and handsome, while Peyer was darker complexioned and had to watch his weight. Muehleisen came from a prestigious family whose name made history books. They were pioneers, sports heroes, military legends. Peyer's family, in contrast, were plain midwestern stock, working class.

Craig Muehleisen rode motorcycles, which among the Chips was considered the most prestigious way to patrol the freeways. Craig Peyer decided he wanted to take up motorcycle riding too and got himself a dirt bike to practice on so he wouldn't make a fool of himself on the massive patrol cycles. Even though Peyer preferred patrolling alone, as a sort of highway Lone Ranger, they even talked about switching beats so they could ride together as partners. It was Craig and Craig, *hermanos*.

Peyer switched to the El Cajon sector in 1984 in the eastern part of the county, rural and wide. But even being with his buddy couldn't make up for the lack of anything to do out there in the boonies on those little country highways. "It was a lot of boring times. It seemed like an eight-hour shift lasted sixteen hours," he said later. After only a few months, he won his transfer back to San Diego sector, patrolling from the U.S.-Mexican border to the northern edge of the city and the closer bedroom communities, to the coastal strip as far as the beach town of Del Mar.

It was easy for Peyer to win his transfers because he was well thought of in the highway patrol. Peyer didn't have the charisma of Muehleisen but he had his own reputation for consistency in his favor. Steady, reliable Craig Peyer. No surprises. By the book. Always the most tickets. Always the cleanest everything. It didn't make him the most popular cop in the barracks, but his bosses seemed to appreciate him for his steadiness. And his reliability was rewarded.

Craig Peyer won the best perk of the San Diego division of the highway patrol, free trips to the Hawaiian islands, just to remind a bunch of sailors not to run red lights when they hit shore. It even had a romantic name, the Ships at Sea program. He would fly to Hawaii and then ride back across the Pacific aboard some aircraft carrier like the U.S.S. *Kittyhawk*, a ship so big it had its own zip code. What he liked best of all about that duty was standing on the deck of the big flattop and looking out at the sailors at attention all focused on him.

Craig always seemed to know what he wanted out of life. He started on his master plan at the end of his stint in the military in 1972, when, four months before mustering out, he married Deborah Zalfen, the sister of his air force buddy. What could be more perfect: her folks even lived down the street from his folks in San Diego.

After the war, he made his living making house calls to homes and businesses, fixing air conditioners for San Diegans who wanted a perfect climate inside to match the paradise outside. But after only a few months, he may have decided something was missing in his life. For Craig, nothing could deliver on his expectations better than one of the most celebrated law-enforcement organizations in the world, the California Highway Patrol. He grew up in the fifties when every kid's hero was Broderick Crawford, the solemn agent of justice in the old TV drama *Highway Patrol*.

From the start it seemed Craig Peyer was destined to be a cop. He had one of the highest scores, a remarkable 95 percent on his entry tests in May 1973, and then in July headed up to Sacramento for four months training at the CHP academy.

His wife, Deborah, attended an orientation for the spouses of highway patrol recruits, where she was told her husband's behavior might change temporarily, maybe for up to a year.

''They are going to act real tough around the house, but

they are just trying to find themselves," the advisor told the worried wives. "They are taken with their new sense of power. But it doesn't last."

When this expected change came over Craig, Deborah was prepared. But she waited and waited for Craig to change back to his old, friendly self. What disturbed her most was a new preoccupation with flirting Craig developed. "His head swelled. He became mister macho," she would tell people. "The badge was a way to flirt."

The patrol sent Craig to start his life in law enforcement in the exclusive Los Angeles–area beach community of Malibu. One thing Peyer learned fast was that when you wore a badge, everyone talked to you, even in a tony movie-star town like Malibu.

As lovely as the southern California coast was, living in a small apartment down the road in less exclusive Santa Monica didn't seem to fit his big plans. And then there was the child to think about. Michelle, who was in the throes of her terrible twos, had outgrown the apartment. It seemed to Deborah that she and Craig were fighting more. Maybe it was the close quarters and the pressure of LA. Craig decided to try moving his family out of the stressful environment into laid-back San Diego. He won his transfer from Malibu to San Diego, but he returned to find his once-sleepy hometown transformed by an unrelenting growth spurt. It wasn't the same town that he had grown up in.

For Deborah, the move did little to alleviate their troubles. She was getting pretty disgusted with his flirting, his ordering her around, and his demanding that she keep a perfect house. She was supposed to polish his brass and his precious badge, 8611. And the way he expected her to listen for the sound of his motorcycle coming up the street so she could push the garage-door opener and he could glide up the driveway coolly and dismount like he was Easy Rider seemed like too much for her to bear.

Deborah Peyer had seen his temper flare before, but for the first time, after she brought up a divorce in July 1978, she later recalled that he started getting more violent. In his rages he threw things and threw her around, she said, sometimes in front of their three-year-old daughter.

One afternoon five years into the marriage, she asked for a divorce. Peyer said nothing for a minute. Then in a quiet voice he told her how much he loved her and that he would always love her. Please, he begged her, please, make love with me one last time. Deborah tried to tell him it was already over, but he was already moving toward her. He was so gentle, but she cried through the whole thing. It felt wrong, false, she told friends, and she tried to push him off her, but he wouldn't stop.

But the screaming matches still didn't stop. She kept telling herself that deep down underneath all the macho swagger was a sweet man who really did love her.

The last straw came during one particularly ugly fight. Suddenly he stalked across the room, grabbed her, and threw her on their bed. He climbed on top of her and started to choke her. She said she felt his fingers on her neck, and she was terrified. Just as suddenly as he started, he stopped and began to sob. That was it for Deborah. She scooped up little Michelle and immediately moved in with her parents.

Even after the separation and divorce, Deborah still relied on Craig. There seemed to be nothing he couldn't do. When her car broke down, he knew how to fix it. When they had lived together, he'd taken care of the checkbooks and bank accounts and always paid the bills on time, putting money aside religiously. So when she needed money, she knew he would always have spare change to lend her. When their daughter started to defy Deborah, she turned to her ex-husband to discipline the child. "The girl thought her father walked on water," Deborah said.

In his new single days he threw a Fourth of July Independence Day celebration, and bragged to his buddies at the patrol and at the San Diego Police Department that his party was going to be a blast—literally. He said he had a bunch of spectacular fireworks, Roman candles, cherry bombs, the works, one of the partygoers recalled later. If Craig had the stuff, it would have had to have been smuggled across the border because fireworks were illegal in San Diego. When the gang showed up at Craig's house in Poway, all he had was a bunch of sparklers. Despite Craig's bombast, there were no fireworks. He explained that he just didn't want to violate the law. That was typical Craig, one of his friends said. A guy who lived by the book.

Four years after his divorce, in May 1983, Peyer married Karen Muehleisen. His second wife, like his first, was the sister of one of his buddies, this time of Craig Muehleisen.

But Karen Muehleisen soon discovered that she was more independent than Craig preferred. She kept her checking account separate, and she insisted on keeping her maiden name as her middle name, Karen Muehleisen Peyer. Not exactly a major blow for feminism, but Peyer never got used to it. For Karen, the Muehleisen name was something to be proud of— they were a pioneer family back when San Diego was still the wild west; they were war heroes; they helped create the military stronghold of NORAD, the North American Air Defense Command built under the Rocky Mountains in Colorado to withstand nuclear war.

Karen soon found Craig too possessive for her taste. He seemed to resent all the time she spent with her friends and family. Once Karen's father, Bud Muehleisen, called to wish her happy birthday, but Craig told him she wouldn't be back until late.

But when Karen came home, he told her nobody had called. She soon found out otherwise and went through the roof. How dare he stand in the way of her and her family!

Things got worse. She didn't like the way he disciplined his daughter, how he yelled at her in the middle of a picnic and would humiliate her by sending her to her room. "Do I really want to have kids with a man like that?" Karen wondered.

At other times Craig could be so sweet. And he was incredibly reliable. She certainly couldn't complain that he wasn't a good provider or that he wasn't interesting to talk to.

Yet at other times she felt even the simplest tasks like grocery shopping would turn into an ordeal. Craig would insist that they go out together. But only he was allowed to choose the food. Even their sex life was suffering. This guy she was once so crazy about seemed to be becoming more and more selfish in all parts of life and now even in bed. "If I claimed that I could not breathe, he took it personally, and it made him angry,'' she said later.

Everything he did started irritating her. "He was always picking faults with everyone else, but if anybody said anything about his hairy chest or his weight, he became furious.'' Karen Muehleisen lasted exactly six months as the second Mrs. Craig Peyer. By the fall of 1983, she had filed for divorce.

After they separated Karen soon discovered that Craig was checking up on her as he did his first wife, going to her house late at night and early in the morning and shining his flashlight into the rooms to see if she had a lover spending the night. Karen Muehleisen became furious when she learned that he had kept her name off the deed to their house, which meant she would not get half the money in the divorce settlement.

True, Craig had owned the house before they married, but by this time Karen was so bitter she would stop by their old house to scream at him. She called him so often at the highway patrol station that the word was out among the Chippies that if Craig Peyer's wife called, it was best to tell her he was out.

The Brown family moved in next door to the Peyers on Via Stephen in November 1983 just in time to watch Craig and Karen's marriage disintegrate.

Karen and Jeffrey Brown were a young religious couple with a new baby. With her husband's support, Karen chose to become a full-time mom and quit her job. Jeffrey had a steady job with a civil engineering firm and there seemed no end to the building going on in this county. But money was still tight. Karen and Jeffrey had their problems as a couple, but none of the strain showed when they dressed up and left for church on Sunday mornings. Craig Peyer could see them go, the proud father, the serene mother, and child.

Karen Brown met the man next door, and they started talking. Her new neighbor was helpful, and reassured her that they were living on a quiet street, but that if anything went wrong, after all, he was a highway patrolman who had a badge and a gun.

She soon learned that Craig, as she was calling him now,

was pretty handy around the house, too. There seemed to be nothing he didn't know about the inner workings of a house or how to raise a child. Craig worked evenings and night shifts, so he was home most of the day.

Karen could listen to him for hours as he talked about his adventures in the world of law and order, and told all his war stories. He lovingly described his life in the highway patrol and how it all began in the seventies as highway patrolman to the stars in Malibu. He had great stories about all the rich people he got to order around.

Craig recounted tales of the great Christmas parties that actor Burgess Meredith, a police buff, would throw for all the local cops. Sometimes Craig would go out to Meredith's house and have a cup of coffee with the man who played the evil Penguin on the old *Batman* television shows and the gnarled trainer in the *Rocky* movies.

Another favorite story was how he'd been invited to actor Larry Hagman's house in the exclusive beachfront fortress of the Malibu Colony and what it had been like to talk man-to-man with the guy who played the immoral oil tycoon J. R. Ewing in the television soap opera *Dallas*.

Eight months after Karen Brown moved in next door to Craig Peyer, she filed for divorce from her husband Jeffrey. It was a week before their fifth wedding anniversary. A lot of people at her church raised their eyebrows at that.

Karen had become so dependent on Craig that she hired the same attorney the patrolman had used for his last divorce. The settlement gave Karen the house, most of the Sears appliances, and the Browns' most precious possessions, the Waterford crystal decanter and the Norman Rockwell statuettes.

It wasn't the community property that was so hard to untangle for Karen and Jeffrey Brown; it was the emotional split. At one point during the breakup they had a fight and Jeffrey told her that they simply could not divorce because they were born-again Christians—hoping that if she wouldn't listen to him, maybe she would listen to God. Karen refused to listen and tried to leave, but she only got as far as the front lawn before Jeffrey tackled her and demanded that she get back inside the house.

That scared Karen enough to go to court and ask for a restraining order against Jeffrey, telling the judge about the tackling and adding that she needed to keep her estranged husband away or he would hide property and money and even might take their son out of the country. In July, she spurned Jeffrey's efforts to reconcile. The final separation granted, the Browns got joint custody of Jason with Jeffrey to give Karen $250 a month child support, until mid June 1985 or whenever she remarried, whichever came first.

Three weeks after her child support ran out, Karen Mary Eich Brown became Mrs. Craig Alan Peyer. The wedding was small, mostly family, and Craig's highway patrol friends. The first Mrs. Peyer and her new husband also attended the ceremony. Within three months of the wedding, the third Mrs. Peyer became pregnant and the following June, a girl was born. They named her Kacey, which was the name Peyer's best CHP buddy, Craig Muehleisen, had already picked out months earlier to give to his child, who was due soon after Peyer's. Then the Muehleisens felt betrayed, as though their friends had robbed them. They picked another name for their child.

Karen and Craig followed the American dream and sold their two neighboring houses, worth almost two hundred thousand dollars combined, and bought another in a posh new neighborhood in Poway called Los Arbolitos—Spanish for little grove. By Christmas 1986, the Peyers had just started settling into a routine family life. Their decorations were complete in their new dream house, all the way down to the cheery welcome mat out front wishing visitors, "Have a berry nice day," a souvenir from Knotts' Berry Farm amusement park in neighboring Orange County.

The Saturday after their second Christmas together in December 1986, Peyer slept late—he loved to sleep—and then they all did chores. The children went outside to play with their new toys and after Karen made lunch, he went upstairs and got ready for work.

11

Badge of Betrayal

BILL Nulton flip-flopped on his bed. It was 4 A.M. on January 16, as good a time as any for another drink of water. He went into the kitchen and paced for a while. He sat down and tried to read the sports page.

"What's wrong, honey?" his wife called out from the bedroom.

"It's okay. I can't sleep. I'll be in in a minute," he said.

How could he explain that, in the weeks since they met, Sam Knott had become like a father to him? How awful it felt to know it was his duty to inform Sam about something so terrible? Nulton kept remembering the Knotts' library with all those clippings about Cara and all those mementos of her life. And now Nulton was going to have to tell Sam that a police officer killed her.

A cop, damn it, a cop.

"I just can't get over it, if this guy did it," Nulton told his pal Olsen as they talked about the case earlier at the police station.

Olsen tried to reassure him. "We did our job, that's all," Olsen said. They commit it. We solve it. Just the facts, just like *Dragnet*. But Nulton couldn't pass this off as just another case, another bunch of papers that should be shoved away in a file cabinet now that their part was done. He kept thinking about how the Knotts were unlike any other victims he had ever dealt with. They met the tragedy like a head-on crash,

96

and they had the guts to stick around and pick up all the pieces. They didn't try to run and hide. Sam was always saying he wanted to make something positive out of this tragedy. Something positive. Jeez, Nulton thought. The Knotts still felt an enormous commitment to Cara. Just as if she were alive. They even talked to their daughter as if she was right there beside them. Olsen couldn't get over that.

Nulton had talked with the Knotts almost daily for weeks, but he had to drop out of contact now that they finally were ready to corner a suspect. Finally. It was tough for Nulton not to mention anything to the family about the police interview with Peyer but he knew they had to keep a tight lid on the information. After the last meeting with Peyer, Nulton knew it was just a matter of time before the patrolman would be arrested.

"When are we going to get this guy?" Nulton asked Jarvis.

"Soon," was all the lieutenant would say.

Now the moment had arrived. Throughout that Thursday, Nulton rehearsed the lines he would say to Sam, how he would tell Sam about this California highway patrolman who was going to be arrested for killing his sweet daughter.

On the morning of January 15, San Diego Police Chief Bill Kolender was due to march in a parade through downtown, honoring Martin Luther King, Jr. He was about to join the throng when his electronic pager went off like an alarm. The chief picked up his cellular telephone and called headquarters. His commanders were ready to move in on Peyer. Kolender resumed the march down Broadway, waving at the crowd, and then a few blocks from the county courthouse he stepped aside. He pulled out his cellular phone again and dialed the Knotts' number.

"Hello, Sam? It's Bill Kolender. We've got some good news for you. We're going to arrest somebody today. We'll have some people over."

"Thank you, we had a feeling," Sam said. "Thank you, for Cara."

It was growing dark Thursday by the time television news editor Mike Workman and his crew pulled into a convenience store in Poway. Workman felt lousy, like something stuck under a shoe. That's what I get from running around snooping for two weeks straight, a stupid cold, he thought angrily as he ran inside the store to buy another box of tissues.

He sat on the car hood next to the pay phones and waited. Finally, a phone rang, and he grabbed the receiver before the first ring finished. "This Workman? We're on our way," said the voice on the end of the line.

Twenty minutes later, Workman saw the big white unmarked police cars pass, so unmistakable with their multiple antennas and short-haired drivers. Two of Channel 8's big white unmarked cars peeled out after them and tailed the cops through the Los Arbolitos neighborhood until they all stopped at the dead-end street called Treecrest.

The editor and reporters Dave Cohen and Liz Pursell ran to the front porch of the house. The cameraman turned his glaring television lights into the front window, illuminating the Peyer family living room.

Workman felt a little queasy, but he didn't stop the cameraman either, telling himself, It has to be done, in case he eats his gun in the front room or runs out the back door, which I bet he does.

San Diego Police Detective Paul Olsen and Officer Jim Clear did the deed. "Craig Peyer, we have a warrant for your arrest for the murder of Cara Knott."

Three detectives in suits led Peyer out of his house and slapped handcuffs on him, while another plainclothes unit stood by for backup. Peyer was silent as he walked out dressed in brown Levi's and a maroon velour shirt. All Karen could do was watch. The kids gathered around her, stunned beyond belief and tears. She instinctively backed into the house, away from the glare of the TV lights and camera. Karen watched police lead her husband around the police cars and push him into the backseat where she knew the doors had no handles. There was no way to get out.

It wasn't fear, but disbelief that masked his face as Peyer struggled to maintain control of himself. Nobody spoke, but everybody watched Peyer's every move, wondering whether he would react like a trapped animal.

"And I didn't even do it," he said quietly, his only words.

Workman whispered to his crew, "Jeez, I feel kinda sorry for him."

Even after all his mental rehearsals about meeting the Knotts, Bill Nulton still felt uncomfortable driving out to their house with his boss, Sergeant Armijo. He liked Ted and thought he was a good investigator, but Nulton wanted to tell the Knotts himself. He wanted to hug Sam and Joyce and the rest of the family, but with his sergeant along, he had to be a by-the-book cop. Ted was going to do the talking.

Sam let them in.

"We heard the news from the chief. It's good to see you," Sam Knott said, looking at Nulton.

"Hi, Sam," Bill Nulton said, trying to keep from trembling. He introduced Armijo, who took over in his business-like way.

"They are arresting a suspect right now," Armijo told the family. "The guy is a highway patrolman who was on duty."

Sam gave a knowing smile. Joyce nodded and sat down on the couch.

"Who else but somebody in authority would my baby stop for?" Sam asked, sounding exhausted. "She was so good. She wouldn't stop for anybody. Isn't that what we told you all along? I thought it might have been some service station guy; somebody who we were depending on."

Armijo and Nulton also felt ashamed that the suspect was a cop. They gently tried to remind Sam that this guy wasn't like all the detectives who were working night and day to solve Cara's murder. This guy was different.

Sam nodded in agreement. Joyce's father, Bud Smith, sat with his hands on his face. He jumped from the couch. "I don't believe a police officer would kill my granddaughter! No, that can't be. We are law-abiding. Why did this happen?"

He broke into tears and ran out the door of the house shouting over and over, "Why did this happen?" Joyce ran after him with Sam close behind. Out on the front lawn they grabbed him and hugged him close. Nulton and Armijo watched them from the doorway.

"My father, he's abided by the law his whole life. He

doesn't understand.'' Joyce said, trying to explain his behavior to the officers.

Once again, Sam found himself in the role of trying to put people at ease when he was the one who really needed to be comforted. ''I'll go get some pizza. Does that sound good?'' Sam wanted to get outside to think, anyway. When Sam returned with two pizzas, everyone gathered around the kitchen table transfixed by the television set as they awaited the press conference broadcast. The others were forcing themselves to enjoy the pizza but Armijo couldn't eat. He kept thinking about Cara and the cop.

Nulton was watching Sam Knott, who seemed so unfazed by the news, and wondered whether Cara's father might have known all along it was a cop.

Once Patrolman Craig Peyer was safely inside the police station and fingerprinted, San Diego Police Chief Bill Kolender and Highway Patrol Chief Ben Killingsworth strode into the police conference room full of waiting reporters. Kolender sat before the bouquet of microphones and made the announcement. ''I am sorry to have to tell you that a law enforcement officer has been arrested in the murder of Cara Knott. It saddens me to tell you that the suspect is a CHP officer who was on duty at the time. Craig Alan Peyer.''

Killingsworth looked even more devastated than the police chief. The California Highway Patrol officers had taken the news hard, he told the press. ''And personally, it's probably the worst thing that has ever happened to me on the job.'' Killingsworth told the crowd that Peyer had a good reputation and an unblemished record in his thirteen years on the force. But he offered no reasons why this stellar cop had turned homicidal. The two chiefs were flanked by Deputy District Attorney Joe Van Orshoven and Homicide Lieutenant Phil Jarvis.

''We'll take some questions, but we don't want to jeopardize the investigation,'' Kolender advised the reporters, making it clear he wasn't going to say much more. Suddenly the biggest local news story had become world news and the reporters clamored for answers.

''Why him? Why such a good cop?'' reporters kept asking, trying to get some hint of the evidence that led them to the cop.

"I received information from the public. I received bits and pieces . . . that we were able to put together," Jarvis explained, not saying exactly what bits and pieces. Instead, Jarvis issued another plea for people to report anything, no matter how seemingly trivial, they might have seen between nine and ten that night near the Mercy Road exit.

Van Orshoven said a fifty-page affidavit was filed with the arrest warrant, but it was sealed from public scrutiny under court order. The warrant was for the crime of first-degree murder.

Chief Kolender lavished praise upon Jarvis and the staff of the San Diego police crime laboratory. "They did an excellent, excellent job," he told the reporters, although he wouldn't say what the laboratory found.

"Everyone who wears a badge feels the pain of an incident like this," Kolender said. "This occurrence should in no way affect the integrity and professionalism of the many, many thousands of law enforcement officers throughout the state of California."

They refused to discuss a motive, to say what might have prompted the patrolman to attack the young woman.

After news of the arrest, reporters raced to the Knotts' house to get their reaction and to see if they knew more. As the first reporters arrived, Sam asked the cops what to do.

"I think maybe you should release a statement after it is all over, maybe not too critical," Nulton said.

"Let's just watch TV," Joyce suggested.

So the family remained closeted in their living room, forcing reporters to watch them through the window as the family followed the developments flashing on the television screen. They did not stir as they listened to details of the arrest.

About an hour later, Sam Knott emerged from the house dressed in a rumpled white shirt. He huddled with his children and son-in-law, all looking as if they were on the brink of tears. Sam read a prepared statement thanking the public for their help.

"We would like to thank the community for all their support. We have been informed of what has transpired and I would like to appeal for any information that would relate to my daughter's whereabouts from about 8:40 to 9:45 P.M. that Saturday.''

Reporters stood there waiting for more outrage from the grieving father. But Sam closed the door.

Workman's film clip of Peyer's arrest ran on the eleven o'clock news up and down California. He backed it up with stories about the bitterness in the ranks of the highway patrol as one of their colleagues was charged with murder. He ran another story showing the public's immediate reaction of fear and anger to the news. Only one woman in a man-in-the-street survey said she thought Peyer was innocent until proven otherwise. The piece ended with a full-frame shot of Cara's smiling face lingering on the television screen until it faded away to black.

Following Peyer's arrest, his many friends and neighbors stepped forward to stand by him. CHP Officer Pete Strayer told reporters that he worked the beat next to Peyer's and considered him a very good friend.

"I don't believe it, I couldn't believe it," Strayer said.

Strayer said that officers looked up to Peyer. "Everything he did, he did right. There's no question about it," Strayer said. "He was a dedicated officer, a good officer, and a good man." Peyer's friends and neighbors agreed that he was a great guy and there was no way he could hurt anybody. They raised money to help the family. St. Gabriel's Catholic Church, where Karen Peyer took her children for a time, also rallied behind the family.

Even though it was mid January, the Christmas lights were still strung up along the Treecrest Street house, a testament to how preoccupied the normally meticulous Peyer had been in those days after the holidays.

The beleaguered California Highway Patrol set up a special hot line for the community to call and discuss its worries and concerns. And the community had a lot of concerns; before the second day was out more than two hundred people called. A highway patrol psychiatrist was brought in to talk to all the officers during their briefings, and arrangements were made for special counseling for those cops especially devastated by the arrest of one of their own.

Craig Peyer's buddy Craig Muehleisen was having trouble sleeping. He couldn't believe the murder suspect was his former brother-in-law. When he heard the terrible news, Muehleisen started questioning himself. Could I have done something? Why didn't I notice any warning signs? He talked often with his old high school classmate, Nulton, the detective investigating the case. But every time he talked to San Diego Police, some of his colleagues at the CHP seemed to give him the cold shoulder. Did some think he was betraying a brother cop? But Nulton would remind Muehleisen that he was the one who had been betrayed. Muehleisen knew Nulton was right. But that didn't make him feel any better.

Two days after Peyer's arrest, at 3:30 P.M. Saturday, Karen Peyer sat in the visitor's room of the San Diego County Jail talking to her husband. He was unshaven, his brown eyes bloodshot, and he wore a blue jail-issue jumpsuit as he sat on the other side of the double-paned glass window. As husband and wife talked via the in-house telephone, Karen tenderly stroked the frame of the bulletproof window that separated them. Peyer fought back tears and bit his lower lip. He tried covering his mouth but he couldn't control the sobs.

His parents, Hal and Eileen Peyer, paced the visitor's room like caged animals. They wore sunglasses in the dimly lit room. They would stop abruptly to pass messages to Craig through Karen, and Peyer's mother tried to smile encouragingly at her only son. Karen put Craig's ten-year-old daughter Michelle on the phone so she could talk to her daddy. After their half-hour visit was up, the Peyer family left.

As reporters confronted her outside the jail, Karen Peyer answered questions in a soft voice and tried to be polite, although it was clear she didn't know what to say. This criminal business certainly was all new to her. She had never seen a jail before, much less been in one. How was Officer Peyer doing in jail? reporters asked.

"He found out that he's claustrophobic," Karen answered. "And he's having trouble falling asleep."

"Do you have a statement for the press?" one reporter

shouted as another cut him off. "Is your husband guilty, Mrs. Peyer?" Karen froze on the sidewalk. Then she pulled Michelle close and tried to smile bravely.

"My husband is entirely innocent of the crime he's been charged with." She tried to keep moving down the sidewalk and get to her car and away from there, but the reporters still pressed in on her. "How does he like his cell, Mrs. Peyer?"

Hal Peyer said nothing as he hustled the family along the sidewalk past the public defender's office where he had spent the last few years of his working life as a civil servant. He knew the criminal justice system well enough to know that getting his son out of jail was going to be very tough.

Hal knew all too well how prosecutors, for the sake of bravado, love to keep their suspects in jail because it makes a difference to a jury if the accused is seen walking in with the rest of the public from the hallway, or being led in from the holding cell shackled and surrounded by armed guards. Hal surely knew this was going to be a long haul, and an expensive one. Peyer would have to be free so he could work to help pay off the bills that surely would become yet another nightmare.

Hal Peyer realized he was going to have to start looking for one damn good lawyer.

12

The Brass Ring

CHRISTMAS 1986 brought another death to Deputy District Attorney Joe Van Orshoven's doorstep, when he picked up Monday morning's *San Diego Union* from his front porch and read about the pain of a father whose golden child was dead. Joe already knew the story without reading the details, for he understood the sorrow and anger that random disaster brings and these people lived right up the street.

All that week after Christmas he spent his days pruning fruit trees and pounding away at projects outside his country house, hard sweaty work that usually helped him get lost from the world. But each day's newspaper brought to his doorstep more and more details about this Knott girl's murder.

Then he read about the family's funeral plans. She was going to be buried almost the same day as Claude. Joe sat in the den with the newspaper and let himself drift back to that Christmas two years ago when life had been so sweet, it could almost make a grown man believe in Santa Claus.

"Who would have thought a smart-ass like me would have done so good?" he used to say. He would smile as he thought back to the times his bluntness had gotten him into trouble. It hadn't been easy getting where he was, there was the army and the Korean War, finishing law school with a wife and three kids to support, getting a job in the district attorney's office, and all those years at the bottom of the heap.

After twenty-plus years of noble but low-paying toil as a civil servant, Joe had worked his way up to the top floor, head of the superior court division, the DA's point man handling all the felonies—murders, rapes, embezzlements. He was a player in the legal big leagues.

That wonderful Christmas of 1984, Joe Van Orshoven was on top of his world. California had a law-and-order governor. Maybe Van Orshoven could even wrangle an appointment to the municipal court judgeship he had always thought was beyond his reach. In those days when all seemed possible, Van Orshoven watched his stepson, Buford "Claude" Montgomery, Jr., blossom into the high school student body president and the star of not only the football and baseball teams but the basketball team as well. And Claude was smart too, only As and Bs that kid got, on top of all those sports.

"He was something," Van Orshoven said.

That Christmas holiday, Claude was home from his next to last semester at California Polytechnic Institute, a respected university up the coast. Saturday night before Christmas, Claude and his buddies headed down to Rosarito Beach in Baja California, Mexico, on the wild party path paved over the years by millions of southern California kids who indulged in Baja's unrestricted camping, legendary surfing waves, cheap Corona beers, five dollar lobster dinners, and border-town thrills. But as the young men drove home along those unlighted chaotic Mexican highways, someone smashed into their car. The driver survived. Claude was killed.

Like most traffic accidents, Claude's was just a matter of life's crap game, and this time it was Van Orshoven who got the bad-luck roll. Everything had been looking like the final scene in *It's a Wonderful Life*, where the hero gets a second chance. But that was all gone now.

As Joe sat in his den two Christmas seasons later he realized he had not completely shaken all the pain from his head yet. For here on his lap was a picture of happy Cara Knott, and when he looked at her it brought back again all his anger over life's random disasters. But this time, he thought, there's something I can do about it.

* * *

District Attorney Ed Miller didn't get elected to enforce law and order in the seventh largest city in America for sixteen years without knowing a hot case when he saw it. This Knott case was smoking. Her death had captured the public's heart, and they were hungry for justice. By the time Van Orshoven's vacation ended and he walked into work Monday, January 5, Miller was preparing to appoint a deputy to be ready the minute police landed a suspect.

The district attorney always considered the personalities of his deputies when he made such important decisions. Miller's top deputy attorneys were tied up with two of the most controversial cases of his tenure, both of them losers, one a racially sensitive shooting case that ended with a cop dead, and the second a Hispanic public official accused of taking kickbacks. Miller consulted his top assistant district attorneys, Brian Michaels and Dick Neely.

"How about Joe Van Orshoven? He wants the case," Neely proposed.

Miller was surprised. "Joe hasn't touched a case in years," he said. Van Orshoven had been his point man on plea bargains, a sort of air-traffic controller for the courts, deciding what case could be squeezed in where in the immensely crowded court system; he handled all the thousands of little cases, little details, little headaches. Now the deputy was in charge of Municipal Court, not even handling murder cases.

Ed Miller had known Joe Van Orshoven a long time. Back when Miller was San Diego's U.S. attorney and Van Orshoven a young deputy district attorney, they always bumped into each other. That wasn't hard in those days, Miller thought. This place was such a backwater that the legal community was pretty small. In those days even Cleveland was bigger than San Diego.

When Miller took over the DA's office in 1971, Van Orshoven was there, and although they weren't close friends, they had a bond. They had a history and loyalty was important to Ed Miller.

"He tried every kind of case that was around," Miller said. Plus, the cops were pushing for Van Orshoven, especially police homicide Lieutenant Jarvis. Miller didn't usually pay attention to what the police said when it came to the courtroom end of crime and punishment. But in the Knott case, the DA decided that law enforcement confidence would be vital, if in fact the defendant turned out to be, God forbid, this highway patrolman they were questioning.

Unfortunately, there was the little matter of the drinking.

Van Orshoven had been arrested for driving drunk only two weeks before Cara's murder. Ordinarily, getting popped for a "deuce," which is the legal slang for drinking and driving charges, would just be a minor embarrassment for someone in the DA's office, resulting in a fine and a little community service time; people, even public prosecutors, are human.

The top brass at the district attorney's office also knew in this case that Van Orshoven would be catapulted into the public's eye, and they knew constant spotlights were not easy to take. Not only had the prosecutor been arrested, but by a California highway patrolman! The irony had to make Miller wince inwardly, but his face remained impassive as he stared out his big windows at San Diego Bay, thinking. Maybe this patrolman would clear himself and they'd find another suspect.

Still looking out the window, the DA said to Neely, "Let's give Joe the case. He's the right choice."

13

Stormy Weather

CALIFORNIA highway patrolman Craig Peyer, a man without a blemish on his record in thirteen years on the force, spent six days in solitary confinement in San Diego County Jail. The charge: murder in the first degree.

Half the town was betting Peyer would do something rash. The cops, especially, figured that any lawman might kill himself to escape the shame of a murder rap. Certainly the county sheriff expected the worst, and put the patrolman on suicide watch under extra heavy guard.

While Peyer spent his days locked inside an eight-by-eleven-foot cell, he was becoming infamous in the outside world. The story of a law enforcement officer being arrested for murder was broadcast coast to coast. How could something like this happen? The order of the world was that the sky is blue and cops exist to protect you. Southern Californians couldn't understand how such a scandal could occur in their backyard; maybe in inner-city Detroit, sure, or in New York where everyone expects the weirdest possible behavior. But San Diego was America's finest city. It was even painted on the police cars. This was supposed to be the place where people came to leave ugliness behind, to escape brutal weather, the unhappy past, the rat race. Suddenly the highway patrolman accused of murder became the only topic in town. Did he do it? Was sex a motive? If you can't trust cops, who can you trust?

With such a reversal of the expected, the norm, people began to panic. They bought extra locks and guard dogs and signed up for self-defense courses. Ex-cop Sandy Strong especially found his self-defense studio besieged with calls, since he was the one who had taught self-defense to Cara Knott. Strong had always told his students to be careful of people posing as police officers. It saddened the former sergeant that now he had to warn students about cops themselves.

Out on the streets, law enforcement officers county-wide were being confronted with outright hostility. People yelled at them, they glared at them, they accused. Women motorists were ignoring officers who tried to pull them over. Law and order deteriorated to such a point that a sheriff's deputy ended up throwing a woman in jail for refusing to pull over where he commanded her to. All she did was drive to the safety of a well-lighted nearby gas station.

Before San Diego erupted into anarchy, the two heads of local law and order, San Diego Police Chief Bill Kolender and Highway Patrol Chief Ben Killingsworth, politely reminded the public that there were more than three thousand law enforcement officers in the county and they could be trusted to protect and serve. But many people failed to be calmed by another promise from men with badges.

On Wednesday, January 21, 1987, almost one month after the murder of Cara Knott, armed guards fetched Craig Peyer from jail and escorted him in handcuffs to the courthouse across the street. After two delays for legal technicalities, it was finally time for Peyer's arraignment, time for him to plead guilty or innocent to first-degree murder.

That same morning, Peyer probably couldn't help but smile to himself when he heard that the man who was trying to put him in prison, Deputy District Attorney Joe Van Orshoven, got his own share of beating by the press. Van Orshoven got his baptism in the public spotlight when the *San Diego Union* broke the story about his arrest for drunken driving in December, and how the pop was made by a California highway patrolman. The question was out in the open—could Van Orshoven's judgment be impartial?

Great, Van Orshoven thought when he saw the morning

paper; here it was his first day in court, and people were already shooting at his kneecaps.

The prosecutor put the story out of his mind as he strode into the packed courtroom and took his seat on the right side. The back door of the courtroom opened and bailiffs led the accused to the defense table. A murmur went through the crowded courtroom as people got their first real look at California highway patrolman Craig Peyer. The accused looked so ordinary, so stodgy and clean-cut, people seemed disappointed. He was certainly no smooth psychopath like Ted Bundy or a killer just oozing evil like southern California's Night Stalker, Richard Ramirez, who murdered thirteen people in a 1985 summer killing spree before being captured by angry residents of East Los Angeles.

Sam Knott watched the patrolman stand with his hands tucked inside his jail-issue pants, and Sam could feel himself seething with rage. Sam wanted to scream, You monster! What did you do to my baby girl? But the big man kept his cool and put on an expression he hoped was dignified.

Sam stood as San Diego Superior Court Judge Herbert Exarhos walked into the courtroom and took his seat behind the bench. Sam was the only person in the audience to raise himself from the seat, but sticking out didn't bother him. His eyes focused only on Peyer.

"The People of California versus Craig Alan Peyer," the bailiff called. The first two orders of business happened so quickly, so coated in legal jargon, that Sam wasn't sure he understood what they were saying. The judge declared that Peyer qualified for a court-appointed attorney. And since the defendant's attorney of choice was Robert Grimes, the court would allow Grimes to defend Peyer.

Surely, Sam thought, his tax money wasn't paying the tens of thousands of dollars it was going to cost to defend this monster? But it was so. The judge determined the accused was technically poor enough to qualify for a court-appointed attorney; it seemed Peyer's $176,000 house didn't count as an asset because it was considered shelter for his four dependents.

For his part, Joe Van Orshoven was pleased with Peyer's choice of defense attorney. The prosecutor considered Grimes a gentleman, a straight shooter, a good match for him in court. Grimes was a forty-year-old local boy with a solid reputation and many big-time cases under his belt: a multiple killer and a San Diego policeman accused of running a prostitution ring.

Still, Grimes hadn't performed any miracles defending one of his biggest clients, con man J. David Dominelli. Dominelli had swindled tens of millions of dollars from San Diego's elite through phony investments and then attracted even more suckers by using their money to pay for his southern California high life, complete with a classy blonde mistress, ocean-front offices, the best champagne, custom suits, convertibles, and parties with the swankest of investors, developers, entertainers, and politicos. When Dominelli fell in 1984, he brought down with him San Diego's popular surfing mayor, Roger Hedgecock.

Grimes was Gary Cooper tall and ruggedly handsome, a big guy who let his hands do his talking and kept his voice gentle. His custom suits draped over a body tanned and toned from battling the waves. He was one of those growing breed of San Diego–style lawyers who liked to slip out of work early Friday afternoons and hit the beach with his boogie board. He lived in the beach town of Encinitas twenty miles up the coast from San Diego, a hybrid of yuppies and avantgarde and kooky southern Californians with its vegetarian restaurants and surf shops, holistic health centers and aerobics workout salons.

With the small downtown practice he ran with his attorney wife, Linda Grimes, he had a smorgasbord of clients, along with many high-profile cases, especially murder and corruption cases. There was plenty of action to go around as San Diego was emerging as the Miami of the West, where vast amounts of crack, smack, speed, and marijuana routinely slipped over the U.S.-Mexico border. With his low-key demeanor and conservative style, though, Grimes contrasted sharply with the flashy lawyers who specialized in drug cases and sauntered around in their Italian suits and German cars worth as much as an assistant district attorney's salary. Compared to the Gucci gang, Grimes seemed like a regular Eagle Scout.

Even Boy Scouts can have a past, and Grimes had had his share of wild times. About twenty years before, he had been joyriding in a small plane over Mexico's rugged westernmost state, Baja California. Grimes didn't know a drug deal had been set to go down on the same airstrip he decided to land on, but the Mexican federal police sure had.

The *federales* had mistaken Grimes for the drug dealers. They'd shot down his plane, and when he'd climbed out of the wreckage, they'd whipped out their guns and arrested him. While he'd stood there bleeding, another plane started to land. Great, he thought, this must be the crook they're looking for, so they'll let me go. Except the *federales* had better aim this time. When they'd shot the newcomer down, they killed him.

The *federales* had thrown Grimes into the infamous La Mesa prison in Tijuana where machine-gun toting guards patroled the roof. In La Mesa prison, how well you eat and live can depend on how much you bribe the guards. Grimes had known enough about Third World justice to deduce his best defense was not truth, but escape.

Grimes had spent four months in La Mesa without ever seeing a judge, until he'd managed to tunnel his way out and slip across the border to the United States. Those terrible months in prison also shaped him forever as a defense attorney, because the gentle Bob Grimes now fully understood the terror of being an innocent man imprisoned by the whims of an eccentric justice system.

Now the seasoned defense lawyer stood in court with his most renowned client yet, highway patrolman Craig Peyer. The lawyers began to debate the most crucial point in the court debut of Craig Alan Peyer—was the accused going to get out of jail on bail?

"On the matter of bail, your honor, we request it be set at no more then one hundred thousand dollars. Officer Peyer has ties to the community, his family lives here, he is still employed in the county of San Diego," his attorney said.

"Furthermore, he was suspended from the highway patrol on January 5. On January 7, he was told he was a suspect in this case," the defense attorney pointed out. "If Mr. Peyer was going to flee, he had ample opportunity to do so. Craig continues to assert his innocence and he intends to fight this case to the end.''

Deputy DA Van Orshoven's voice boomed full of strength and assurance as he argued for bail of no less than half a million dollars. The lawyers went through the arguments, the DA pointing out the seriousness of the offense, the defense noting Craig Peyer's strong ties to his hometown and his clean record as a cop. Judge Exarhos settled on a three hundred thousand dollars bail, steep but low enough for Peyer to make and stay out of jail until his trial. The Knotts filed out of court quietly, uneasy that Peyer would likely soon be free.

Karen Peyer stood in the hallway and made her first official statement to the assembled crush of reporters, cameras, and microphones blocking the hallway. ''I love my husband. God willing, the court system will set him free,'' she said, and pushed through the crowd.

Sam wasn't sleeping. His nights and days were full of thoughts of Cara and how he should have protected her. He was adamant that he would do everything he could for her now. All the little details passed through his mind one by one, while he tried to work, while he tried to sleep.

Sam had done everything in his power to help the law flush out the monster, and now that the law had him, it was out of his hands. Sam had already complained about the flaws in the police system to the mayor, the city manager, several county officials, two state assemblymen, two police chiefs, ten newspapers, four television stations, the Junior League, and a crime victims' support group.

But to Sam, there was still one more job he could do. That was close the Mercy Road exit.

''That freeway exit never should have been there,'' Sam told Joyce again and again. ''There's no road there, there's no construction. There's nothing but trouble.''

The head of the local office of the California Transportation Department was a little surprised to get a call from Sam Knott. Like everyone else, he had heard about the murder and felt great sympathy for the girl and her family. Sam wanted a meeting with the top transportation brass. A citizen doesn't usually go around telling the state of California how to run its freeways. But within days Sam sat across the desk looking straight into the highway commissioner's eyes.

"That freeway exit is a disaster. It is a danger to the public," Sam told the state officials. "The police say it's the number-one crime spot in that area. It should be closed unless you're ready to really start building Mercy Road." Already, the men were painfully aware, people had nicknamed the exit "No Mercy Road."

Within the week, Sam won out and the state Transportation Department announced it would temporarily close the exit. Soon the words "Mercy Road" were covered over on the green freeway signs like giant Band-Aids over a wounded public psyche.

It took Karen Peyer a week but she and the Peyer family managed to raise the three hundred thousand dollars needed to bail her husband out of jail by pledging their house, her parents' house, Craig's parents' house, and some of their neighbors' homes. But no sooner had they raised enough property to pledge for the bail bond and get Craig free, than more bad news hit.

Deputy District Attorney Van Orshoven announced that "new evidence" had surfaced in the case and he was going to ask the judge to raise bail to one million dollars. It was Mafia kingpins who usually were slapped with million-dollar bails. It was drug lords, serial killers, not guys with squeaky-clean records like Craig Peyer. If the judge went along with the prosecutor's request, that would make the patrolman's bail the highest ever in the county for someone not in line for the death penalty. This case was making history on yet another front.

California had just resurrected its death penalty law, but only for murders committed under so-called special circumstances, what lawmakers determined were the particularly egregious violations of morality such as lying in wait to kill, killing for financial gain, and especially brutal slayings. Prosecutors did not seek to make history by being the first to seek the death penalty against a highway patrolman.

The court hearing was set for Tuesday, almost one week after the first one. Into the fray stepped yet another lawyer,

Judy Rowland. Rowland had met the Knotts when they came to the California Center for Victimology looking for guidance about their rights and the legal system. Now Rowland wanted the right to argue in court, on behalf of the victim's family, that Peyer should never be freed on bail.

If the judge allowed Rowland to appear in court, her appearance would be unprecedented. The ever-traditional legal community was in an uproar. Legal experts declared that adding a third voice in the courtroom would topple the delicate balance of prosecution and defense that had served American justice for centuries. Not only that, it would be two against one.

Before the hearing, Judge Exarhos took the three attorneys into his chambers to hash out the issue privately. Grimes argued vehemently to keep the third lawyer out of the arena, saying, "A public statement by Miss Rowland is neither legal nor appropriate. Her participation would be catastrophic to my client's right to a fair trial."

Deputy District Attorney Van Orshoven was trying to remain neutral. The prosecutor believed that the Knott family was turning into the proverbial eight-hundred-pound gorilla; he had never seen a victim's family so in the forefront. If they wanted Rowland to speak for them, well, he did not want to upset them any further. Besides, Rowland was a former colleague; she had left the San Diego County district attorney's office to join the victims' rights movement that had swept the state four years earlier.

"Though I may personally find the participation of these people less than comfortable," Van Orshoven began carefully, "it's extremely naive of us to ignore the fact that the community is interested in hearing from these people."

Judge Exarhos pointed out that under the law the victim's lawyer was the deputy DA. "Don't you represent the people of the state of California?" he asked Van Orshoven.

The prosecutor agreed. "I represent all the people of the state of California."

The judge focused on Van Orshoven. "Shouldn't her comments and her thoughts be more appropriately directed to you, so that you can present them in court?"

Van Orshoven hit the ball back into the judge's court saying, "Whatever your honor decides."

What the judge decided was to let Rowland into court for the second bail review hearing. On Tuesday, January 27, the third lawyer officially argued in state court that Craig Peyer should never be freed on bail.

In the end, Judge Exarhos sided with the prosecution and more than tripled Peyer's bail to one million dollars. The judge never said whether the appearance of the victim's lawyer swayed his decision to stiffen the bail. But the appearance by Rowland made legal history; the Knott case was just starting and already it had allowed a new and controversial precedent concerning the issue of how and when the crime victim's voice should be heard within the legal system. One official at the California Center for Victimology, where Rowland worked, bragged to a reporter that when it came to the Knott case, "The center has more information than the district attorney." Just what Van Orshoven needed, more shooting at his kneecaps—this time from people who were supposed to be on his side. Now the prosecutor was reduced to having to publicly insist that he had control of his case.

"Nobody knows more about the evidence than I do," he told reporters in response to the center's contention. "If they have information they haven't shared with me, I wish to heck they'd share it with me."

The next morning at his El Cajon home, Sam read the little exchange in the morning paper. "I don't care if the bar association gets their feathers ruffled. That monster should never be loose again," he told Joyce.

The name Peyer had never been spoken in the Knott household. Banning the name was not something they talked about doing. It just happened by instinct, as if they all knew that uttering that name would be like speaking a curse in a sacred place.

It seemed every morning she woke up, Karen Peyer faced another mountain to climb.

Now her test was to raise one million dollars—why, it takes weeks to even *count* to one million. Where was a substitute gym teacher going to raise that kind of money?

Craig's parents sent letters asking for financial help from their friends at Singing Hills Country Club where his mother, Eileen, had played golf for years. Karen sat down and wrote out a plea to her neighbors to help.

Craig has pierced me through my being with his urgent pleas for his release from jail as quickly as possible. With these cries for help, the Lord has placed it upon my heart to do whatever is necessary to raise that almost impossible amount.

Karen tried writing to actor Burgess Meredith for financial help, pouring out her heart on notebook paper and hoping his fondness for law enforcement might sway him. Meredith's response was to forward her letter to the district attorney's office.

While his family devoted themselves to raising the million, Peyer remained in special segregation inside the massively overcrowded county jail. Then on March 5, seven weeks after his arrest, the patrolman was quietly bailed out of county jail at 9:30 P.M. after posting a bond for one million dollars.

Craig Peyer's father had an idea.

They would write a book about how a respected police officer was railroaded by prosecutors, picked as a scapegoat because the cops couldn't pin the murder of the all-American girl on anyone else. The Craig Peyer story certainly was compelling, as the Peyers knew too well, living inside the nightmare as they did.

With a book, they hoped to get their side of the story out to the public. Hal and the Peyers agreed that the media had already decided Craig was guilty and were taking every kind of cheap shot available. They felt there was no way he could get fair news coverage.

Maybe they thought a book could help raise money to pay for Craig's defense. Hal called some local literary agents and found one with a client who was a lawyer and a part-time writer. Attorney Rohn Robbins and his agent met with the Peyer family several times to talk about the possibility of writing a book. Robbins remembers vividly meeting over at Hal's house in a solid middle-class neighborhood of ranch-style houses, with an RV parked in the driveway.

Robbins found the family friendly and forthcoming with background information, but to him the father was overbearing. "Hal did all the talking. He always sat at the head of the table. Everyone always deferred to him," Robbins said.

Craig Peyer seemed to Robbins to be a likable guy and very talkative. But that was as far as the project went. First, Robbins decided there wasn't enough money involved. And secondly, he said, there was the matter of Hal Peyer wanting to control the story.

"I found their story compelling," Robbins said, "but I felt uncomfortable just signing away creative control like that."

Sam Knott sat in his favorite easy chair next to the fireplace. From across the room a life-sized photograph of Cara's face smiled at him. Over his head, hung her watercolor painting of a mother sea otter with her babies. On his lap sat his poetry notebooks dating back to his army days that he had dug out of some old boxes. Now he was never without them. Writing poetry eased the roaming pain in his heart.

Sam wrote to keep the lonely thoughts away during those weeks and weeks they waited for justice. Meanwhile, downtown in the police laboratories detectives were meticulously analyzing the clothes taken from Cara and Peyer. They took fifty samples from Cara's bloodstained white sweatshirt and came up with three gold fibers. Now they had to figure out where those bits of gold thread had come from.

They analyzed the drops of blood under their microscopes, blood from the sweatshirt, blood from her boot. Whose blood was it? They analyzed fingerprints they found inside her car, six fingerprints. Who did they belong to?

The lawyers meanwhile started filing documents, stacks of documents concerning who would be allowed to testify in court, where the trial was to be held, and what kind of genetics experts should be included.

January turned to February and Cara's birthday passed quietly. Sam wrote her a poem to commemorate the day Cara would have been twenty-one years old, a full-fledged adult, ready to graduate from college and start her own life. The *San Diego Union's* popular city columnist Tom Blair reprinted part of Sam's birthday poem:

> *You are my daughter and I'll always protect you*
> *You are my sleeping beauty, with an instant smile*
>   *and a happy laugh*
> *For you are spirit song.*
> *And endless summer sunshine*
> *And ocean spray.*
> *I will always celebrate your life song of giving*
> *And your triumphs of joy*
> *For you are my morning and evening star*
> *And now you are stardust and you will live forever.*

Just when Karen Peyer thought there were no more catastrophes left in the world to strike her family, short of disease or devastating earthquakes, there came another blow.

On May 28, five months after the murder—and five months before the trial was set to begin—the California Highway Patrol officially fired Craig Peyer. Even though Peyer still was an innocent man in the eyes of the law, the CHP conducted its own internal investigation and declared, without a trial, that Peyer was guilty of violating a dozen CHP policies, and of killing Cara Knott.

The Peyers were stunned. Craig was arguably the most conscientious cop in the barracks and had given his life to the highway patrol. Now they were betraying him and the sacred right of the judicial system, that every accused man is presumed innocent. He had been suspended since his arrest but still drew his $36,000 a year income. The firing cut that salary out just when the Peyers needed it the most. Since Karen had no full-time job, there was now no health insurance for them or the three children.

How was this firing going to look to prospective jurors; Craig's brethren wouldn't even stand by him? Up until this announcement, there had been thousands of people, even hundreds of thousands, rooting for Craig. Karen knew it, she saw their looks when she went to the supermarket. They sent her cards of encouragement and called her on the phone. All Karen Peyer could do now was turn her worries into prayers.

Just when he was about to take center stage in the greatest case of his career, life handed Joe Van Orshoven two more sorrows. His mother's Alzheimer's disease had recently gotten worse and her physical health had also deteriorated. Since she no longer lived with her husband, Joe was left to care for her. At about the same time Joe's ninety-four-year-old father started losing his health as well. Eight months after Van Orshoven took the Peyer case, his mother died. And within one month, old Joe Van Orshoven died in his sleep.

Van Orshoven handled details of funerals and sorted out estates while trying to overcome his grief over the loss of his father, who left some very big shoes for Joe to fill. Old Joe had been a wild west cowboy and a heroic fighter in World War I; he had joined the U.S. Border Patrol back when they still patroled the border on horseback. He rose to the top of the patrol, eventually running the entire San Diego sector.

The burden of living up to his father's image weighed on Joe who was by that time deep in major pretrial motions and legal research that required his complete attention.

The outside world did not see the conflict inside Van Orshoven. District Attorney Ed Miller was pleased with his deputy's progress. Van Orshoven kept him up on all the pretrial motions, which he was winning. Two victories stood out. Van Orshoven defeated Grimes's bid to move the case out of San Diego County because of the defense's fear that all the publicity surrounding the trial might prejudice jurors. Grimes had even hired a pollster to measure local opinion, and came to court armed with poll results that indicated the majority of county residents believed that Peyer was a killer. But the judge ruled that there was insufficient proof to support the defense argument that he couldn't find twelve citizens among the county's populace that would give the former highway patrolman an even chance at guilt or innocence.

And in a second pretrial skirmish, over Grimes's protests, Van Orshoven won the right to bring to court all of the two dozen women Peyer had pulled over on Mercy Road for long and often intimate talks in the months leading up to the slaying.

The trial date kept moving back until finally a date was set for right after the Christmas holidays. As the time drew closer, Van Orshoven was increasingly confident he could win Peyer's conviction. "I'm going to get a conviction," he told Ed Miller in a meeting soon after Thanksgiving. Miller looked across his big wooden desk at the bantam-sized prosecutor. Joe's white hair was slicked into place, his face was browned from working outside, and he wore his sober gray suit well. He looked like a man with a mission.

Van Orshoven stayed up to all hours of the night in his den preparing to wrap a legal noose around his enemy the way he imagined Peyer had ensnared Cara. But the question remained, would the prosecutor's legal rope be strong enough?

Courtroom 22 sits on the fifth and top floor of San Diego County Courthouse, a squat civic affair from the sixties built with plain stucco walls. The room is paneled in a dull brown wood and includes wall-to-wall shelves of law books. Civic planners of yesteryear failed to prepare San Diego for its tremendous population growth and thus built such courtrooms with only thirty seats. The New York City court facilities bathrooms are usually bigger than courtroom 22. It was in courtroom 22 that, exactly one year and one week after the death of Cara Knott, the State of California—Craig Peyer's former employer—officially began murder proceedings against him.

Van Orshoven was about to lead, for the state, one of the most complex kinds of trials in law, a case built entirely on circumstantial evidence. All he had to tie the accused killer to the victim was a nickel-sized drop of blood, a dirty yellow plastic rope, six microscopic gold threads, a set of extrawide tire tracks on Mercy Road, a doctored speeding ticket, and a cop with weird habits. With the absence of eye-witnesses, the state's case had to be pieced together with the help of police work and scientific analysis. Blood experts had determined that the little drop of blood taken from Cara's white boot matched Craig Peyer's blood type and two key genetic markers.

The police also had what they believed was the murder

School picture of
Cara Knott.
(Photo courtesy of the Knott
family.)

Cara with her mother,
Joyce Knott, three
years before her death.
(Photo courtesy of the
Knott family.)

Cara with boyfriend Wayne Bautista at a local waterskiing spot on San Diego's Mission Bay. The couple were very athletic and often spent their time at the beach, working out at a health club, or running. (Photo courtesy of the Knott family.)

Cara and Wayne on prom night at the famous Hotel Del Coronado.
(Photo courtesy of Boyd Anderson Photography.)

Cara as a bridesmaid at her sister's wedding one month before her death at age 20.
(Photo courtesy of the Knott family.)

Cara and her father Sam at a fashion show held at her high school.
(Photo courtesy of the Knott family.)

The old highway bridge and creekbed at the Mercy Road exit. The middle of the bridge is the approximate spot from which Cara was thrown the night of her death. (Photo courtesy of the Knott family.)

The bike path leading to the old highway bridge. The desolate surroundings are clearly apparent. (Photo courtesy of the Knott family.)

Sam and Joyce Knott, Cara's parents, listen to
testimony during the first trial.
(Photo courtesy of the Knott family.)

Craig Peyer, a 13-year
veteran of the
California Highway
Patrol, during
arraignment on
charges of murder.
(Photo courtesy of
San Diego Union.)

Deputy District Attorney Joe Van Orshoven holds the murder weapon during closing arguments of the first trial. (Photo courtesy of *San Diego Union*.)

Craig Peyer standing with his defense attorney, Robert Grimes. (Photo courtesy of Roni Galgano, *San Diego Union*.)

Prosecutor Paul Pfingst holding up a school picture of Cara in court during the second murder trial.
(Photo courtesy of Charles Starr, *San Diego Union*.)

Photo of Craig Peyer taken off a television set as he appeared on a segment titled "Safety Tips for Stranded Motorists," just a day after Cara's murder.
(Photo courtesy of Associated Press.)

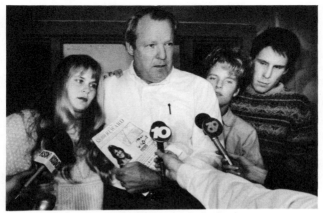

The Knott family gathers on their doorstep for the media on the night Craig Peyer is arrested. Left to right: Cheryl Knott, Sam Knott, Cynthia Knott Weick, and her husband Bill Weick. (Photo courtesy of Bruce Huff, *San Diego Union*.)

The Knott family reads statements at the sentencing of Patrolman Craig Peyer. Seated before them are Paul Pfingst and Joan Stein. To the right are seated Defense Attorney Robert Grimes, defendant Craig Peyer, and attorney Diane Campbell.
(Photo courtesy of Roni Galgano, *San Diego Union*.)

weapon, the yellow rope they found in Craig Peyer's patrol car. The rope braid generally matched the scars on Cara's neck; it was definitely not CHP-issue equipment and the way it was stuffed under the spare tire in the trunk was certainly suspicious. Peyer had to have put it there himself.

The best solid evidence the state had were six small threads, Van Orshoven thought. The experts told him that three gold fibers found on Cara's body matched those taken from the CHP patch on Peyer's uniform. What made those fibers even more distinct was that they were from a kind of patch that was no longer made; only veteran CHP officers would have such gold-trimmed patches.

Van Orshoven had no eyewitnesses, but he did have a young couple whose limousine had broken down at the off ramp probably minutes after Peyer brought Cara down into the darkness of Mercy Road. The couple had seen a police car speed away from the scene and he would put on the stand another young couple who drove farther down the canyon to make out at about 9:30 that night, and they had passed by Cara's car parked near the bridge. Those young lovers had seen little else because they had decided, ironically, that the place was too spooky to be romantic, and had left soon after they'd arrived. That gave him a time of death, he believed, between 8:45 and 9:30.

The state also had the scratches on Craig Peyer's face that had appeared the night of the murder. Plenty of witnesses would testify to that. And Van Orshoven felt Peyer's excuse, that he fell against the fence at CHP headquarters, was so thin that any jury could see through it. The extrawide tire tracks found at the scene matched the wheelbase of a CHP cruiser. That put Peyer at the scene.

Finally, there was the matter of Craig's little games with pretty women he pulled over from the freeway. There was credible testimony that Peyer had talked endlessly to these women about their jobs and feelings, boyfriends, lots of things wholly unrelated to the motor vehicle code. Van Orshoven was going to call twenty women who spent up to ninety minutes at Peyer's mercy below that lonely off ramp.

The prosecutor had the thirteenth ticket Peyer had written that night, with the time crossed out and back timed an hour.

How convenient that the new time just happened to be close to the hour when Cara Knott was slain.

Van Orshoven had an ominous pattern of behavior, and he had fiber and blood evidence based on the newest scientific techniques. But the presentation wouldn't be easy. He knew the evidence was not only complicated to grasp and to explain to juries, but also legally controversial, and behind it all he had a reasonable motive—that this cop was so regimented that he would do anything to save his nice and neat little life—including kill anyone who threatened to expose him, as Cara must have done when she refused to submit to his power games.

The district attorney had nothing, Peyer's defense team contended, but a big pile of puzzle pieces that had to be forced together to frame an unlikely suspect, a good father and husband, a Vietnam war veteran, an experienced and stellar cop.

Grimes figured the best weapon he had would be testimony from homicide investigators themselves. He would offer a chilling prospect to the jurors—that the public was so hungry to get the murder of the all-American girl solved and police were so desperate to get a suspect, any suspect, that they framed one of their own. It was, Grimes figured, the ultimate betrayal.

He was outraged by the police's claim that nobody else had the chance to commit the crime except Peyer. That was certainly not strong enough to convict a man of murder. Especially when the accompanying evidence was so flimsy. Not only did authorities fail to pinpoint something as crucial as the time of Cara's death, but the coroner never sorted out the order of her injuries. Was Cara alive when she was socked so hard in the right eye that her skull cracked? Was she beaten up first, or did the awful damage come from the sixty-five-foot fall?

How could the patrolman have engineered the murder? Cara's car had been parked a quarter mile from the old highway bridge. How could Peyer have carried dead weight that far and thrown her off the bridge without leaving any marks behind? Police had found no indication that anyone had been dragged across the bridge, and they'd found no blood in or on his car. If he'd used the yellow rope to strangle her, why had there been no blood or skin tissue found on it?

Yes, the defendant had his face scratched the night of the murder. But Cara had no traceable skin residue under her fingernails to prove she had scratched him. And Craig had an explanation of the scratches. Plus he hadn't tried to hide the scratches; he even had had his supervisor write out an injury report. Would a guilty man have called attention to himself that way? And if he had just murdered somebody why would he bother stopping to help the Iranian man whose car had broken down on another freeway that wasn't even on Peyer's beat? Even though his shift was over and he should have been checking in at headquarters, he had taken the time to push the man's car to a nearby gas station.

The extrawide tire tracks at the murder scene could have been made by any big car braking at high speeds. That night Peyer had put so many miles on his car, about 250, how could he have racked those up and disappeared as the state contended and still been able to kill someone?

And those fibers. The lab found bits of purple fibers on Peyer's gun and uniform, but they didn't necessarily come from Cara's clothes. They could have been from his kids' coats. Or for that matter from the dry cleaner's where police had picked up Peyer's uniform a week after the murder.

Most of all, Grimes contended, the state had no motive for this by-the-book lawman wanting to kill the girl. There was no proof they'd even met.

The first day of trial, January 4, 1988, was a typical sunny winter day under the palm trees, but for a change San Diegans were not distracted by the balmy weather. They remained riveted to the unfolding legal duel. The highway patrolman on trial for murder was the talk everywhere from the attorney-filled tables at John's Diner two doors from the courthouse to La Costa, forty miles to the north, the fat farm of the rich and famous.

If this courtroom drama were a late-night movie, the opposing stars would be Robert Young and Gary Cooper. It featured Van Orshoven in the Young part, the dapper career prosecutor with a booming voice and an old-time addiction to cigarettes, an oddity in a health obsessed town where it seems everyone else quit ages ago. In contrast across the aisle was Bob Grimes as Gary Cooper, his voice gentle and his manner amiable.

Beside Grimes at the defense table sat his co-counsel, Diane Campbell, a stunning and tall woman, with long dark hair, big eyes, and elegant clothes. Some said she resembled television's Wonder Woman, Lynda Carter. Between them sat thirty-seven-year-old Craig Alan Peyer, in his wide-collared shirts, his pale yellow sweater tight against his barrel chest, his maroon polyester sports coat with its lapels just slightly too wide. He looked like the kind of guy who got a new suit at Sear's every couple of years whether he needed it or not. Campbell and Grimes didn't try too hard to soften Peyer's image with, say, a tweed sports coat. As Campbell said, "He's a cop. There's no way to change him."

When Sam Knott arrived in courtroom 22 that first day of the trial, he wasn't sure where to go. He was deeply concerned with courtroom rituals, like where it was proper for the Knott family to sit in the courtroom. There was one thing he didn't want to do. He wanted to make sure he didn't sit next to Peyer's family. What a horror that would be. So, on this day, as he led his family into courtroom 22, he took the middle row on the right side. He just followed his instinct. He was relieved when the prosecutors came in and sat at the table in front of the family, Assistant District Attorney Joe Van Orshoven and his assistant, Jim Atkins, a rookie prosecutor who bounded across the courtroom in his cowboy boots. Sam turned to his family, pleased that everything seemed in order. Things were starting off well. He was in the right seat.

The Peyer family quietly filed into the middle row on the left, behind the defense. The Knotts and the Peyers made it a point to look everywhere around the courtroom, at the jurors' box, the witness stand, the judge's chair. But never at each other. And so it would continue for the next eight weeks in a not-so-private battle of emotional wills.

Sam Knott sat stiffly in his seat and looked over the judge. He had read up on this man, San Diego Superior Court Judge Richard Huffman, who was pretty new to the bench but was no debutant to high-stakes cases. Both Sam Knott and Joe

Van Orshoven were pleased that Huffman, a onetime assistant district attorney, was assigned to take the Peyer case. Joe Van Orshoven told Sam that Huffman had prosecuted an array of defendants—from Mafia hitman Jimmy "the Weasel" Frattiano to Mayor Roger Hedgecock, who was forced to resign from office after being convicted in connection with the mishandling of campaign funds.

Huffman, the son of a Los Angeles fire captain, had the reputation of being a brilliant attorney. He was the first lawyer in California history to win that most unusual of murder cases—a conviction in which the body of the victim was never recovered. Since the body often provided most of the evidence in the case, that meant he had relied on circumstantial evidence. With that background, Van Orshoven assured Sam Knott, the judge certainly knew his way around the logistical mine fields of circumstantial cases.

Huffman was also a law professor with heavy-weight political connections, including one to one of the most powerful men in the nation, then-U.S. Attorney General Edwin Meese. For Sam, it was keen irony as he watched the mild-mannered judge with square glasses and iron-gray hair, that Huffman had once been turned down for judgeship because he was considered too aggressive. Now Judge Huffman sat in his black robe on the elevated judicial easy chair and seemed to Sam Knott more like a wise grandfather, ready and eager to judge the evidence fairly.

From the start, Judge Huffman made clear he was going to take extra care with this historic and sensitive case. His first move was to order the two hundred potential jurors to be prescreened to see if they had picked up too much prejudicial information from the exhaustive media coverage of the case.

For most lawyers, the ideal situation would be that no jurors had ever heard of the case being tried. But Van Orshoven had explained to Sam that both he and the defense lawyers were heading into the trial knowing it would be nearly impossible to get jurors who knew nothing of the Peyer case. "The best thing we can hope for is to get jurors who are open-minded," the prosecutor told him.

During the prescreening process, the prospective jurors bore out Van Orshoven's predictions. "I don't think there's anybody in this state that hasn't heard about the case," said one blunt banker, who ended up on the jury.

Another man questioned by the lawyers said he knew beyond a shadow of a doubt that Peyer was innocent. How did he know? the judge asked. The prospective juror answered, "I'm a doctor of psychology and I am trained in parapsychology." The good doctor was excused from jury duty. Some prospective jurors had other problems. One complained that he was too claustrophobic to sit in such a tiny courtroom all day, and he too was shown the door.

In the delicate science of jury selection, each lawyer relies on his own complex system and pored-over theories, a gamble not unlike that of a tout at the race track. As Grimes prepared his case, his main worry was the testimony of all those women Peyer had pulled over near Mercy Road. He had lost his legal maneuver to keep them out of the court, so he decided to announce to the prospective jurors that those women would be testifying about their meetings with Peyer, thereby softening their impact since the news was coming from him, the defense. For Grimes, the strategy was simple: remove the element of surprise and make it seem commonplace.

At the same time, Grimes wanted to choose panelists who would not be too sympathetic to the testimony of these women. Grimes didn't want jurors who would seriously question the image of Peyer as a law-and-order family man. Grimes was not only concerned about what the women would say, but also with how they looked. The women stopped by Peyer near Mercy Road were all beautiful—a major factor that could alter the image of Peyer from the model husband to major swinger. With that, Grimes started on the offensive, tipping the prosecution's hand. "What if," Grimes asked the pool of jurors, "woman after woman comes in, and it starts to look like the Miss Poway pageant? What if you decide he was the Gary Hart of the highway patrol?" Grimes referred to the former Colorado senator whose highly publicized fling with model Donna Rice ended his chance at the White House in 1984. Not a bad comparison for a stodgy highway patrolman accused of murder, to be put up against a sexy presidential candidate whose most serious crime seemed to be the fact that his libido got out of hand.

Judge Huffman also warned the jurors about the upcoming testimony of the women stopped by Peyer. "Their testimony can only be used to determine whether it is likely that Mr. Peyer stopped Cara Knott, and not to decide whether he has a bad character or had a disposition to commit crimes. It is not an indication that he is a Jekyll and Hyde."

Van Orshoven revealed a glimpse of his tactics early. This was an emotional case, and he wanted jurors who would feel for Cara Knott, a woman who was brutally slain, and not get lost in the confusing information about DNA genetic testing and the legal hairsplitting that would come with it. The prosecutor asked the prospective jurors if they would mind if he became angry on occasion, saying, "You understand that it is my job and that I may become emotional in my presentation of the case?"

Clearly the prosecutor wasn't the only one emotionally involved with the case. One prospective juror asked to be excused because the whole scenario upset him. He had a sister the same age as Cara, he explained, and he knew how crazy he would be if anyone hurt her. "In all fairness to the defense, I don't know that I would make a good juror," the young man said. The defense agreed, and he was dismissed.

As the juror left the courtroom, Sam maintained the same sober expression, but inside he felt a surge of pride. He had done his job; he made people in this town understand who Cara was and feel her loss as deeply as if she were one of their own family. But was this going to backfire on him now? What if all the good jurors who related to Cara got kicked off, and only those who were insensitive and aloof remained?

Just then a forty-one-year-old mailman in the jury pool told the judge he believed that Peyer was probably guilty. That made Sam feel better. But the mailman added, "I can give Mr. Peyer the presumption of innocence." The mailman made the jury.

Another possible juror Victor Dingman said he knew all about the murder because his skiing buddy was a reporter who had covered the case and had shown him Cara Knott's autopsy report. The guy gave Cheryl Knott the creeps from her vantage point in the audience. "Who in the world reads an autopsy for fun?" she whispered to her father.

Cara's middle sister waited for Van Orshoven to say "thanks but no thanks." Dingman knew all about the Mercy Road dead end, since he worked an early-morning shift and often pulled off the freeway to nap there so he wouldn't fall asleep at the wheel.

The monster's lawyer must love this guy, Sam thought, looking over at Grimes, who held a poker face as the potential juror continued talking.

"How many conversations have you had with the reporter about this case?" Van Orshoven asked Dingman.

"Two or three at the most."

"How familiar are you with the case?"

"Only [that] there's some question about the blood test. He wanted to find out how the blood tests are done. I don't even know what blood tests are, what's involved."

The prosecutor nodded, apparently satisfied with the response. Judge Huffman turned to the defense table. "Mr. Grimes?"

"I'll pass, your honor," the defense attorney said.

And so Victor Dingman was left in the pool for the final cut.

Cheryl and Sam rushed over to Van Orshoven as he left for the recess. As they walked hurriedly down the hall, outside earshot of the reporters, they told him how uneasy they felt about Dingman's possible presence on the jury.

"It doesn't seem to me he would be very good," Sam said. The rest of the family added their apprehensions.

After the break, a confident Van Orshoven went back to work. So certain was the prosecutor of his case, he only challenged a few potential jurors, although he had the chance to reject more than a dozen. He was like a basketball coach who was so sure of his game he didn't bother using all his time outs as seconds ticked away. He figured, why tamper with something that's solid? With a speed that surprised everyone in the courtroom, the Peyer jury was picked in only two days.

The lawyers selected a jury of eight men and four women to judge Craig Peyer, their former public servant. They ranged in age from twenty-four to seventy-three and included a flight attendant, two mailmen, a retired engineer, a teacher, a banker, a computer company executive, a corporate auditor, a retired navy man, and a self-employed computer programmer who had a daughter Cara's age. And the juror who had read Cara's autopsy report, Victor Dingman.

Cheryl Knott was fuming. "What happened?" she asked Van Orshoven later. "Why didn't you take that Dingman guy off?" She tried to remain calm as she reported back to her family, "He told me he forgot."

That weekend a freak storm blasted into usually sedate southern California, whipping the winds up to sixty-four miles per hour, wiping out trailer parks, ripping the roofs off houses throughout the southland. It was deemed one of the worst storms of the century, and in its wake left eight people dead one hundred miles to the north in Los Angeles. A hotel collapsed along the beach in neighboring Orange County. The storm damaged San Diego County so badly a state of emergency was called. Roads were flooded, businesses closed, roofs of buildings ripped off, even the renowned San Diego Zoo, where Cara Knott had worked one summer, was forced to close for the first time in its seventy-five-year history.

The killer storm was still pelting rain down on the city when testimony in the murder trial of Craig Alan Peyer began.

"The people call Wayne Bautista." Van Orshoven uttered those words and the battle commenced. Bautista walked up to the witness stand as everyone stared at the dark-haired young man Cara Knott had planned to marry, a man police once listed as a suspect in her murder. Bautista was as handsome as Cara was lovely. As a couple, their complementary good looks had turned heads.

The prosecutor warmed the witness up with basics—his age—twenty-one—where he lived—in northeastern Escondido—where he was the night of the murder—at home with his sister and stepsister.

"In citing your attention to a photograph that has heretofore been marked as the people's evidence number one, do you recognize the person in that photograph?" asked Van

Orshoven as he flashed a framed eight-by-ten color glossy of Cara's smiling face.

"Yes I do," Bautista answered.

"On the twenty-seventh day of December nineteen-eighty-six, what was your relationship with that person?"

"She was my girlfriend. I was her boyfriend."

"How long had you been in that relationship?"

"Approximately three years."

"Had there been any discussion between the two of you regarding marriage?"

"Yes, we were planning to be married as soon as we graduated from college." The audience expected Bautista to finish with the phrase, "and live happily ever after."

Bautista was a testament to what a virtuous young woman Cara Knott was, nursing her sick boyfriend instead of taking it easy on her vacation, the dutiful daughter who called her parents and stopped for gas instead of risking the trip home on anything less than half a tank of fuel.

"During the period you and Cara Knott were going together, you were familiar with her manner of response to authority figures, and more importantly, to her parents?"

"Yes. She always kept her parents aware of what she was doing and where she was."

"I take it you had gone places with her in her automobile?"

"Yes."

"At anytime had she stopped to pick up any hitchhikers?"

"Never."

"Had she ever suggested that you do so?"

"She told me that I shouldn't."

Another crucial point was established in Van Orshoven's mind, a likely response to the defense's argument that a weird hitchhiker sought by police had actually killed Cara Knott.

Bautista told how he had driven up and down the freeway unable to find Cara and then had headed back to the Knotts' house around 2 A.M. He described how he'd driven to Cara's friends' houses after that, and then returned at 5 A.M. to the Knotts' to regroup. During his search, he said he even got off at Mercy Road.

"I drove to the bottom of the off ramp and observed a

trailer and a tractor on the right-hand side enclosed in a fenced area, and on the left-hand side there were signs posted CLOSED. All there was was mounds of dirt and I assumed that's all there was, so I drove straight back up the freeway and took I-15 south.''

Van Orshoven didn't belabor the point, and handed his first witness over to the defense. Grimes unfolded himself from his chair and walked up to Bautista on the stand.

"Mr. Bautista," he began in his gentle voice, "did you have any conversation with Cara at the time she was leaving? In other words, did she say good-bye or anything like that?''

Wayne related the last conversation he had ever had with his girlfriend. He told how he'd stood at the door and watched her drive away. There was no way, he said, that anyone had gotten in the car with her.

"Okay," Grimes asked, "what part of the house were you in?''

"In the family room," Wayne answered.

"You weren't on the phone when she left?''

"No, I was not.'' Wayne wasn't going to give the defense lawyer much beyond yes or no answers to any questions if he could help it.

"What kind of mood was Cara in when she left the house December twenty-seventh?'' Grimes asked.

"Cara was a little concerned for me, being that I was sick.''

"Was she upset at all about anything?''

"No, she wasn't.''

Grimes couldn't get the boyfriend to say Cara was mad at Wayne for staying cooped up all weekend, and maybe she went off for a little fun before she started for home. The defense attorney tried a new tack.

"Were there places in the area that you two used to go, like places you [might] go dancing or anything like that?''

"No, there wasn't.''

"There was no place in Escondido you danced?''

"We drove to one place to dance, but we ended up not going.''

"When was that?'' Grimes wanted to know.

"I believe it was February nineteen-eighty-five, or some-time in nineteen-eighty-six."

"Do you remember the name of that place?"

"It was After Dark."

"But you ended up never even going inside?"

"It wasn't our type of place."

The boyfriend didn't leave much of an opening, but Grimes played it up for all its worth. Maybe the jury would believe Cara got restless and decided to try the place out.

"Then, in the early morning hours of December twenty-eight," Grimes asked, "did you pick up any hitchhikers?"

"Yes," Bautista answered and Grimes paused, letting the jury get the full effect.

Grimes was ready to give the jurors an opening for doubt. Now, if the boyfriend picked up hitchhikers because he's a good soul, perhaps the jury would believe Cara might have picked up the weird hitchhiker before meeting her death.

"He was at a gas station where I exited," Bautista said, referring to his hitchhiker. "And he said his car had broken down. And I had noticed his car, so I just drove him down the off ramp to his car."

Grimes believed he'd made his score and wanted to let it sink in to the jurors. So he retreated. "Thank you, Mr. Bautista, nothing further."

Judge Huffman nodded to the prosecution. "Mr. Van Orshoven, any redirect?" Van Orshoven asked Bautista to elaborate about this bar, After Dark.

"It wasn't your type of place then?" he asked.

Bautista seemed grateful to be able to explain without seeming a snob. "I didn't feel comfortable there. The people there weren't my type of people."

"Rough crowd?" Van Orshoven asked.

"Yeah." Bautista nodded.

Van Orshoven looked at the jurors and stood near the prosecution table where Cara's picture stared at them, as if to say, how could they believe a sweet girl like this would go dancing alone at some rough place?

"No further questions," the prosecutor said.

Van Orshoven was presenting the case sequentially, retracing Cara's last steps. He brought up the Chevron gas station clerk to verify the computer record of Cara's last known stop, the credit card slip showing she'd bought six gallons of gas. Then the person who found Cara's car took the stand, her brother-in-law, Bill Weick.

Van Orshoven began: "Did you have a close relationship with Cara?"

"Yes, I was her big brother."

"What was her habit having to do with keeping family rules and regulations?"

"She's—" Bill started to answer in present tense, so intent was he to keep Cara alive. "She *was* very precise. She would do what she said she would do," Weick said.

"What was her attitude toward authority figures in general?"

"She was one to have respect for people who had authority."

Van Orshoven asked how he had found Cara's car so far down the Mercy Road dead end.

"I saw that I could not go to the right because there was construction. . . . I drove to where the road stopped. There was a wall of dirt there and I saw a curve. It looked new and I asked Cindy what she thought we should do.

"It was dark and foggy, something out of a movie," Weick testified, recounting how they'd called Cara's name for a half an hour and then headed back up to the freeway to find a phone, and how easy it had been to slip his car around the construction barricades that blocked the way down the dead end.

When it was Grimes's turn, he only had one point to make.

"Mr. Weick," the defense attorney asked, "was one of the items you were looking for a white coat that belonged to Cara?"

"No, it really wasn't."

"You weren't looking for a white coat?"

"No."

"Did you ever find a white coat?"

"No."

With that, Grimes raised a little doubt, a little mystery in the case—the white leather jacket that disappeared. It was not key, just provocative enough, he hoped, to make the jury wonder where it went and why the cops had never found it. Grimes moved on to everything Bill Weick took out of Cara's car and put into his own—the shopping bag, Cara's net bag, her purse—in order to show the evidence had been disturbed.

"Did someone put those bags back in the car?" the defense attorney asked.

"Yes."

"Who did that?"

"Cynthia and the police officer," Weick answered, like Wayne, trying to minimize his answers.

The questioning continued, and through it all sat Craig Peyer, as quiet as stone. The jurors stole glances at him, to see if he would give anything away. He kept staring straight ahead at the witnesses, never even blinking, it seemed.

Following Bill Weick was his wife, Cynthia, Cara's oldest sister, who identified the bags found in Cara's VW. Then her middle sister, Cheryl, identified Cara's white purse, her makeup bag, her white wallet with the driver's license still inside, the shopping bag from Nordstrom's. They were both on and off in a flash. Van Orshoven was counting on delivering a more powerful unspoken statement, that these were walking, breathing replicas of their murdered baby sister.

Cara's mother, Joyce, followed her daughters. The jury saw a pert woman in her late forties with graying light hair. There was no mistaking the pain in her face. Joyce explained how a friend of hers had taken a self-defense course from a former police sergeant, Sandy Strong, and loved it so much she was taking her own daughter. That's when, Joyce testified, she suggested to Cara that they both take the class. The self-defense teacher taught them to always strike out when attacked or threatened, she explained. "One of the things he taught us was to go for the eyes with the fingers. To scratch and kick." With shouts and jabs, they had practiced simulated attacks with men instructors.

She talked about the friendship she had with her youngest girl, a picture-perfect mother-daughter relationship, rare indeed. "She was my buddy," Joyce said softly.

Grimes knew better than to pounce on a grieving mother. He passed on the cross-examination. The way things were going the worst statement that he could elicit from Mrs. Knott would be that Cara didn't make her bed enough. And Grimes doubted he could even get that out.

"The people call John Samuel Knott," Van Orshoven announced.

This is it, Sam thought as he walked carefully through the little gateway that separated the spectators from the participants. He climbed up the two steps and sat down in the witness chair to the left of the judge. The jury box was so close, he felt he could almost touch the jurors. Sam ignored the lawyers and the gallery and looked the jurors right in the eye. He wanted them to understand and remember him. All his work to get the monster who had killed Cara had brought him to this moment of truth. Nothing was going to stand in his way. He turned his attention, concentrated and alert, to the deputy district attorney.

Van Orshoven took his time with this witness. He had no choice, because the victim's father gave lengthy answers to every question. Sam was definitely going to speak his piece. Unlike the others, Sam was eager to go beyond the yes and no answers. He wanted to elaborate and illuminate the dozen jurors with the truth, as he saw it.

Sam sensed quite correctly that there was no way Grimes could contest much of his testimony. It would appear somewhat cruel, and it just didn't seem to be the defense attorney's style.

"First, I got a call to my soul about ten o'clock," Sam began, "a call to my soul. I jumped up from my chair and I kind of startled my son-in-law. I got up, got my coat, and went out to get the car. . . ."

He talked about searching, stopping the California Highway Patrol and asking for an all points bulletin on Cara, stopping sheriff's deputies twice, having Cheryl call the police all over the county, contacting the San Diego Police.

"I was out looking for my daughter because police would not respond because they had this twenty-four-hour policy, which is obscene. . . .

"Then I drove down the Mercy Road off ramp, and I looked to the left and there were barricades, to the right there was some equipment, so I was kind of taken by the fact that there was a car abandoned there and thought maybe she was in the car. I looked out under the bridge and the bridge was totally black and had these barricades, so I didn't envision the possibility that they were available to drive through. So I then proceeded back onto the freeway. . . .

"So I made another call. I called the highway patrol, the head dispatcher, the dispatcher on duty, around five-twenty and it was a terrible, horrible phone call."

"Okay, Mr. Knott," Van Orshoven interrupted, trying to gently pull the reins in on his witness, to keep up the momentum of the tale of dread. "Tell us what the weather that night was like."

"It was cold, the coldest night of the year," Sam answered.

"And you spent sometime from ten o'clock in the evening to five o'clock the following morning attempting to find your daughter?"

"I left about five-thirty and went out again," Sam resumed his tale. "I left the same time Wayne left and I actually followed Wayne so that he would be able to get home. And so I left him at the gas station. I decided to search around the park, which was right behind the shopping center. So I searched all the cars, just to see if she was hiding in there, for safety reasons.

"And then about six-thirty I was coming down one of the side streets and I saw my first San Diego Police car, black-and-white, so I chased after it. . . . I actually followed the first responding unit to the Mercy Road area.

"I jumped out of the car, I saw my car—my daughter's car there a mile off the freeway. . . ." And the big man sobbed unabashedly on the stand, in front of the audience and the television cameras. Van Orshoven was gentle with his last question, just one final emphasis on the size of the loss that brought them all to court this day.

"Mr. Knott, how old was Cara at the time of her death?"

"She was twenty years old," Sam answered.

Grimes certainly didn't want to keep open wounds in front of the jury any longer than necessary. "No questions, your honor," he said.

Quietly, trying not to break the spell Sam Knott had cast,

the prosecutor said, "I have no more witnesses prepared, your honor."

The crowd broke thirty minutes early after the first morning of testimony with the words of Cara's father lingering in the courtroom air.

But that was all the jury heard about Cara Knott for a long time. Van Orshoven was betting that the jury was intelligent enough to size up what kind of woman Cara was without his having to dwell on her. He didn't want to risk overplaying his sympathy card with the jury. But to reinforce Cara's presence, Van Orshoven kept her school picture in a gold frame propped up on the prosecution table, so Cara's sweet smile could be seen by the jurors throughout the entire gruesome proceeding.

Next, the prosecutor prepared to show how the accused and the victim crossed paths that night. Highway patrolman Craig Peyer was known to write a lot of tickets in his time. The night of the murder, he wrote thirteen. Van Orshoven brought in the twelfth and thirteenth people who had received tickets from Peyer before and after the prosecution's estimated time of the murder, 8:45 P.M. The deputy DA wanted to emphasize the ninety-minute gap when no one had seen or heard from Craig Peyer.

The second-to-last ticket went to Elise Hegret, caught speeding down Interstate 15 on her way to meet friends at a disco about 7:45 P.M, December 27. Hegret testified that Peyer had been quick and businesslike when he wrote up her ticket at the side of the freeway. There was one oddity, she said. He wrote the wrong birthdate on the ticket, as if he were distracted.

Teenager Jean-Pierre Gulli came to the stand to testify about getting the thirteenth ticket of that evening. Gulli had spent the day with his twin brother and their older sister at Miramar Lake in northern San Diego, and then had gone back to her apartment for dinner. There, they watched a videotaped movie.

"What time did you leave your sister's house?" Van Orshoven asked.

"It was nine-thirty, between nine-thirty and nine-forty-five."

"How do you know that?"

"Because we started the movie at eight and it was approximately one and a half hours long."

"After you left your sister's house did you have contact with a California highway patrolman?"

"Yes, I got a citation for my taillights; they were out and so he stopped me."

"How long after you had left your sister's house were you stopped?"

"I'd say fifteen minutes."

"So what would you estimate the time to have been when you received the citation?"

"It was ten."

"I show you a document that has been heretofore marked people's number forty-four for identification, and ask if you recognize that document."

"That was the citation I received."

"Inviting your attention to the portion of that document at the top that shows the time. It appears that one time has been scratched out and another time put in. Did you make that modification to the document?"

"No, I didn't."

"Who made that modification, if you know?"

"The officer who issued me the ticket."

"The officer who gave you the ticket?"

"Right."

"Do you see that individual in the courtroom today?"

"Yeah, he's sitting right over there," Gulli said, pointing to Peyer seated at the defense table.

"At the time and place where you received that ticket, what was the lighting?"

"It was pretty dark and it was a pretty foggy night."

"Did you get out of the car and check the taillight?"

"No, I didn't. I took his word for it."

"I beg your pardon?" Van Orshoven wanted to bring this home. After all, this was what the trial was all about—whether people trusted this cop.

Gulli repeated his answer loudly. "No, I didn't. I trusted him."

"When did you first notice the change of time at the top of the citation?"

"When the officers came to my house and pointed it out to me."

"Some police officers came to your house and talked to you about it?"

"Right."

"Was it after you had seen on the TV that some twenty-year-old girl had been killed?"

"It was like the day after."

"The day after?"

"Right."

Now it was Grimes's turn to cross-examine. "Mr. Gulli," the defense attorney began, "when the officer approached you to give you the ticket, I take it he came to your driver's side?"

"Yes, he did."

"And he stood there, and you had a conversation?"

"He asked for my license and registration and I gave him my license."

"You identified Mr. Peyer in court, here," Grimes pointed out.

"Right."

"Is that from having seen him on TV or is that from having a pretty good look on that evening?"

"That was mostly on the TV because before it was really dark. I really couldn't make out his face."

"So, then you didn't notice any type of scratches or marks on his face, did you?"

"No, like I said it was fairly dark."

"Well, did you look at a photo lineup of some subjects that the police officers showed you in January nineteen-eighty-seven?"

"Yeah, I did. I told them I remembered him having a mustache and he showed me a bunch of pictures and none of them looked like the one, but I picked out a couple that looked like it."

"Did you pick out [one] that you felt confident it was the officer?"

"I think so."

"And when you picked the officer out of the photo lineup

at the San Diego Police Department, that wasn't based on TV, was it? Wasn't that based on having seen him at the scene?"

"Yes."

"Now, I assume, Mr. Gulli, that when you stated that you felt you could identify him, his face, that's because you had seen facial features—"

"Right."

"When he gave you the ticket."

"Right."

"Now at some point during this event did the officer and you exchange things? For example, you handed him your driver's license."

"Yes."

"Did you see anything on his hands?"

"Not that I remember."

"When he handed back your driver's license, was there any type of bloodstaining on his hands?"

"Not that I remember."

Grimes had succeeded in flipping the witness totally around. At first Gulli said he didn't see him well enough to describe him, then Grimes had him saying he got a long look at Peyer and saw no scratches, no blood, nothing suspicious. The cross-examination of Gulli was vintage Bob Grimes. His technique relied on the regular-guy gee-whiz image, not like the aggressive, jaw popping, vein thumping lawyers advocating their end-of-the-world stands on television.

In the courtroom, the witnesses gave Grimes the we-like-you look. With that reasonable way of his, like bait on a hook, Grimes's technique was to lead witnesses along the path of agreed-upon fact, and then when they got to the place in the forest where the paths split, the defense attorney would gently nudge them down *his* path.

By the time he left the witness stand, Gulli felt like he was lying but he couldn't figure out what had hit him. The teenager knew he'd ended up saying things that he didn't want to say, and he didn't like it.

In the world outside courtroom 22, storms continued to rage. A half dozen fishing boats capsized off the coast of Baja

California, Mexico, and four people drowned. The research tower at Scripps Institution of Oceanography up the coast in La Jolla snapped in two. Inside courtroom 22, the storms were Craig Peyer's as the prosecution opened the second day of testimony in his murder trial. On the second day, Karen Anderson held the courtroom audience in her grasp when she testified that this highway patrolman had stuck in her mind that night precisely because he was acting so strangely.

On the night Cara was killed, Anderson was working at a Shell station when Peyer came in. The highway patrolman seemed out of sorts. "It looked like he had been in a fight. I noticed claw marks on his face. The one on his left side was bleeding," she testified. After she had given him an inquisitive look, he'd told her, 'It's been a hell of a night.' Then he'd handed her a blue-and-white state credit card and told her he wanted five dollars worth of gas, which struck Anderson as unusual since she had never seen the highway patrol gas up there before. They had their own pumps at their office.

She'd looked up Peyer's CHP credit card to see if they honored it. Anderson explained in court that she always did that because if it was her mistake, the boss would take money out of her paycheck. But before Peyer had pumped his unleaded gas, Anderson said, he'd opened his trunk. Inside the minimart in the station, Anderson had been talking to her daughter and son-in-law, an off-duty San Diego police officer. While chatting, she'd noticed this strange highway patrolman on the other side of the plate-glass windows, reaching in his trunk and wiping off his big black flashlight with a grease rag.

She'd seen him taking his hat from the trunk and bringing it around to the front of the car. Then she said she saw him taking out his nightstick from the trunk and wiping it off before relooping it through his heavy black leather gun belt.

Grimes's gentlemanly calm was visibly shaken by Anderson's testimony, as the middle-aged woman sat up on the stand in her black rayon dress and her pinkish oversized Sophia Loren–style glasses, with her bright blonde hair pinned back in a bun. Grimes held copies of her previous interviews and testimony right in his hand. "You never told police about this before," he said accusingly. He read her police statements out loud to her. "They say nothing about seeing the officer at his trunk." The defense attorney accused her of reading about the case in the paper and then exaggerating what she had seen.

"No," Anderson protested. Since Peyer's arrest, she said she had been away from home and hadn't been reading about the case.

"Where were you at the time of the arrest that there were no newspapers?" Grimes asked, annoyed.

Anderson hesitated and turned to the judge, "Do I have to say where, your honor?" she asked plaintively.

"I would appreciate it if you did," Judge Huffman replied.

So she confessed to the courtroom full of strangers that she was in a women's crisis center from January 13—two days before Peyer's arrest—until almost the end of the month of January. Inside the shelter she didn't pay any attention to all the news on the television and newspapers, she insisted to Grimes. "I was concentrating on my own problems, not his." But Grimes caught her. He referred to an interview she had with police on January 21—while she was in the shelter and six days after Peyer's arrest—when she said she had seen Peyer's picture in the newspaper.

Van Orshoven's next item of business was to bring up Peyer's fellow officers and friends on the patrol to testify against him. By bringing CHP Sergeant Joe Riordan to the stand, Van Orshoven brought the jury to Peyer's last official contact with his headquarters the night Cara Knott was killed. Riordan was an amiable fellow, but like Peyer's other colleagues, was not eager to elaborate on what he saw and heard. He stuck to the facts as he knew them, and that was all. When Peyer came back to the CHP station that December night, Riordan related from the witness stand, the patrolman had looked disheveled.

"What happened to you?" Riordan testified he'd asked Peyer. And Peyer told him how he slipped and fell at the gas pumps out back behind the station.

Even though Grimes started out with his disarming, "Good morning, Officer Riordan," the defense attorney made no dent in this witness.

CHP Officer James McCoy, who was best man at Peyer's wedding, testified that on the night of the murder, Peyer walked right past him, ignoring him, even after McCoy tried to talk to him.

"He was walking toward me. I said, 'Hey, hi, Craig,' and he had the uniforms up at his face level and looked straight back toward the back door and just walked right out of the building, not even acknowledging."

"How far away did he pass?" Van Orshoven asked.

"About two feet," the officer answered.

"Did you notice anything unusual?" The prosecutor was hoping he'd bring up the scratches, but McCoy clearly was more hurt by the snub.

"No, other than Craig and I have always been very good friends and I was surprised he didn't acknowledge me or say hi or something. He just was looking straight at the back door, just walking by me."

McCoy and his partner ended up taking out Peyer's patrol car for their graveyard shift. Van Orshoven asked him if he had seen the yellow rope in the trunk or noticed anything unusual about the car. But McCoy couldn't be sure whether he even checked the trunk, though procedure calls for them to at the beginning of every shift.

"If anybody's car that I looked into or wouldn't bother checking, it probably would have been Craig's car because he's real thorough," McCoy answered.

What followed was a platoon of cops to testify against Peyer. None of the CHP officers who drove Peyer's car recalled seeing the yellow plastic rope that the prosecution claimed was used to strangle Cara Knott. The rope was not CHP issue, the officers agreed, and none of them knew when or how it had gotten under Peyer's spare tire a week after the murder.

Then, Van Orshoven brought a couple who were the closest thing to witnesses he had. They placed a law enforcement officer at the scene around the time of the murder. Duane Clinkscales told the jury about how he had surprised his then-fiancée, Ann Pascarand, that night for her twenty-first birthday by coming around in the chauffeur-driven limousine and taking her down to San Diego for a fancy dinner. The night turned out to be a surprise, all right. The luxury machine broke down two freeway exits from her house, Duane testified. They sat at the Mercy Road off ramp for close to an hour waiting for help.

Both Duane and Ann saw a police car flash by, and they both paid attention because they hoped the officer would come to their rescue. Sam Knott was ecstatic to hear this testimony. That's it, they've fingered the monster at the scene of the crime, he thought. But Sam was less hopeful as their testimony continued. Each testified that they had seen a different kind of police car coming from a totally different direction.

Duane Clinkscales admitted that he had vision problems and had trouble distinguishing colors. Van Orshoven pressed him on his vision, suggesting that maybe it was Duane who mistook the color of the car and its direction. But on cross-examination, Grimes got Duane to say his "vision trouble" was just nearsightedness.

"Nearsightedness, like most of the rest of us?" Grimes asked.

"Yeah," agreed Duane.

The trial was full of thousands of little details like what Duane Clinkscales might have seen and why, details given to the jurors to consider for the prosecution or defense, or to reject completely. Every day for weeks the two sides battled a hundred times over which side would claim victory for each of those little details.

Sam Knott noticed his own little detail. The courtroom was so small and the crowd to watch the trial was so large that the bailiffs always let the families into the courtroom first, to make sure they got seats. And as he was sitting there, he watched the Peyers come in from lunch and Karen reach into her purse and pull out some gold-rimmed eyeglasses that Peyer had been wearing during the trial.

"Look at that," he whispered to Joyce. "I bet those glasses are fakes. They're just trying to make him look harmless. See how they had him put on all that weight. He looks about as dangerous as a pharmacist!"

The trial was moving so fast now that Deputy District Attorney Van Orshoven had to ask the judge for a break because he was having problems assembling witnesses fast enough.

Certainly, this was a natural problem when a lawyer is handling more than one hundred witnesses, but the little lapse did nothing to help Van Orshoven's image to the jury as the man in control.

Judge Huffman nodded and turned to the jurors. "It's always good to take a break and let the mind absorb that which the backside could no longer withstand," he said.

Day two ended two hours early. Day three began with the announcement of more delays. There would be no court next week on Wednesday and Thursday.

Van Orshoven's assistant, Deputy District Attorney Jim Atkins, started questioning witnesses. Atkins had only been a lawyer for two years, and he had never done a murder case alone before. Now here he was all alone in a courtroom on a case of this magnitude. It was like sending a rookie up to bat at the bottom of the ninth inning with the bases loaded. In the play-offs.

Van Orshoven left Atkins to handle the complicated and often bone-dry scientific evidence portions of the trial, because the senior man said, "He had an interest and knowledge in science." Sam Knott didn't mind; he liked the way Atkins handled himself in court.

Atkins started questioning an important prosecution witness, Deputy Coroner Dan Matticks, an ex-cop and former paramedic now with San Diego County Coroner's office. Matticks testified that he had found Cara lying on her back, three hours after her body had been discovered by police. The body was cold, in full rigor mortis. Her joints and blood stiffened in what is called lividity, which usually occurs eight to twelve hours after death.

He ordered the ambulance drivers to put plastic bags on her hands, head, and feet, to preserve any fibers or skin tissue found there. He examined her briefly and determined the preliminary cause of death was likely ligature strangulation, that she was strangled by a rope, a cloth, something around her neck.

"Can you give us an exact minute of the day when she died?" the prosecutor asked.

"There is no scientific method available to state an exact time of death," Matticks answered. "She died no later than four A.M. December twenty-eighth. She could have died any time after midnight the previous day.''

On TV Perry Mason always found things out like time of death and that was in the fifties. Surely forensic science had come a little way since then. Grimes wanted the jury to think that too.

The defense attorney asked the deputy coroner about the procedure of measuring the liver temperature of the recently deceased. Matticks explained that the liver retains body heat for longer periods than outer surfaces, so measuring internal organ temperature at the murder scene where some body heat can be detected can allow a closer approximation of time of death, so the theory goes.

When exactly did Cara Knott die? Was there a liver temperature taken? If so, what happened to it?

These basic questions were hanging over the courtroom like storm clouds. There was a liver temperature taken, it turned out, but it was taken hours later in the morgue, not at the murder scene. And then any temperature measurement record had been lost. Grimes wanted to make the most of the investigator's blunder, while the prosecution was naturally trying to stop him.

In fact, forensics, the science of death, is much like life— it is not perfect. Current accepted pathology techniques still can't pinpoint death down to the minute, no matter what Quincy and the superstar cops on TV say. They can measure the fluid in the eye, or they can take the liver temperature. Liver temperatures can pinpoint death down to the two-hour range if taken in optimal conditions, but other variables come into play, like wind, moisture, how clothed the body was, and whether the night temperature differed drastically from the day temperature.

''We know that one was taken but we have not been able to determine who took it,'' Van Orshoven told Judge Huffman out of hearing of the jury. ''We know that it was taken because there was an incision on the abdomen of the victim.''

Judge Huffman allowed some discussion on the liver temperature, leaving the two lawyers to slug it out in open court about how far each could go.

Grimes tried to get Deputy Coroner Matticks to say that a

liver temperature had been taken, so he could show that the investigators had lost the important fact, and build on his own defense argument that police who make such mistakes could also end up making a mistake about who they blame for the crime.

"Did you take a liver temperature?" the defense attorney asked.

"No," the witness answered.

Grimes took a stab: "Did you observe anybody else take a liver temperature?"

"A liver temperature was taken," Matticks replied quickly and firmly.

At the same time, both prosecutors Atkins and Van Orshoven objected to Grimes's question.

"One at a time," Judge Huffman told the deputy district attorneys sternly, a warning to the veteran Van Orshoven to keep his case organized. The coroner Matticks went on to explain how they take liver temperatures. They cut open the right side of the abdomen and stick in a thermometer.

"Describe what the liver temperature probe looks like," Grimes said.

The witness complied. "It's a thermometer at the top with a trocar probe or metal probe that inserts, similar to that which is used in measuring the inside temperature of meat cooked in an oven."

The probe was the size of a half dollar, he said, and a foot long.

Grimes finally got the deputy coroner to say that a liver temperature had been taken, but that no one remembered exactly who had taken it or what happened to the temperature reading itself. Sam Knott felt his stomach tightening.

Grimes highlighted yet another lapse in the investigation. He called San Diego Police Detective Gene Back to the stand. Back, a twenty-year veteran of the force, was the detail man of the crime scene investigation, the one who catalogued the hairs, the fibers, the fingerprints, the tire tracks found at Mercy Road on December 28, 1986.

The tire tracks, Back said, measured fifty-three inches apart, exactly the width of Peyer's police car. Why didn't investigators do anything with those tracks besides measure them? Grimes asked Back. Why didn't Detective Back make imprints or collect samples and examine them under more scientific conditions? Grimes wanted to know. Why didn't police perform tests to approximate dew residue on dirt? the defense attorney asked.

Back sat in the witness chair looking like a man having trouble biting his tongue. You can bet he had a few answers he would have liked to have given Grimes as the defense attorney peppered him with questions.

"Would you like to have that to do over again?" Grimes asked the investigator.

Van Orshoven managed to say "I—" before Judge Huffman cut in saying, "You object to that."

"Yes, I object," Van Orshoven said.

"Sustained." Huffman nodded.

The jury never heard whether Detective Back thought the tire tracks were a big enough clue to really concentrate on if he had it to do over again.

Grimes then seized upon another piece of evidence left lying in the dirt, a footprint found in the mud on the bridge. It, too, was only photographed and not analyzed or imprinted in a cast. If it matched Craig Peyer's boots, the defense attorney told the jury, you can bet the police wouldn't gloss over the footprint. But, he said, no one will ever know for sure.

By the end of the day, the defense had successfully magnified three flaws in the police investigation into the murder of Cara Knott—the lost liver temperature record, the mysterious footprint, and the tire tracks—to Godzilla-sized proportions.

14

The Brethren

To walk among men who live by their wits, to know life and death, to have the world depend on you, to be a cop: it's all Craig Peyer could have wanted.

Cops live by their own rules; as protectors of the civic mores they are under attack by the worst that life has to offer. It's the world against them. Only brother cops could understand what it was like to put their lives on the line every day and square off against the forces of evil. Often they live alone among themselves, tell their own jokes, marry each other. Craig Peyer lived his life that way. His best friends were cops; he partied with cops; and he had married into a cop's family. Yet the most important rule in that most sacred code that cops uphold is the one that says the brethren do not turn against one of their own.

Cops could put up with bending the rules a little, maybe hard drinking, hanging out with hookers, a little betting on football. But Craig Peyer was accused of murder, a crime even the flexible lines of the cop world would not tolerate, and many of his brothers cast him out. He was on the outside now. But whatever he was, he was one of them.

On the third day of the trial, the prosecution brought in a police officer who didn't play by the old unspoken rules, because her sex made her an outsider to that tough and loyal fraternity. San Diego Police Officer Jill Oglivie walked up to the witness stand in her crisp khaki uniform, wearing over her heart a silver badge etched with the words, "To Protect and Serve." She began by explaining how she had met Craig Peyer near the murder scene on New Year's eve, three days after Cara Knott's body had been found.

Patrolman Peyer had said he'd stopped two possible suspects in the Knott murder, and Oglivie and her partner, also a woman, answered his call for backup. Oglivie's partner had talked to the drivers in two pickup trucks carrying all-terrain bikes, while she'd stood behind and covered her.

"I exited my vehicle and Officer Peyer, seeing me, motioned to my coat, he said, 'Oh,' perhaps thinking that it was a ranking insignia of some sort. He walked over to me," Oglivie testified. "He stood next to me and began questioning me."

Van Orshoven led her along. "Questioned you in what regard?"

"He wanted to know about the murder case involving Cara Knott," Oglivie answered.

"What did he ask you, and what did you respond?" the prosecutor asked.

"He asked me what the scoop was, what homicide was telling the patrol force. And since I was a patrol officer and this was my beat, surely I must know the inside scoop."

Oglivie was off and running without any more prompting from the prosecutor. "And I told him, I didn't know. That it had been on my days off and I knew basically just what was in the newspapers and little bits of rumor that was going around. He insisted that I must know something, surely they must be giving something on the hot sheet or something.

"I said, 'No, I didn't know.'

"He said, 'Well, I hear they're doing an autopsy.'

"I said, 'Yes, they are.'

"He says, 'Why would they do an autopsy?'

"An autopsy is done on anyone who is found dead for any circumstance, unless it's natural causes," Oglivie explained for the sake of the jury, in a disgusted tone suggesting just how naive his questions had been for a veteran law enforcement officer. "And he began asking me questions about it in a very immature, sophomoric, juvenile fashion, in my opinion."

"Just tell us what the questions were and what the responses were that you gave," Van Orshoven interrupted, trying to keep the speeding train of Jill Oglivie on track.

The cop nodded. "He was very excited and was saying, 'Well, what's the real scoop? Did you hear anything about the possibility that some guy was waving money in Escondido and he jumped in the car?'

"I said, 'I heard about that, but I don't know anything about that.'

"He said, 'Well, I heard that they found a piece of ear in her mouth.'

"I said, 'I heard that rumor too, but I didn't know it to be true.'

"And he took both of his hands, grabbed his ears and he said, 'Well, I got both of mine.' "

The policewoman wore her blonde hair pulled back tidily into a bun, accenting her earlobes. Suddenly she reached up and tugged on her ears to demonstrate how Peyer had grabbed his. Her dramatization, so simple, brought gasps through the courtroom gallery. They were at complete attention and hanging on her every word. Oglivie seemed pleased by the reaction. She looked over at Sam Knott and gave him a slight nod of recognition as she continued telling her version of that New Year's eve beside the murder scene.

"I looked at him and I said, 'Well, I don't think you have anything to worry about.'

"He said, 'What else can an autopsy show?'

"I said, 'Well, if there's skin underneath the fingernails, they can determine a lot from that.'

"He said, 'Like what?'

"I said, 'You know this stuff.'

"He said, 'No, tell me.'

"I said, 'Well, if there's a good substantial amount of skin, that they could determine certain things, like skin type or blood or anything like that.'

"He said, 'What if there is hair?'

"I said, 'If there is hair, obviously you might be able to determine if it was blonde hair, short hair, long hair, Afro, different style.'

"He said, 'They could get all that, huh?'

"I said, 'Yeah.'

"He said, 'Well, if there is skin under the fingernails?'

"I said, 'Yeah.'

"He started cleaning his fingernails," Oglivie said, a hard edge to her voice. "I again said, 'You don't have anything to worry about.'

"But then he said to me, 'What do you think happened down there?'

"I said, 'I really don't know. I said all I know'—and I motioned to the bridge. And when I motioned, I motioned to the west side of the bridge. He turned to me and he said, 'No, you don't know what you are talking about.' " Her words dripped with contempt as she recited the conversation. " 'She was put out on the other side of the bridge.'

"I looked at him and I said, 'If you know so much, then why are you acting like you don't know? And why are you asking me?'

"He said, 'Well, what do you think they will do with the guy when they find him?'

"I said, 'Well, who knows that it's a guy? It may be a woman.'

" 'What do you think they will do with him?' " she quoted Peyer as asking her, the courtroom audience hanging on her every word.

"I said, 'Well, I hope he dies a slow and painful death.'

"He said, 'Well, you don't know what you are talking about.' And 'It could have been an accident' and 'Maybe there is different circumstances you don't know about.'

"But at that point he got very angry with me. He changed his personality. He stood taller. His voice inflection changed. He became angry. He displayed a rather perturbed manner. And he turned to his vehicle and he said in a very loud voice, 'I'm out of here. I'm leaving.'

"I said, 'Do you want these suspects' names? Do you want your name on it or anything?'

"He said, 'No!' He went to the car, went to his vehicle, slammed the door, and accelerated directly into traffic without paying any attention and two vehicles had to slam on their brakes.

"His exact statement was, 'You don't know what you're

talking about. Maybe it was a situation that got out of control, maybe it just went too far.' ''

San Diego Police Officer Jill Oglivie was vivid, confident, and attractive. If the jury believed this cop, she could do more to bury Peyer than any of the other one hundred prosecution witnesses who would swear to tell the truth so help them God.

Grimes rushed up to repair the damage that Peyer's fellow officer had just wrought. "How do you remember this so well?" the defense attorney demanded.

"Easy," Officer Oglivie replied. She then launched into an explanation about how she wrote the conversation up on a police report.

"What happened to the report?" asked Grimes.

"Homicide didn't want it," Oglivie testified. "They preferred to do their own."

Grimes didn't seem surprised that homicide detectives would reject what seemed like an important piece of evidence. Hadn't this been what he was saying all along?

"Officer Oglivie," he began pleasantly, suddenly changing the subject, "did you also stop a young man by the name of Leaverts in the area around January eight?"

"I don't recall," replied Oglivie stiffly, an odd memory lapse for a woman who had just remembered every monosyllable from one year before about the Knott homicide.

Grimes closed in. "Did you talk to a young man on about January eight in which you wrote a report saying the young man acted very bizarre and strange and did strange things?"

"I may have; I don't recall," Oglivie replied cautiously.

Grimes pounced. "Did you have a conversation with a young man after which you wrote a report saying that while you were discussing the Cara Knott homicide he was—the young man was touching his genitals and staring off into space?"

The audience stirred. Suddenly the star witness didn't seem so impeccable. Was this lady for real, or was she just paranoid? Why would she think this other guy was a murder suspect just for staring off into space?

"I don't recall the date," the policewoman answered. But

her face took on a resigned look as she watched the defense attorney turn to his desk and pick up a sheaf of papers.

"And in that report, did you state that this young man had asked many questions regarding the homicide . . ." Grimes asked.

"I don't recall, sir," Oglivie said blandly. "I did a report. May I see the report to refresh my memory?"

Grimes handed her the report. "Does that refresh your recollection, ma'am?"

"Yes, sir, it does."

It seems, she testified, that homicide didn't want that report on the flaky guy either. Clearly Oglivie was wishing the whole matter would disappear. But she couldn't avoid Grimes, who kept pressing her for details.

"Could you tell us about the conversation you had with the young man January eight?" the defense attorney asked.

Van Orshoven had had enough of how the defense attorney was pushing his witness around. The prosecutor cut in with his booming voice, "At this point in time, I have to interpose an objection as to relevance, your honor."

Grimes turned to the judge, "Your honor, I submit the descriptions of this young man's behavior will sound strikingly similar to what Officer Oglivie described as attributed to Officer Peyer."

"What are you offering it to prove?" Judge Huffman asked.

"Offering to prove in fact that this witness perhaps might read certain things into behavior, and is perhaps pretty much fixated on this incident," Grimes answered.

Huffman looked down through his square glasses at the defense attorney. "Let me see the report," he said thoughtfully. Huffman scanned the police report. "The objection would be sustained." But it didn't matter to Grimes; he had made his score already. He moved his questioning to the report she had written on Peyer, hoping that stacking them up side by side in testimony would make the one look as silly as the other.

"Officer Oglivie," he continued, "regarding the report you wrote on Officer Peyer. When did you write the report regarding this incident?"

"Within one or two days of the arrest," the witness answered.

"One or two days on or before the arrest?" Grimes asked.

"Within two days *after* the arrest," she replied curtly.

"Within two days after the arrest?" Grimes repeated her concession, to make sure the jury understood she was saying she wrote up her conversation with Peyer as suspicious only after he was arrested.

"Yes, sir," the patrolwoman said.

That was all he needed. Grimes turned to the officer in conclusion, and said, "Thank you."

15

The Hanging

BOB Grimes was on a roll, but he had a problem. The presence of the Knotts in the tiny courtroom was making him uncomfortable. Juries always watch families of victims during trials and he was used to that, but the Knotts were being treated like royalty. The press, other courtroom observers, and even some witnesses would talk to them and glance at the victim's family while they testified, and Grimes was worried the jury might be swayed. Everyone the jurors could see in the courtroom—aside from the defendant and his family—seemed to be on the Knotts' side.

Grimes brought the issue up in a closed-door meeting with Judge Huffman and the prosecution. He couldn't risk the chance that his complaints about the family's presence might become public and compound the Knotts' already powerful influence in the case.

"Your honor, I would like to make two comments," Grimes began. "The first one is that certain witnesses seem to acknowledge Mr. Knott, Sam Knott, as they leave, in various ways. One witness shook his hand after testifying for the prosecution. I believe that Officer Oglivie and Officer Spears were smiling and nodding to Mr. Knott while they were giving testimony."

Grimes continued, "I know that a lot of these officers have gotten pretty close to the Knott family during the course of the trial. In fact, during motions, I think Officer Back was seated with the family during certain pretrial motions.''

The judge listened, his hands folded together almost as if praying as he absently pressed his fingertips together.

''I think it might be appropriate,'' Grimes said, ''if the witnesses and perhaps the Knott family are asked not to have any displays or familiarity either in court after the witnesses have testified or out in the hallway where the jurors are waiting. As the court is aware, the jury does tend to mix among the people standing outside the courtroom.''

Van Orshoven did not like the way Grimes's arguments were going. ''I'm a little nonplussed by the suggestion that I should further restrain these people.'' Judge Huffman also wasn't happy about muzzling people's emotions so easily. ''I'm not in a position at this moment to assess,'' he told Grimes, but promised, ''I certainly will look for it as we continue on.''

Huffman acknowledged that he had noticed the Knott family was different and more involved in the proceedings than any other victim's family he had seen. ''I know that the Knott family is here all the time,'' the judge added. ''Mr. Knott stands up every time the jury goes in and goes out and is the only person in the audience that does so. But I'm reluctant to do anything about it.''

Van Orshoven took the judge's words as a warning, and before court resumed, he took Sam aside. Try to blend in with the rest of the courtroom audience, the prosecutor suggested politely. Just because it was proper courtroom decorum for the lawyers to stand when the judge and jury entered the room, that didn't apply to anyone else in the courtroom.

Sam had had little contact with the prosecutor about strategy and evidence during the trial, and now he was amazed at how the legal world was worried about such triviality as whether he stood or sat. But Sam took the little directive to be a sign that he was making an impact, and his spirits lifted slightly. I must be getting under somebody's skin, he thought.

The courtroom battle recommenced as Van Orshoven brought in one of the most crucial of the scientific experts, Dr. Lee Bockhacker, the county pathologist who conducted the autopsy on Cara. Bockhacker was a tall and thin man with glasses, and he approached the witness stand with a distracted air of a scientist. And indeed when the doctor opened his mouth his answers came out in a long and complex flow of scientific jargon way over the head of most laymen.

The prosecutor began with questions about the marks on Cara's neck from the strangling, and it took several tries before Dr. Bockhacker answered that Cara had one ligature mark over the right side of the neck, multiple ligature marks over the left side of the neck, and one mark, in particular, that shifted up and down erratically on the neck.

"Shifting up and down caused by what, doctor?" Van Orshoven asked, hoping that his expert would launch into a tragic tale of a woman trying to fight against a relentless attacker for every last breath.

"Can only theorize about that, but struggling or movement," Bockhacker responded, for once briefly.

The prosecutor tried again. "Struggling on the part of either the person who is applying the ligature, or on the part of the person to whom the ligature is being applied?"

"One or both," the witness answered.

Not exactly conclusive but the DA shifted to another more general topic. "How would you describe the injuries?"

Bockhacker spent what seemed like a long time detailing the dozens of bruises and scrapes on the victim's chest, abdomen, on the back of her upper left arm, on her left elbow. "There was a scrape mark noted over the left anterior abdomen laterally, and there were abrasions as depicted in the diagram noted over the front of the upper extremities. Namely the thighs and the vicinity of the knees," he concluded.

Van Orshoven held up a morgue photo of Cara's body and showed it to Bockhacker. "Inviting your attention, doctor, to the victim's head, and more particularly her lip, did you form any opinion with respect to whether or not that particular injury was sustained before or after death?" the prosecutor asked.

"My opinion, it occurred before death. . . ." the doctor said. But before the DA had a chance to say anything else, Bockhacker asked him, "Could I see that other photograph again please?" The pathologist looked over the photo, and then to Van Orshoven's horror the expert backtracked on his testimony. "I would not be able to say whether the laceration of the left lip occurred before or after death. I did not see that before," the pathologist announced calmly.

Van Orshoven tried to hide his disappointment and hastily tried to steer Bockhacker to his side of the facts. "During the examination of the remains, doctor, did you ascertain that there were internal injuries that had been suffered by the victim?"

But Bockhacker would not budge. "First of all," the witness answered, "I might add before I list the injuries, there was very minimal amounts of hemorrhage noted about these injuries. Ordinarily in life one would expect an appreciable amount of bleeding at these sites if it had occurred before death. So on the basis of that, I concluded that these were—these injuries had occurred after death."

Eventually, Bockhacker answered the question in his own way, detailing the grisly facts: Cara Knott's right collarbone was broken, ribs one through ten snapped, the lungs lacerated, the pelvis fractured in two spots, the lower leg bone fractured, multiple cracks at the base of the skull, several lacerations of the liver, multiple tears of the right lung, multiple bruises of the lungs.

The Knotts could feel people in the audience watching them for any reaction during the pathologist's cold litany of death. The family stared ahead. They never flinched.

Finally, Grimes took over the unpredictable witness. He quickly tried to corner the pathologist, suggesting that the coroner's office could not pin down the time of death because it failed to take the liver temperature that might have given them the answer.

"Did you take a liver temperature?" Grimes asked confidently. He was all set for one answer: no. Instead, he got a surprise.

"Yes, I did," Bockhacker answered.

The defense attorney looked startled because Bockhacker had denied taking any such temperature during Peyer's preliminary hearing that preceded the trial. "I would like to correct that during the preliminary hearing I was asked regarding this, and I had forgotten that." Bockhacker said his notes suggested otherwise. Once again, Bockhacker started to apologize: "Even though I did not feel that the liver temperatures—"

Grimes recovered in time to stop the doctor. "Objection, nonresponsive," the defense lawyer said.

Judge Huffman looked down at the doctor from his elevated judicial chair and supported Grimes. "Let the attorney ask questions," he sharply told Bockhacker.

Grimes resumed. "What was the liver temperature?"

"Sixty-four degrees Fahrenheit," Bockhacker answered.

"What time was that taken?"

"I'm not—it would have been approximately when the victim came to the coroner's office. I would say in the vicinity of one o'clock."

"Did you make a notation of what time you took it?" the defense attorney asked.

"I dictated this, since I was wearing gloves of course at the time. . . ." the doctor began. Grimes moved closer to the witness stand to take a hard look at the paper Bockhacker was reading.

"May I please look at your notes, Dr. Bockhacker?"

"For what purpose?" the pathologist asked suspiciously, guarding his notes.

The judge told the doctor he had to show the defense attorney his notes. Grimes glanced at a crumpled yellow sheet of legal paper full of numbers and asked, "Now was this something that you prepared at that time?"

"That was something I dictated, because this is not my writing," Bockhacker replied.

"Whose writing is that?" Grimes asked.

"I don't recall," the pathologist said.

Grimes must have felt like he was wrestling Jell-O. He paused and tried again to elicit from Bockhacker exactly the source of the liver temperature. "When did you find this note?"

"As a matter of fact, it was sometime after the preliminary hearing," Bockhacker said. "I went through some miscellaneous papers and found it at that time."

Grimes reminded Bockhacker that he testified at a preliminary hearing in 1987 in which a judge ordered that Peyer be bound over for trial.

"At that time, was your answer that you had no knowledge

of a liver temperature being taken other than seeing an incision in the abdomen?'' Grimes asked testily.

"I don't believe those were my words," the witness said.

"Dr. Bockhacker, referring to a transcript of preliminary examination.'' Grimes picked up a stack of papers and read, "Question, 'You didn't take a liver temperature?' Answer, 'I did not take a liver temperature.' ''

He looked sternly at the witness, "Does that accurately reflect your testimony at that time?''

"Yes," Bockhacker mumbled. "Okay, I did not say that one had not been taken. I did not think that I had taken it. But I didn't recall if there had been one taken or not."

"Well, you testified that you personally did not take one; is that correct?'' Grimes said.

"That's correct."

Grimes shook his head slightly and tried again to pin the witness down. "What is your present belief? Are you telling us today that if it was you that took it—''

Bockhacker interrupted, "That I took it, yes, sir."

"So," Grimes asked impatiently, "why didn't you tell anyone?''

"I brought it here to correct it today," the witness replied.

That was it. As Bockhacker was excused, the lawyers and the judge retreated into the judge's chambers. For Grimes, Bockhacker's rambling testimony had raised plenty of questions about how much he knew about the liver temperature and when he had first learned about it. This was a crucial bit of evidence. Suddenly, Bockhacker had just discovered his notes. Grimes found that nearly impossible. It just proved, Grimes told the judge, that the prosecution was flouting the rules.

"Your honor," Grimes said, "I am quite concerned that there may be a violation of the discovery order in this case." Under the state's rules of evidence, the prosecution is supposed to notify the defense about evidence. The exchange of evidence prior to a trial is known as the discovery process.

Van Orshoven looked in the distance, as if to say it's not my fault. Huffman seemed upset over the surprise statements and asked the prosecutor to explain Bockhacker's testimony. "The last I heard from him before I came to court," the deputy DA said, "was that a liver temperature had been taken and somebody had provided him the results on a piece of paper."

Judge Huffman sat thinking for a moment, the fingertips of both hands still pressed together as if in prayer. Finally, he declared, "Mr. Grimes, I would be certainly willing to allow you to postpone the cross-examination of Dr. Brookacre or whatever his name is."

Huffman turned to Van Orshoven and told him he was not going to allow the government's objection to any testimony that focused on the time of death, particularly relating to the liver temperature. "We had the issue of liver temperature raised at the preliminary hearing," the judge said. "It's been there from the outset. The coroner's office took it. They took vitreous potassium from the eyes and testified to it."

The tangle dissolved as the three men broke for lunch. An hour and a half later, Bockhacker returned to the witness stand and remained there under Bob Grimes's grilling for most of the afternoon.

Sensing he'd won a victory over the issue of the liver temperature, Grimes hoped for another opening from Bockhacker. The defense lawyer pointed to the rope encased in a plastic bag on the evidence table. He picked it up and walked toward Bockhacker. "Is it your testimony that this rope is consistent with having inflicted these injuries, is that correct?"

Bockhacker was silent for a moment. "Could you say that again more slowly?" the pathologist asked.

"Well, is this rope in exhibit thirty, is it consistent with having inflicted the injuries that you observed as ligature marks on the neck of the victim?"

"Yes," Bockhacker answered.

"Now, by consistency, you aren't telling us this is the rope, are you?"

"That's correct," Bockhacker replied.

"As a matter of fact, there are a wide range of ropes that could be a little thicker, that could be a little thinner, that could have inflicted the ligature marks," Grimes said. By his comments, the defense attorney seemed more intent on making a statement to the jury than seeking a response to the question.

Bockhacker agreed. That particular rope on the evidence table didn't have to be the murder weapon. But the pathologist felt the need to amplify his answer, and Grimes let him, hoping the doctor would tangle himself further in his long-winded testimony. "A little bit thicker and a little bit thinner, but the diameter of the rope is very close to the—is between— let me think for a second," Bockhacker said. Yes, the pathologist repeated, that the diameter of the rope was "very close" to whatever instrument was used to strangle Cara Knott.

Grimes pressed on. "Did you ever examine this rope to determine if it had any blood or skin or anything like that on it?"

"No," Bockhacker answered. From the prosecution table, Van Orshoven waited for Bockhacker to explain that his job did not include examining the rope for forensic evidence, but the pathologist remained silent.

Grimes kept going on the rope. "Have you ever seen it other than in court?"

"No," Bockhacker replied again.

"Right," Grimes said, clearly in control again. "In taking the histories of cases where people have died of ligature strangulation [and] there has not been those types of scratches and attempts to withdraw the ligature, does history sometimes show [that] that's because there were multiple assailants, one person pinning down a person's arms while the other applied the ligature?"

Van Orshoven sensed he was losing his own witness to the defense side and he spoke up. "Excuse me, your honor, I would think that question was without foundation."

"Sustained," Judge Huffman ordered.

Okay, Grimes decided, he had to abandon the theory on multiple assailants for now. So he returned to one of his key themes: the mishandling of the mysterious liver temperature record.

He turned to Bockhacker. "You still didn't really remember who took the liver temperature on December twenty-eighth?"

"Not until I really looked down and saw that my name was there," Bockhacker answered.

And so it went. By the time the defense attorney had finished thoroughly confusing Dr. Bockhacker, the jurors were already privately nicknaming him, Dr. Bodyhacker.

It was a great relief to everyone in the courtroom when late in the afternoon, the awful Polaroids from the morgue were put away and the Miss Poway pageant began.

That's how Grimes satirically described the portion of the trial in which Van Orshoven introduced twenty of the twenty-four young women who testified that Patrolman Craig Peyer pulled them off the freeway down to the remote Mercy Road off ramp late at night.

Van Orshoven wanted the jurors to understand that this was no straitlaced police officer they were dealing with, but a man who played sexual power games with women—and had gone too far. A twenty-year-old manicurist testified about being stopped by Peyer for driving with a burned-out headlight after midnight. Likewise, twenty-three-year-old Sarah Lundburg testified how she was brought down to the Mercy Road dead end for the vehicle code infraction of changing lanes without using her blinker.

Ami Hoeppner, a twenty-two-year-old department store guard with long dark hair, was stopped twice in the same month for crooked headlights. To humor Peyer, she testified, she adjusted her lights the way he suggested the first time, and then he stopped her again ten days later for the same infringement. As he wrote her up, Hoeppner told the court, Peyer asked the security guard if she ever watched women changing their clothes in the store dressing rooms.

The seven California girls brought the first week of trial to a close. The next began with thirteen more pretty women, who took their turns on the witness stand telling the jury how they had spent up to ninety minutes in the dark at Mercy Road talking and even driving around with Officer Peyer.

Their conversations with Peyer covered subjects as varied as the women's love lives, divorces, the housing market, freeway driving, and their jobs. Some of the women told the jury that they left Mercy Road expecting the friendly highway patrolman to call them up for a date. In the back of the court-room, Karen Peyer dropped her gaze and looked at the floor. Cheryl Knott stole a glance at the woman. What was going through Mrs. Peyer's mind, Cheryl wondered, when she heard in court how flirtatious her husband was and how he had told a total stranger that his "girlfriend" lived nearby?

With the Miss Poway pageant, Van Orshoven felt he was back in control of the trial. Even Grimes believed that the women were making some connection with the jury, breaking through what the prosecution contended was the facade of Craig Alan Peyer as the all-around family man.

Before the women finished testifying, Grimes felt it was time to talk to the judge again about problems he was having with the government investigation and its apparent failure to tell him about certain information. As the trial wore on, Grimes was making note of the increasing list of not only surprise witnesses, but also surprise statements and reports he wasn't given. Were the cops, and the prosecution team by default, hiding things from the defense in violation of the state discovery laws that required them to turn over all results of investigations?

After Huffman shut the door, Grimes got to the point. "Your honor, I'm extremely concerned about what I believe has become a pattern of noncompliance," the defense attorney said.

He reviewed how Bockhacker had testified about new information he'd previously denied having. "As it developed, the way I asked the question—he surprised me very much with his answer—we found out there was a liver temperature taken. It developed that very likely what he gave us was, might have been, hearsay or otherwise objectionable if we'd known it in anticipation and had been able to prepare."

Then Grimes brought up another new prosecution report that contradicted previous testimony. A San Diego police detective, Sal Salvatierra had a report from Karen Anderson, the gas station attendant, in which she told the officer she did not see Peyer go into his trunk and retrieve items. The report, which Salvatierra said was given to him sometime the previous year, contradicted Anderson's testimony during a preliminary hearing, Grimes said.

Grimes said he wanted a court remedy to his problems, which were denying his client a fair trial. The defense attorney told the judge he didn't mean to castigate the character of Van Orshoven or the prosecution team. "Mr. Van Orshoven informs me that he never received this report, and I believe him."

Before the pageant continued, the defense lawyer told the judge he had just received the name of another witness, Sharon White, who claimed to have been stopped by Peyer. "I have never heard her name before this morning," Grimes said. He complained that he learned about her only from that morning's lineup of prosecution witnesses. Then he found out the woman had called the district attorney's office a full week ago to say she had been pulled down to Mercy Road by Peyer for a registration violation.

"And so there is basically a surprise witness we're not at all prepared to cross-examine," Grimes told the judge. "I think that there are a couple more situations where I suspect this type of thing has occurred. That information has not been given to the prosecution because it would then go to the defense."

Judge Huffman decided it was time to straighten this discovery business out once and for all. "Where is Mr. Van Orshoven today?" he asked pointedly.

Assistant District Attorney Jim Atkins spoke up. "I'm sorry, your honor, there's been a problem with the subpoenas so he is busily tending to that matter personally."

Judge Huffman's tone made it clear he did not want to hear any more surprises. He told both lawyers, "If there are other loose ends out there, tie them up."

The judge warned Atkins that any more slipups in not providing the defense with discovery information could mean that the prosecution would have to forfeit their witness. "You go forward at your peril," the judge said.

Go forward they did. At Atkins's direction, the Miss Poway pageant continued in court. The prosecutors wanted to call as many women as possible to tell the jurors variations of the same theme: that Craig Peyer had a thing for pretty young women, even if he had a wife and family at home. The possibility was that Peyer had been leading up to something, keeping the women on the dark off ramp for increasing periods of time, forcing them into his patrol car, driving them even deeper into the canyon. It was only fate that Cara Knott was the one he killed.

A tall blonde named Ann Tolgaard testified that she was driving her VW late on Halloween night when Peyer pulled her off the freeway at Mercy Road. She got in his patrol car and he drove her to her baby-sitter's house because he had told her her car wasn't safe enough for the trip.

Kathy Deir, looking every bit a reasonable professional in her business suit and flowered tie, talked about how Peyer had given her a ride in his cruiser to show her the old Highway 395 bridge. Her little ride came two weeks before Cara Knott's body was thrown from that very bridge.

Radio disk jockey Shelly Sacks testified about how Peyer had wanted to hear about her break-up with her boyfriend, and how he had her get into his patrol car with him while he'd written up the ticket. "I just felt uncomfortable with all those little shooting side glances," Sacks said.

Officer Peyer's longest late-night meeting was with a perky blonde nurse named Cheryl Johnson, who was forced by Peyer to back up on the freeway in order to take the Mercy Road off ramp. On the witness stand, Johnson appeared shaken, even more than a year after the encounter with Peyer. She testified that Peyer had spent more than an hour and a half making small talk with her. She said he had even turned off his police radio, severing contact with the outside world, which had scared her.

Peyer had told her Mercy Road was not a safe place for a woman late at night, she testified. "He said, 'Somebody could get raped or murdered down here, and nobody would ever know.' I said, 'At least I'm with you,' " Johnson recalled.

Grimes worked hard to deflect the damage these women were doing to the defense. He made sure the jury heard in great detail from each witness that Peyer had never touched one of them. Peyer had never asked any of them out on dates or taken their telephone numbers. He'd never said anything unseemly.

The defense attorney even made it seem that the women

enjoyed the time they spent with Peyer. None of them testified that they'd told the patrolman they felt uncomfortable, Grimes said. So how was Peyer to know they were scared, if they didn't say anything? Grimes reminded the jurors often of that point.

As he cross-examined Cheryl Johnson, Grimes asked, "Did you ever tell him that you were frightened, that you wanted to leave?"

"No, it didn't seem the right thing to do," she answered.

Grimes managed to highlight positive points from some of the women. Peyer was friendly and helpful, they agreed. Somehow he managed to get answers to the effect that they were pleased that in such an urban place like San Diego with its two million people, an officer would take such an old-fashioned concern for their safety.

If Grimes was upset about surprises, he probably was not imagining that the biggest bombshell of them all was next on the agenda. And it was delivered by the milkman.

Robert Calderwood was a sharp figure of a man in his sixties, sporting freshly barbered iron gray hair, a trim physique, and a well-fitting light colored suit. Calderwood was not only a milkman for Hollandia Dairy, he was an Amway salesman, an ex-cop from Massachusetts, a retired career marine. And an enigma.

Here it was, more than a year after one of the most sensational criminal cases in San Diego's history was underway. Then on the day the trial began, Calderwood suddenly called the district attorney's office claiming he held the missing puzzle piece that definitely linked Cara with her accused murderer.

Up until Calderwood entered the picture, the only evidence linking Peyer to Knott was the drop of blood and six pieces of fiber, and even those were in much dispute.

Calderwood said he had been on his way to San Diego that night to recruit someone for his Amway business, in which he and his associates went door to door selling cleaning products. Calderwood had been driving his truck about sixty-five miles-per-hour down I-15 when he'd been startled by a CHP loudspeaker in front of him ordering a VW beetle to pull over. Calderwood had kept driving for three more freeway exits, and then pulled off I-15 into a roadside restaurant named Brian's for some coffee and to call his prospective salesman. He had decided it was too late to make an Amway house call. From the coffee shop, he'd gotten on the freeway north and headed back to his home in the rural town of Fallbrook, one of the loveliest towns in the county which also happens to be home of notorious white supremacist Tom Metzger.

Calderwood testified that on his way home, he had seen a CHP cruiser speeding, with its lights off, down the frontage road beside the I-15 freeway.

Grimes demanded to know why Calderwood had waited so long to get involved. The defense attorney was relentless. Why? If you are telling the truth, why now? Grimes asked. Calderwood had a ready explanation. "The speed of the investigation and the arrest led me to believe that if, in fact, a highway patrolman had killed a young lady under that exit that he must have done a terrible job of concealing evidence because they must have had something very strong to arrest him," Calderwood testified.

"You felt that they had enough and that they didn't need you?" Grimes asked.

"Yes, sir," Calderwood replied.

"But surely what you saw seemed important?" Grimes asked.

"It became apparent to me that I had observed more than I had cared to," he answered.

Calderwood also maintained that he hadn't come forward earlier because when Peyer was freed on bail, Calderwood was afraid the patrolman would hurt any potential witnesses. "I saw no reason to place my family in any jeopardy for an entire year," he told the defense attorney.

"Why did you refuse to talk to the defense investigator?" the defense attorney demanded.

"I was concerned that the statement wouldn't be used in the interest of justice," Calderwood responded primly. "I would be concerned that a true statement would be twisted so it didn't appear as it really was."

Grimes hoped the jurors would catch the contradictions in

Calderwood's testimony. Now Calderwood was saying he was worried about his family. Minutes earlier, he said he didn't come forward because he didn't think his story was important enough.

The defense attorney had had enough, and, for the first time in the trial, lost his cool. He faced off with Calderwood and said accusingly, "You're making this up to wrap it up and put a bow on the case for the prosecution!"

No, Calderwood insisted, and he pointed out he had a corroborating witness. Right after the murder, Calderwood said, he related everything he had seen on the freeway to one of his customers on the milk run, a Betty Bahnmiller. It was Betty who had urged him to come forward and tell the district attorney, Calderwood said. Betty Bahnmiller took the stand and confirmed the milkman's story.

Later that night, over at Channel 8, editor Mike Workman was skeptical about this Calderwood character and decided to check the milkman's story out for himself. Workman drove a truck from the television station north to Mercy Road and speeded up to sixty-five miles-per-hour, seeing if he could really notice the cars passing by as Calderwood said he had. It was mighty tough at that speed in the dark to notice anything but the road in front of him. But then again, Workman thought, if the milkman did hear Peyer call Cara over to the side over the CHP loudspeaker, those things are loud enough to give anyone within half a mile a jolt and maybe cause someone to take notice of who got caught.

Then Workman crossed over to the northbound side of I-15 to see if it was possible to see a police car speeding away. But from the high perch of the truck, Workman couldn't even see the frontage road.

There was no way that milkman saw anything, the newsman decided.

Calderwood's startling testimony unfolded on a Friday, two days before the Denver Broncos and the Washington Redskins squared off in the Super Bowl being played in San Diego. And even in the midst of the overwhelming hoopla of the main event, between all the hype and the parties and the Rockettes and the Goodyear blimp, people paid attention when the milkman's tale hit the weekend papers and news-casts. His testimony packed quite a punch.

Van Orshoven had had enough of the surprises too. He let Calderwood's story sink in to the jury. Now the prosecutor was ready to weave the final thread that he believed would legally hang Craig Peyer. It was time to deliver the scientific proof—from the former highway patrolman's own uniform—that would place him near Cara Knott in her final hours.

The prosecution brought San Diego police criminologist John Simms to the stand to give the jury a science lesson, one of the most important in the trial. Simms testified about the tiny fibers found at the scene and why the police believed so strongly that Peyer was the killer.

Sam Knott and others in the courtroom listened intently as Simms explained how police found two gold fibers on Cara's white sweatshirt. Those fibers, Simms said, matched fibers taken from Peyer's CHP jacket shoulder patch—his gold-edged CHP emblem. Plus investigators also found purple fibers on Peyer's black police boots and his gun which, Simms said, resembled fibers from Knott's purple sweat-pants.

Finally, there were dark blue fibers found on the dead woman's hands, the expert said, which matched the fibers from the border of two CHP shoulder patch jacket emblems found on the uniform Peyer wore that night. Those fibers had, Simms said, "overwhelming microscopic similarities."

Simms explained how each fiber seen under a microscope had distinct markings and colorings, and when light was shone through the fibers they showed different characteris-tics. Under questioning by prosecutors Van Orshoven and Atkins, the expert said that the gold fibers from Peyer's CHP emblem and those found on Cara's sweatshirt were an exact match.

But after Grimes had finished his questioning of Simms, he had the fiber expert very confused about where the gold fibers came from.

"In fact," Grimes asked the witness, "you cannot even say with any certainty that the fibers, as identical as they appear, were even made in the same factory."

The fiber expert conceded that was so.

"How big are these fibers we're talking about?" Grimes asked Simms.

"Microscopic sized," the expert replied, "less than a quarter-inch long each."

"Okay," Grimes said, "if I have something on my clothes or you have something on your clothes that we commonly call lint, is that what we're referring to as fibers?"

"In a manner of speaking," Simms concurred.

Grimes continued. "What about the hair investigators found on Cara's dashboard?" he asked Simms. "That hair didn't belong to Cara or Peyer or anyone in the Knott family."

"That's true," Simms said.

"Was there any attempt to find out who the hair belonged to outside of that group?" Grimes asked. And again Simms conceded that no attempt had been made to further identify the hair.

Likewise, Grimes asked, "What about the yellow rope found in Peyer's car?" The defense attorney had Simms tell the jury he found no blood or skin residue on the rope.

Grimes had Simms talk about all the tests the police evidence team had performed on the hairs and fibers found on the victim and the accused. There were purple threads found on the yellow rope, Simms admitted, that did not match anything Cara had worn. But police did not search any further to see where those purple fibers came from.

Grimes was using the witness to further his own theory that the police were framing all their evidence in order to convict Peyer. "Did you take all the information away from the crime scene and compare it with everything else available from Mr. Peyer and his environment and select everything you could come up with that would match?"

"To a certain extent," Simms answered.

Sam was shaken as he overheard the exchange in the courtroom. It was as if Grimes was running over the witness, flattening anything of value that he had to say. The invaluable police evidence of fibers was solid proof that Peyer was Cara's killer, Sam was certain of that, and he worried that it was all going to be lost on the jury if they dawdled over superficial evidence that the police might not have pursued.

The Knott family reviewed the morning's testimony over the lunch break and Sam expressed his dismay over Grimes's treatment of Simms's testimony. "Ah, nobody's going to believe that garbage," Cheryl Knott said confidently, dismissing the defense lawyer's cross-examination. She scoffed at Grimes's characterization of the fibers linked to Peyer as lint. "Lint? How could he call that lint, like it was some particle floating in space? It was evidence, and he's trying to pass it off as nothing!" Cheryl was beside herself.

"So, the cops didn't find any fibers on the rope, what's the big deal?" Cheryl asked. There were plenty of others from Cara's clothes that were found on the monster. "Yeah, well the rope was real slippery plastic. It wouldn't absorb anything." Cheryl was waving her fork around like she wanted to stab a certain defense attorney whose name also had been banned from the Knott household.

The Knotts were seated at yet another restaurant reviewing the case over cheeseburgers. Every day a new restaurant, every day rehashing the trial. As they sat around the restaurant table, Sam, Cheryl, Bill, Cynthia, and Joyce Knott tried not to think about how much this ordeal was costing them, or how they would pay the financial bill for staying away from work once the emotional and legal ends were finished.

Sam was doing some financial consulting work, but Joyce was on a leave of absence from her job at the nutrition-dietary department at the University of California's San Diego Medical Center. Without her income, and with Sam barely putting in a minimum of hours, the household bills were piling up. Thank God, Joyce thought, for all those wonderful friends and neighbors who left casserole after casserole on their doorstep. But Joyce wasn't eating right, and she was feeling sluggish and tired. What irony, she told her family, looking down at her lunch. "Look at me, a nutritionist, eating cheeseburgers every day."

They downed their lunch and trudged back through the littered city streets, passing under construction scaffolding and talking over the pounding of jackhammers and equipment grinding away at new high rises going up around the courthouse on Broadway, the main street of San Diego's downtown. They tensed as they passed the little green patch of park where the homeless hung out, dozens of ragged men among the estimated five thousand homeless wandering the few square miles of downtown that butted up against the bay to the south and the freeways and suburbs to the east. Sam always found it ironic that the homeless lived there among the flowers and wrought iron benches smack against the whimsical outdoor shopping mall of Horton Plaza, the Disneyesque architectural contortion of pink and other pastels, the favorite spot of tourists.

The Knotts walked back inside the dingy courthouse, took the elevator to the fifth floor, and resumed their seats on the right side of courtroom 22. For the next two days, the defense and prosecution debated the impact of the six pieces of microlint, fibers so small that when put end to end they barely measured an inch. But this was a trial of inches. These fibers could very well decide whether or not Craig Peyer would ever be a free man again.

As San Diego cleaned up the wretched excesses of its first Super Bowl, the murder trial of the highway patrolman was in its third week and still front page news. The days of debating fiber evidence wound down and the courtroom turned into a mini police convention. The prosecution trotted out twenty-nine law enforcement officers from the more than fifteen police agencies throughout the entire county who were working the night of Cara's murder. None of them admitted being near Mercy Road on December 27.

From his seat in the audience Sam watched the dozens of uniformed men and women wearing badges take the witness stand, and he couldn't help but wonder which of them had refused his desperate pleas to help find Cara that December night. Sam was surprised the feelings of anger he still felt. He still wanted to jump up and slug the cops on the witness stand who had ignored his requests for help. After all that had happened over the past year, he had developed a great respect for San Diego Police Department homicide squad because they had taken the case to heart and wanted to find the killer just as much as he did. But that respect for a handful of detectives still didn't erase the bitterness in his heart for the other law enforcement people he felt had betrayed his family.

Joe Van Orshoven had been around juries long enough to know that they could only take so much talk about fiber evidence, no matter how significant. He wasn't sure how he'd scored with the fiber match, considering that Grimes had appeared to do some damage. But the prosecutor knew science was on his side. There were enough issues to go around to support the truth as he saw it. If the jurors were a bit confused about how closely the fibers connected Cara and Peyer, then there were other chances to convince them. Van Orshoven felt they wouldn't be mixed up when the blood evidence was presented. The killer left his bloody imprint on this girl, and Van Orshoven was convinced he could get that message through clearly to the jurors. Blood coursed through everyone's veins. Blood was emotional, yes, and this beautiful young woman had been bloodied by her killer.

For this part of the science lesson, Joe Van Orshoven and Jim Atkins called another San Diego police criminologist, Walter Fung, to the stand. Yes, Fung said at Atkins's prompting, bits of blood were found on Cara's new white boots. He said the blood definitely was not Cara's. She had type O. The blood on the boot was type A.

"Was it the same type as that of the defendant, Mr. Peyer?" Atkins asked.

"Yes," Fung replied.

The prosecution didn't drag out Fung's testimony. They wanted a direct hit, as clean and surgical as a smart bomb. But Robert Grimes was ready. He hammered away at the expert and his contention that the police had conducted a shoddy investigation, a probe that targeted one man, Craig Peyer, and never veered from that course.

"Let's assume Peyer was the killer," Grimes suggested to Fung. "Was there blood on his patrol car? On his flashlight? On his jacket? On his gun?"

"No, no, no, no," Fung said. The defense attorney wanted the jury to wonder how the patrolman could have killed Cara without getting blood anywhere else.

Fung explained how he had analyzed blood samples. He had measured enzymes and proteins called genetic markers. If the blood sample had been fresher, he could have calculated up to sixteen genetic markers and narrowed down the number of people who could have dripped that blood on her boot. But the blood was not fresh, and Fung had been able only to find two genetic markers, PGM type 1 and esterase D type 1.

Grimes suggested that explanations were fine, but where was the proof? Fung sheepishly admitted that he didn't have photos of the most important blood tests he'd run. It seems the police expert had run out of film for his camera.

Fung vaguely discussed a blood spot on the door of Cara's car, and how tests had been unable to type the blood. During the seventy-five minutes of testimony and arguments about genetic markers and blood spots, Grimes kept asking: what happened to the blood spot on the door of Cara's car?

Finally, Grimes got the police expert to admit they had tested the smudge of blood on the door and the results had shown nothing. Which, it would turn out, was not exactly the case. The experts had tried to preserve the spot of blood for future evaluations, so they had only tested a portion of it. But the amount they'd taken was too small to show any results and the remaining spot was too small to test. By not testing the entire sample, they had lost their chance to crack what may have been a very important clue.

Still, the prosecution had other blood samples and analyses that clearly focused on Peyer, Van Orshoven pointed out to the jury. One was an analysis of the blood on Cara's boot. An independent expert from a private laboratory in northern California was prepared to testify that its testing had narrowed the possible donors of that blood to 1.3 percent of the white population. A category that fit Craig Peyer.

Blood typing expert Gary Harmor explained to the jury that a genetic marker is a substance found in blood or other bodily fluids which is inherited. The markers are derived from the DNA in a cell and are reproduced throughout the body's cell structure. If a person has blood with an ABO marker, for example, that individual can be a type A, type B, type O, or type AB. Harmor testified that he found Cara's genetic markers to be type O, GLO inconclusive, esterase D type 1, conventional PGM type 2-1.

Peyer's genetic markers, he testified, were type A, GLO type 2 and ESD type 1, conventional PGM type 1, and PGM subtype of 1+.

Harmor said he used one of the most sensitive markers to analyze each of the bloodstained areas found by police to trace individual differences. The analysis, Harmor testified, showed a difference: "Miss Knott is type O, and so I surveyed the sweatshirt looking for ABO type other than O at first to try to find some bloodstain that would give me an indication it was not from her."

"Did you find such a stain?" Atkins asked.

Sam Knott watched how the young prosecutor was careful to keep the complex testimony as simple as possible. Simple questions that would be rewarded with declarative yes and no answers.

"Yes," Harmor answered. "After marking and looking at fifty-four different areas of bloodstain, I found an area that gave me a result of ABO type A. . . . It was a fairly small area of bloodstain present on the left shoulder of the seam between the sleeve and the yoke of the sweatshirt. It covered an area of approximately—it was around the . . . size of a penny."

The stain, unfortunately, was not large enough to type for every genetic marker system, Harmor said.

"At that time and with just that marker alone, were you able to exclude Craig Peyer as the one who donated that type stain?" Atkins asked.

"My conclusion is that Mr. Peyer could have donated that bloodstain and he was not eliminated," Harmor replied.

The blood matched, but Atkins didn't leave it at that. He wanted this match grounded deeply in scientific fact. "In no genetic marker system was there not a match?" he asked the expert.

"That's correct," Harmor said. The percentage of people with that very same genetic marker system included Peyer, he testified, and roughly 1 in 161 people in the Caucasian population of San Diego.

Grimes was ready for the prosecution's damaging percentages. "Would that mean," the defense attorney asked Harmor on cross-examination, "that perhaps there would be around thirteen thousand people in San Diego County that could have these genetic markers indicated in your general population?"

Harmor was an experienced professional courtroom witness. He wasn't going to let the defense just wrap up his testimony by giving a simple yes or no. He was a scientist after all. It was time to be precise. "I get twelve thousand eight hundred," Harmor answered.

Grimes shot back with his own analysis, adding a little hometown touch. "Enough to fill the San Diego Sports Arena?" the lawyer asked. Surely, Grimes figured, the jurors, like most San Diegans, had visited the local stadium at least once in their lives to see the Sockers, the professional soccer team play, or the circus, a concert, or the Ice Capades. The jurors would know how big a crowd that 12,800 could be inside such an arena, and what an awesome task it would be to narrow down to one murderer among them.

Despite Grimes's challenges, Van Orshoven was comfortable. He had covered the emotional arguments, the weird habits of Peyer, the blood and fiber evidence. On the tenth day of trial, just before noon on Thursday, February 4, Van Orshoven announced: "The people rest."

When court reconvened after lunch at 1:30, the defense of Craig Alan Peyer began with attorney Robert Grimes immediately trying to shoot down the prosecution's big surprise witness, the milkman Robert Calderwood. As the prosecution witness, Calderwood had insisted that he'd told a friend that he'd seen the CHP car and that she had advised him to call authorities, even though he'd waited for a long time to do so.

Grimes, however, picked up where the milkman left off. He brought in four of Calderwood's coworkers who were ready to challenge the milkman's story. One employee of the Hollandia Dairy testified that Calderwood had come into her office looking for a 1986 calendar around January 19 of 1987, which was to be the first day of testimony in Peyer's murder trial.

This dairy worker's testimony strongly hinted that Calderwood was swayed to come forward because he'd seen what big attention the trial was getting. Another dairy worker who had trained Calderwood took the witness stand and said there was no way the milkman could have talked to his corroborating witness, Betty Bahnmiller, about having seen a highway patrolman at the crime scene right after the murder. Calderwood hadn't even started working the milk run that included Betty's store until almost nine months after Cara's murder.

A third coworker, Maribel Flores, testified that Calderwood had talked about the murder at the dairy while he was reading the newspaper account of it. As Flores recalled, Calderwood had told her that he had seen a cop car with its lights out speeding away from a road on his way to work one morning, and he needed to know the date Cara was killed so he could decide if that was when he was there.

"I told him that wouldn't matter because the newspaper said she was killed at 8:30 at night, not in the morning, and he said, 'Well obviously someone was going back to check the crime scene to make sure there was nothing there,' " Flores testified.

After Flores finished making shredded wheat of one of the prosecution's star witnesses, Van Orshoven let her walk away from the witness stand. He had no questions for her. By the time Grimes finished putting the dairy workers on the stand, it looked like he had completely torpedoed the prosecution's surprise witness.

Grimes was fired up. He then proceeded to present witnesses to advance his theory that others besides Peyer had had the opportunity to kill Cara. Grimes began his own parade of witnesses who he was sure would punch holes through the prosecution's testimony. He began with testimony about the mystery hitchhiker, a man described by witnesses as jumping out at cars and waving money at them in apparent desperation to get a ride at around eight o'clock on the night of the murder. The weird hitchhiker had stood on the side of the parkway Cara would have driven down to reach the freeway on ramp south, toward home. Donna Bodine was Grimes's first witness who said this mystery hitchhiker was no mirage. Under Grimes's gentle questioning, the young woman said she'd seen the hitchhiker that Saturday night as she'd passed by the North County Fair shopping mall in Escondido right off the I-15 freeway. Bodine had been driving a Volkswagen, and had had to swerve to avoid the guy.

"We were turning right onto the on ramp and a man jumped in front of my car," Bodine testified. "He was on the curb and he jumped onto the lane of traffic where I was. He was just standing there in the middle of the road lunging at my car."

"What time was this?" Van Orshoven asked, taking over his cross-examination.

"Around eight o'clock," she answered. That would make it thirty minutes before Cara passed by.

"How was he attired?"

"Dark pants, dark shirt, bearded," the witness responded. The encounter shook her up enough to stay in her memory.

"How would you describe the individual as to age, young, old?" Van Orshoven asked.

"As middle-aged, I would say. I hope I won't offend anyone," the young woman said. "I would say in their forties."

"You might," the judge observed drily, and laughter rippled through the courtroom.

Under cross-examination by the prosecution, Bodine admitted that she'd never told the police about the hitchhiker, which was Van Orshoven's way of saying to the jury that maybe that was because the incident wasn't important enough. Surely, the prosecution wanted the jury to believe that if she thought this hitchhiker was a murder suspect, she would have called. And since she didn't call the police, that cleared them because they didn't know the hitchhiker existed, so how could they have caught him and questioned him?

But Grimes was ready for that argument. On the redirect, the defense attorney was able to get Bodine to say she had tried to tell police about the hitchhiker, but they hadn't seemed to care. She testified that she had called a TV station Sunday after she'd heard about Cara's murder; certainly it must have given her pause to know a girl her own age who also drove a Volkswagen down that same road had been killed. Bodine said she had called police again the following day, but the authorities never contacted her about what she'd seèn. Here was strong fuel for Grimes's favorite defense theme: that investigators threw away all the other clues that didn't fit into the Peyer-did-it theory.

Bodine's roommate was also in the car that night and she took the stand to corroborate her testimony about the hitchhiker.

After her came an even stronger witness to testify about the odd actions of that hitchhiker on the night of the murder. The witness was a former navy pilot who testified that he had been so suspicious of the strange hitchhiker that he'd called police.

"I heard that there was someone missing, and it was after that I certainly put two and two together," the retired aviator said. "It was such that it was implanted in my memory that there was somebody on that corner that evening."

Grimes had unearthed yet a fourth witness who had seen the hitchhiker, a young woman named Kim Vito, who got on the stand and told the jury that she also had had to swerve to avoid the wild lunging of the man. "It was kind of scary," Vito testified. That was a familiar sentiment coming from a woman on the witness stand in this trial, except this time Grimes offered something new. Young women might have been frightened chatting for a long time with a highway patrolman, but that wasn't the only situation that scared people along the Interstate 15 route. There was this mystery hitchhiker, Grimes wanted the jury to remember, and he still might be out there.

Now Grimes was ready to plant another seed of doubt into the collective minds of the jurors: maybe Cara didn't go straight home from her boyfriend's house as everybody said she would have.

Grimes was moving confidently through the courtroom arena like a quarterback who has just run for two touchdowns. He called San Diego Police Detective Paul Olsen to the stand. As the cop approached the microphone, Olsen looked like he wanted to be anywhere else except testifying for the defense. He looked across the room at Sam Knott helplessly, as if to say, I was subpoenaed, I have no choice. Forgive me.

Grimes questioned Olsen about his early conversations with

Cara's boyfriend, Wayne Bautista, who was one of the first suspects police ruled out in the homicide.

"I asked him if there was any nightclub or favored location where they would go," Olsen testified. "He said that Cara liked to dance, and that she liked a place in Escondido called After Dark."

"Okay," Grimes said, "so he indicated that After Dark was a place that they liked to go to dance?"

"Apparently, yes," the detective said.

"Okay, Detective Olsen, was there any discussion with Mr. Bautista as to whether or not on December twenty-seven, nineteen-eighty-six, Cara was upset about anything?"

"Well, if I recall, she wanted to go to the wild animal park and was getting maybe a little bit antsy because he was sick and had been in the house a couple of days."

"Just getting kind of bored?" Grimes asked.

"Apparently," Olsen agreed.

So maybe everything hadn't been all roses between Cara and Wayne, and maybe that night she had just felt like doing something else. So maybe she'd dillydallied, stopped somewhere. From there, she might have picked up the strange hitchhiker, and Grimes tried to leave the other possibilities to the imaginations of the jurors.

There were other holes in the ship to fix. Grimes was still reeling from the repetitious testimony of all those women that Peyer pulled over, the Miss Poway pageant. Grimes wanted to show that Peyer really didn't mean any harm. After all, these people were Craig Peyer's constituents. At least that's how the highway patrolman saw it.

Two of Peyer's CHP colleagues were called to the stand to tell the jurors what a straight arrow cop the accused murderer was. Highway Patrol Sergeant Richard Dick testified that he and Peyer had responded to a fatal car crash on the I-15 freeway a quarter mile from the Mercy Road exit on October 13, 1986. It had been a particularly memorable crash, Dick said, because one of the cars had exploded and burned to a crisp on the freeway shoulder. A motorist had been trapped inside by the flames.

Dick told the jury that Peyer's investigation had found that bad lighting had caused the crash, because the car's headlight and taillight had been burned out, so the driver of the car that hit it hadn't been able to see the vehicle. Without saying so directly, Grimes, through his questioning, hinted that it was Peyer's years of experience that made him so finicky about proper vehicle lighting. This could be a reasonable explanation for why he pulled women over with crooked headlights. Of course, it may also have explained that Peyer pulled over Cara that night because her license-plate bulb was burned out.

Sergeant Dick went on to say what a meticulous cop Peyer was, that he constantly led the shift in helping clear away road hazards, issuing tickets, and following up on traffic accidents.

Grimes asked Peyer's former highway patrol colleague, "Would you consider it a violation of department policy if another officer took a violator to proceed down the off ramp and then gave the citation down on Mercy Road?"

"Yes, sir, it would be all right," the patrolman agreed.

Grimes echoed him, looking right at the jury, "It would be all right?"

"Yes," said Dick.

"Would it be all right even if it was at nighttime?"

"Yes, sir," the patrolman agreed. "But it probably wouldn't be highly recommended," he added. The yes would have been enough for Grimes's purpose, but he was stuck with a solid maybe anyway.

Patrolman Dick testified that many officers spent time at the Mercy Road dead end because it was a quiet place to sit and catch up on busy work and write police reports. For the first time, jurors got to hear from Peyer's colleagues that he seemed to be a reasonable, conscientious patrolman who, despite his talkative manner, didn't stray from highway patrol rules.

Van Orshoven walked across the courtroom, hoping to get the patrolman back to the notion that what Peyer did at Mercy Road was definitely not by the book.

"Isn't it true that it's kind of dangerous for an officer riding alone to take an unknown violator into a dark place?"

"It could be, yes," Dick said.

"Not only dangerous for the officer, it's dangerous to the citizen, isn't it?"

"It could be," the witness repeated.

"Specifically during hours of darkness?" Van Orshoven asked, and the patrolman concurred. He seemed a pretty agreeable cop, agreeing with the defense, agreeing with the prosecution. In the end, one of the only highway patrolmen to testify for the defense who didn't do much for either side.

Next Grimes turned his attack on the state's scientific evidence. The defense had its own experts to refute the prosecution's contention that blood and fiber linked the victim to the accused. Grimes even used police investigators to make his point.

Under Grimes's questioning, San Diego Police fingerprint expert Ralph Bukowski testified that investigators had found nine fingerprints on Cara's car, none of them belonging to Peyer. Three of the prints had been Cara's, but the other six had not matched any of her relatives or Wayne.

"Did you check to see if those other fingerprints matched any of the known felons in the justice department computer in Sacramento?" Grimes asked Bukowski on the witness stand.

"No," Bukowski answered. Once again, Grimes had another example to prove his theory that investigators simply ignored all evidence that didn't incriminate Peyer, and therefore blew their chance to find the man or woman the defense contended was the real killer.

Grimes called his own experts to the stand to debate the complex science of analyzing fiber by fiber. But first Grimes had another much more touchy issue to deal with: the overwhelming presence of Cara Knott in the courtroom. On Friday, the eleventh day of the trial, Grimes approached the judge's bench while the jury was out of the courtroom. "Your honor, I want to register an objection to some of the prosecution's evidence, especially exhibit one," the defense attorney said quietly. Exhibit one was the color portrait of smiling Cara Knott that the deputy district attorney kept propped up on his desk throughout the trial. "It's so big," Grimes complained. But the judge ruled that the picture of Cara stayed.

From his seat in the audience, Sam smiled. The monster's lawyer was rattled.

The jurors were ushered back into their box and the second day of defense testimony began. There would be thirteen witnesses.

Grimes fueled his theory that maybe Cara didn't go straight home as she told her daddy she would. How else to explain the nurse who Grimes called to testify about seeing a blonde girl in a light-colored VW bug stopped on the freeway shoulder beside three guys—a full hour after Peyer got off duty? Nurse Wanda Dobbie testified for the defense that she had seen a girl who fit Cara's description on the freeway a few miles south of Mercy Road on the night of the murder. Dobbie said she'd seen the squabble on the side of the highway around 11:30 P.M., which meant she would have seen the victim an hour *after* Peyer had checked out for the night.

Dobbie said she'd seen an old brown Datsun blocking the VW's path on the roadway shoulder. And, the nurse testified, she had told the police the same story when she called them the next day, as soon as she'd heard about the Knott slaying. She said police had come to interview her three days later.

She described the cars as being a light colored VW bug and an older model Datsun. "Did you see any people?" Grimes asked.

"I saw a girl standing beside the Volkswagen," the nurse answered.

"What did she look like?" Grimes asked.

"Well, as far as I could determine, a young girl, probably shoulder length hair. And a male had her by the shoulders up against the car."

Dobbie recalled that the girl had worn a white top, and that she definitely had white shoes or sneakers on her feet. "She kicked out, and that's what really drew my attention at the moment," Dobbie said. She said she couldn't really identify the man involved, because his back had been to the road when she drove past. "He appeared to be Hispanic," she said. The prosecution failed soon after to shake much from the nurse's testimony.

The next big question on everyone's mind in the courtroom, in the courthouse, and in the county, was whether

Craig Peyer was going to get up and testify in his own defense. Up until now, the patrolman had remained completely silent on every issue. Very few people even knew what his voice sounded like. He was like a mystery man. His face remained inscrutable no matter what was being said on the witness stand.

The defense lawyer had two other specific matters to clear up, but they were among the most important images that he wanted the jury to think about. He wanted them to see Officer Jill Oglivie not as a competent, hard-working cop, but as a maverick, ready to step on anybody's career to get to the top. And he wanted to end his case leaving the jury with an image of Craig Peyer as the straitlaced family man and supercop. He wanted Karen Peyer to testify about what a wonderful husband she had, and how on the night Cara Knott was killed, her husband had just done his job, come home, turned on the TV set, and gone to bed. He had had his usual snack of cookies and an apple.

Grimes believed he was ready to finally upset the prosecution's neatly organized puzzle when he finally handed it to the jury. The pieces that Joe Van Orshoven fit together so carefully maybe didn't fit so well after all. Maybe there was a mystery killer. Maybe it wasn't so bad that Craig Peyer took women down to Mercy Road. With enough maybes, there was room for reasonable doubt. The jury might think this wasn't the guy.

As he marshalled his witnesses along with their testimonies, Grimes always ended up trying to leave that image of reasonable doubt in the jurors' minds.

In hope of discrediting Officer Jill Oglivie, he called one of her former partners on the police force, Gregory Dotson, to the stand. The policewoman who had done so much damage to Peyer's defense turned out to have hurt this former cop as well—she had gotten him fired, Dotson testified, by complaining that he used profanity.

Officer Oglivie was not to be believed, Dotson claimed. "She exaggerated the truth. She exaggerates a lot. She likes to be in the spotlight." As Dotson's testimony lingered in the minds of the jurors, Grimes called Karen Peyer to the stand.

Earlier witnesses had done minor damage to the highway patrolman's credibility when they had testified that Peyer had told them at a CHP New Year's eve party, four days after the murder, that he suddenly wanted to get out of town. Grimes set out to repair that damage with the patrolman's wife.

Was there ever a time, Grimes asked, that the Peyer family discussed the possibility of moving in 1986, say the possibility of moving out of San Diego?

"Yes," Karen answered, speaking clearly, her head up, her blonde hair curling softly about her round face. "Yes, there was. We started discussing it in the fall, like September." Which would have been four months before Cara died.

Karen talked on the witness stand about how she and Craig had dreamed of building a house in the country and having a big property with horses. "We just felt that it was getting a little too crowded here. So we decided. We started looking at CHP offices in the real northern California areas, Redding, Truckee, Susanville, Ukiah, those offices. Because we were thinking about maybe he could transfer to that office and not lose any of his seniority and pay and we could have our property." That was something surely everyone in the courtroom could understand, that even a solid salary like the $36,000 a year that Peyer was earning at the highway patrol didn't go very far in the southern California real estate market. In San Diego property was so astronomically costly—an average two-bedroom home going for $160,000—that only one-fourth of the population owned their own homes. People could identify with those American dreams of Karen and Craig Peyer.

"Was there any other feature of being in a smaller community that was discussed?" the defense attorney asked.

"Well, we just, being from here, we just felt like it was getting much too crowded and it was losing the one-to-one relationships between people and we felt if we moved to a smaller community that there would be that one-on-one," Karen testified. "And Craig was really looking forward to being called the town sheriff, that he knew people by name and they knew his name."

She spoke smoothly and clearly, looking often at her husband and the jurors. Grimes led her to events right up to the night of the murder. Just before Christmas, she testified, her husband had burned his right hand adjusting a hot valve on his motorcycle. With that comment, Karen Peyer offered an explanation for the source of Craig Peyer's blood and scratches seen on the back of his hand the night Cara was killed.

That night had been like any other, Karen said. Craig had worked a normal shift and come home for dinner and she explained what normal was in the Peyer household. "Well, everybody runs to greet him, the kids were all there, we probably met in the hallway of the kitchen."

"What did he do?" Grimes asked.

"He took his jacket and his gun belt off and sat them on the couch. Next to the baby's purple jacket." That statement offered another counterargument to the prosecution's puzzle, giving a possible source of the purple fibers that investigators had found on his gun, purple fibers that the experts said didn't match Cara's clothes that night.

Karen related to the jury how the family had sat down to dinner before he had left for his shift that night and how her husband had seemed his usually chipper self, but a little tired.

Then after eating dinner, what did he do before he went out the door?" Grimes asked gently.

Karen raised her head high, looked right at her husband sitting across the room, and said, "He gave us all a kiss good-bye."

After his shift ended, Karen said, Craig Peyer had walked through their front door at precisely 11:15 P.M. Karen knew because she looked at the clock, which was her habit. "He got undressed for bed and we looked at the marks on his face," she said. Peyer had been exasperated with himself as he related how he had fallen against the fence in the CHP back lot and scratched himself. To her, Karen testified, the scratches had looked like a crisscross pattern on the right side of his face. She had put ointment on his wounds for him.

Then, she testified, "He climbed into bed and he always— he had a snack. He had a piece of fruit. I think it was an apple and a couple cookies." She concentrated fully, determined to tell her story as accurately as possible. "And he climbed into bed and turned on the TV and he watched TV and ate his snack and I laid next to him in the bed," she testified. Everything about the day was, she said, perfectly normal.

Karen Peyer's unwavering belief in her husband's innocence was the last thing jurors heard before they left for lunch. With her, the defense rested. Craig Peyer would not be taking the stand in his own defense.

It was twilight when the judge, jury, court staff, lawyers, and gun-toting bailiffs climbed into the vans at four o'clock outside the county courthouse. By the time they drove twenty miles north on the I-15 freeway to Mercy Road, the scene of the crime, night had fallen.

The jurors slowly climbed out of the van and stood together for a moment in the eeriness of the dead end. Victor Dingman, the juror who had given Cheryl Knott the creeps, got on his hands and knees and put his ear to the ground. The reporters watched him and wondered if he expected the earth to reveal some secret message. The courtroom had moved from the county courthouse to the murder scene so the jury could see the spot the witnesses had been talking about and pointing to on maps. A police officer stood in the creek bed where Cara's battered body had been found and shined a flashlight up to the jurors standing on the bridge sixty-five feet above so they could see where she'd been thrown.

Craig Peyer walked the death scene with defense attorney Diane Campbell stuck to his side, delivering a silent message to the jury that women have nothing to fear around this proud former lawman.

After the tour of the crime scene in the cold dark winter night, the climax was to follow the next morning in court—the final arguments. But it was a drama delayed. On February 10, all the players gathered expectantly, but Deputy District Attorney Joe Van Orshoven had broken his tooth, it was announced, and he was in too much pain to continue. Everyone went home before lunchtime. The next day the courtroom remained dark. It was February 11, Cara's birthday. She would have been twenty-two.

Bob Grimes was dragging from sitting all day in the courtroom and working all night on his strategy for the last six weeks. His days were getting so long that his four-year-old daughter complained to her mother, "I don't think Daddy likes me anymore." Finally on February 15, Grimes and Van Orshoven were ready for the conclusion of one of the most sensational murder trials in California history.

"First of all, let me apologize to you for disappointing you last week," Van Orshoven began his summation by explaining to the jury about his broken tooth. "I was a little disappointed myself. It was only an English muffin."

To begin closing statements with an apology was not auspicious. But Van Orshoven was an old hand; he hit his rhythm within the next two sentences. His recitation was dramatic, stark. The jurors were riveted.

"Murder, premeditated murder," boomed Van Orshoven across the courtroom. Planning a murder means far more than going out and buying a gun and hatching a plot, he told the jury. "There's another kind of premeditation, and that is a premeditation that goes on when you're engaged in a course of conduct. A habitual course of conduct that may, at any time, explode in a manner that will result in you losing the few things that you have in life that are important to you: losing your family, losing your job, losing your position in the community."

He was delivering his summation as Robert Young might have, sharp, in control, bearing down on the jury. "So what are you going to do if this course of conduct results in a confrontation with another human being that, quote unquote, gets out of hand? You're going to have to get rid of that person. Can't have that person going and telling somebody, complaining to somebody. . . .

"Now you got a gun, got a flashlight, you got a nightstick. But people that shoot other people are often found out, because you know that those bullets we can trace back to the gun. And beating a person to death is a messy proposition," Van Orshoven said.

He picked up the dirty yellow rope, what the prosecution contended was the murder weapon, and began to twist it as he spoke. "So you equip yourself," the deputy DA went on as the jurors' eyes stayed glued to the rope. "You equip yourself so that if something does happen, you can take care of it. And you know," he held up the rope with his right hand, "people's exhibit thirty, it's neat because it doesn't take up much room and it could go into a pocket or up a sleeve or maybe stuck in a gun belt."

Van Orshoven's summation went from murder weapon to murder scene to physical evidence. He pointed to the photo of Cara on his desk and talked about Peyer's way of taking women to Mercy Road who fit the type and who had minor equipment violations.

"We know that Cara Knott had an inoperative license-plate light in her little VW. We also know that something was the matter with the baffle in her exhaust pipe. We know that. We know it was loose in there. And what is more characteristic of Mr. Peyer than to take up some of the time he spends with these young women, showing them what's the matter with their car?"

Van Orshoven stopped pacing and let silence fill the courtroom. He turned his attention to Cara Knott. She had been different. She wasn't like the other women. Cara Knott had been worried about her personal safety and had taken self-defense classes. "And these classes," Van Orshoven continued, "taught her that if she couldn't get away, the thing for her to do was to explode, explode toward the face.

"And it's a terrible thing to observe, but that may be what resulted in her death. That she became anxious, that she couldn't get away. And finally she exploded. She scratched the face of her assailant. And as a result of that scratching, she couldn't live anymore."

He picked up the picture of Cara's smiling face and showed the jury. "And she was turned from that," he said solemnly, "into this," glancing from one photo to the other picture he held in his other hand, the image of the girl's bloody body. The sight of the two pictures side by side proved too much for Joyce Knott. For the first time during the trial, she burst into sobs.

The assistant district attorney turned to Peyer's actions that night, the way the perfect cop appeared disheveled at the gas station and CHP headquarters. And with scratches on his face, and such a lame excuse about where the scratches came from, Van Orshoven said. "If you fall into a chain link fence, and you have really lost your balance, you're not going to tattoo the side of your cheek with the chain link fence. You're going to hit it and you're going to skid down that fence and going to scratch the dickens out of the side of your face. And it isn't going to look like fingernail scratches."

He didn't dwell on the complex fiber evidence, conceding that nothing about the matches made was absolute. But he emphasized that the gold fiber found on Cara's boot was identical to that in the CHP shoulder patch on Peyer's uniform, and that that particular patch had not been manufactured in eight years. It was more than just coincidence.

The prosecutor theorized that Peyer tried cleaning up after his deed but he wasn't smart enough to wipe away all evidence. "Peyer didn't know that his own boot would yield a fiber that was indistinguishable from the fabric in Cara Knott's purple sweatpants," Van Orshoven said, "and he didn't know that police would find two more fibers on his gun that also were indistinguishable from fabric found in Cara's pants." Those fibers may seem small but they were the link that proves that Craig and Cara met that night.

Van Orshoven ended with his kicker, "As you reflect on the evidence here, ladies and gentlemen, I would like you to ask yourselves, as we have asked ourselves, for whom, for whom would Cara Knott stop on the way to her father's house after already reporting her impending arrival? For whom? When her car is found, the passenger door is locked.

"Yes," Van Orshoven said, "she might have stopped for her boyfriend, Wayne Bautista. But everyone knew where he was. Yes, Cara would have stopped for her father, but he was at home working on a puzzle with her brother-in-law. She might have stopped for her brother-in-law or for a policeman. Or for a policeman. And she did stop for a policeman. And the policeman killed her. And that policeman is Craig Alan Peyer."

The prosecutor sat down. Forty minutes had passed since he apologized to the jury.

Defense attorney Bob Grimes unfolded his long body from the chair and buttoned his gray suit coat. He had no intention of hitting only the dramatic highlights of the case in his closing arguments. When he was through he would leave no stone unturned.

Like his opponent, Grimes began by turning toward Cara's photo on the prosecutor's desk. ''They have this picture in front of you again and they talk about Cara Knott's broken body. That's an issue that we've got to get right out in front and deal with.

''Some of you have daughters this same age. And if there's one thing we have to do right up front it is get the emotional content of this case out on the table, deal with it, feel bad about it, feel the tragedy and then go on and be objective about the facts.''

He talked about the democratic ideal that all people are presumed innocent, and it was up to the prosecutor to prove the accused was guilty beyond a reasonable doubt. ''If the prosecution has not provided the burden of proof, they lose. It's as simple as that,'' Grimes said. ''But where is the proof?'' If Cara Knott had scratched Peyer, why wasn't there blood or skin under her nails? If he had strangled her with the yellow rope, why was there no blood or skin on the rope?

One by one Grimes went through what he considered the inconsistencies in the testimonies of each of the twenty women Peyer had pulled over to Mercy Road. One of them had the wrong date. Another claimed it happened on a night that Peyer wasn't working. ''Some of them were dead wrong about what they've said. Some are right and some—most of them, I'm sure—are honest, doing their best to give their honest recollection of what happened.''

He did not touch on every issue, but dwelt only on holes in the prosecution's trial testimony. He leaped from point to point in a rambling manner, but his methodical recitation, his soothing voice, his Gary Cooper manner, kept the jurors spellbound.

The prosecution failed to provide the burden of proof on logistics, Grimes contended. ''Mr. Van Orshoven's got to explain to you not only why Mr. Peyer would do this crazy thing, but *how* he would do it.'' How did the Volkswagen get from the bottom of the off ramp, where all the other women were stopped, to the spot one-third of a mile down the bike path? How did Cara's body get from the car another three tenths of a mile to the bridge?

"Why is there no blood on the highway patrol car?" he asked the jury. "How did he get Cara Knott to the bridge without getting blood in his California Highway Patrol car or on his uniform? If their theory is that he carried her, remember the expert testified the blood on Mr. Peyer's uniform jacket was consistent with Mr. Peyer's and you could rule her out."

Not only was there no explanation of how Craig might have gotten Cara to the bridge, he said, "You kind of wonder why. That's one of the big issues in the case. Why thrown off the bridge? No good reason for it. It seems an act of craziness or perhaps a disturbed person."

Then there was the time element, Grimes said. "Cara gets in her car around eight-thirty from the gas station, passes the bizarre man right before she gets on the freeway. It takes fifteen minutes to get to Mercy Road. The limo is there at eight-forty-five. How does Craig Peyer get her in there?"

There was Cara's character. "This is a cautious young lady," the defense attorney continued. "You've been out to this scene. The road says right on it, 'This is Not a Through Road.' It's clearly not an area that she's going to want to go down. She's not going to drive down there by herself unless there's someone—like perhaps the hitchhiker—that's forcing her to."

There were the scratches on Peyer's face. The defense lawyer recited testimony from three CHP officers who said Peyer's explanation, that he scratched his face on the fence, was consistent with their view of the injuries.

There were fibers and fingerprints unaccounted for, and Grimes launched into great detail on each one, the fibers on the fender of Cara's VW, fibers beside her body in the creek bed, six fingerprints in her car that failed to match Cara's, her family's, her boyfriend's and his family's, and Craig Peyer's.

And finally he moved toward his conclusion. Just like his opponent, the defense attorney started with the photograph of the living Cara Knott and concluded with that of the dead Cara Knott.

"The autopsy in a circumstantial evidence case is the single prime piece of evidence. If we want to be cold and objective about it, [there] is the victim, there's nothing more central to the case. In this case, of all the witnesses that you've heard, including some people that are clearly either fantasizing or just lying—and that includes at least Mr. Calderwood—perhaps the most disturbing witness of all was Dr. Bockhacker.

"He didn't care whether injuries were predeath or postdeath. He just didn't care," Grimes said. "He did such a horrible job that we'll never know certain things that we really need to know in this case."

Grimes moved to make his final plea to the jurors. "I think now having looked at the evidence in this case, the circumstantial evidence rule and the circumstantial evidence all point to someone else doing it, not Craig Peyer, and the flimsy evidence that causes us to speculate, that he definitely causes us to be suspicious," he acknowledged. "But . . . we have to speculate to see it from the prosecution's point of view."

It was up to the jurors now to decide whether the state provided that burden of proof of Peyer's guilt, he told them. "And that's to a moral certainty in your mind, an abiding belief, an abiding conviction that will not last today and tomorrow, but for the rest of your lives." He paused, to let the weight of their duty sink in and in his soft voice he concluded, "I think you agree with me that there's an abundance of doubt in this case."

The defense attorney finished his summation nearly five hours after he had begun.

After the lawyers wrapped up speeches, routine rebuttal arguments filled up another day of court. On Tuesday, February 16, 1988, after 154 witnesses testified and 102 pieces of evidence were piled up on the table, all the talking was over. The jury recessed into their dingy lounge in the belly of San Diego County Courthouse to deliberate on the guilt and innocence of former highway patrolman Craig Peyer.

A day passed quietly. The Peyer family awaited the verdict at Craig's parents' home in suburban San Diego. But since the Knotts lived further away, they had to stay close by if they wanted to be sure to be in the courtroom for the verdict.

It burned Sam to know that the court would only wait for the defendant, because it was considered his trial. The court system provided no lounge for the victim's family to wait. And so the Knotts sat in the hallway on the long wooden benches against the wall. And they waited.

On that first day of jury deliberation, San Diego was slapped with another vicious storm, freezing temperatures and heavy winds that blew in from Alaska. The courthouse hallway, usually bright with the sun pouring in from outside, turned dark and ominous.

A second day passed quietly in the courthouse hallway. On the third day, the jury asked for transcripts of testimony from seven key witnesses, among them the milkman Calderwood. On day four of deliberations, the jury asked for Officer Jill Oglivie's testimony about Peyer grabbing his ears and grilling her about the homicide four days after the slaying.

The fifth day ended with no verdict. The jurors looked weary as they piled into the courtroom to be dismissed and again hear Judge Huffman's admonitions to stay away from news reports of the case and refrain from discussing it outside. Day six passed quietly.

Joe Van Orshoven spent the long days awaiting the verdict at a friend's house a few miles away in Ocean Beach. He sat on the deck watching the waves wash back and forth on the shore, and waited for the phone to ring.

Finally, at the end of day seven, the phone rang.

Van Orshoven and Grimes and the Peyers and the Knotts and an avalanche of news crews poured into the courtroom and awaited the decision. At 4 P.M. on Thursday, February 25, the jury foreman handed the bailiff a note. The bailiff stood before the judge and read out loud the one line written there:

" 'Your honor, we are a hung jury.' "

A shout went up and people started talking at once. All hell broke loose. Karen Peyer was crying. Joyce Knott gasped and grabbed for Sam's hand. The Knott family sat perfectly still, as if they could freeze time by not moving themselves.

But Craig Peyer was going to go free. The jury couldn't unanimously decide whether the highway patrolman killed the college student, and so the whole trial was voided, as if it hadn't happened.

Across the street the former cop's newer colleagues, the jail inmates, heard the news somehow the instant it happened. They started screaming and banging on their bars, from the basement to the roof the roar went up, ''He's guilty, he's guilty!''

But they were wrong. Craig Peyer was a free man.

16

The New Yorker

CRAIG Peyer felt good for the first time in months.

Although his face had remained as impassive as stone during the trial, the tedious days in the courtroom must have taken their toll. It must have been depressing sitting there, listening to all the former friends and colleagues on the highway patrol testify against him, and hearing those exaggerations from women he had escorted down Mercy Road.

He was guilty, sure—guilty of liking people too much. He was a big talker. He tried to impress the importance of safety on people. Was that a crime?

It was hard to go out anymore. When Craig walked out of the courtroom, people's stares clung to him like a hot muggy night. Even his neighbors—people he loaned his tools to and fixed cars for, people who always smiled and said hello—now avoided him and frowned whenever they met him on the street.

With the mistrial, Craig must have felt that at least a good part of the world agreed with him, that he was an innocent lawman set up, framed.

His wife, Karen, was a deeply religious woman, and the jury's decision must have seemed to her like a gift from God. The spirit of renewed faith seemed to enter Craig too. Once a sporadic churchgoer, Craig now embraced Jesus Christ with the passion of a budding minister. After all, hadn't the King of the Jews been misunderstood and condemned by his own peers? Karen took her husband to the Christian Horizon Fellowship church near their home many nights during the trial, and there among other born-again Christians, Craig made some good friends.

Craig prayed fervently. When other congregation members saw tears streaming down his cheeks, they were amazed that such a good man could have been betrayed by the law he had worked so hard to enforce.

Craig kept busy during those precious days of freedom bought with the one million dollar bail. He had always loved working with his hands, and after the California Highway Patrol fired him, his friend Bruce Johnson gave him a job installing electrical systems in swimming pools and spas. It was good to get outside and to be doing something useful, and the four hundred dollars a week he earned helped ease the money worries. The bills were mounting and he was forced to live on his retirement money from his state pension, but how long would ten thousand dollars last? His dad had offered him his pension, but they all hoped the situation wouldn't get that desperate.

Bruce Johnson believed in his friend, and it upset him when people called and threatened him for helping Peyer. The calls were coming all the time now that the newspaper had found out, but after all, Peyer was a man still innocent in the eyes of the law. Johnson just hung up when hecklers called.

Johnson's wife, Cecilia, helped run the pool-building company and she told friends that Craig Peyer was a tremendous help. She was also happy to see Peyer was not the kind of man who sulked about his misfortune. Despite all those pressures, he was still trying to earn a living for the people he loved. "Most people admire him for supporting his family in time of trouble," Cecilia told reporters.

That kind of talk riled San Diego's longtime district attorney, Ed Miller, who certainly wasn't feeling as upbeat as Craig Peyer must have been these days. The way his prosecutor Joe Van Orshoven had been talking to Miller during the first trial, Craig Peyer's hide should have been mounted like a trophy in the DA's office. Van Orshoven thought for sure he would get a conviction. Now Miller had to refile murder charges against Peyer and go through the whole thing all over again. The Peyer mistrial compounded the DA's troubles because after twenty years as the top law enforcement official who routinely ran unopposed in elections, it looked like Miller was on a real losing streak.

Just before the Peyer case, Miller's office lost a highly publicized corruption case against the county's registrar of voters, a Hispanic whom the DA accused of taking kickbacks. Once-quiet minority groups began to vent their pent-up anger at Miller, charging the DA with selective prosecution tinged with racial overtones because the registrar was one of the few Latinos in local office. Only a few months before that, the DA had prosecuted a San Diego city councilman, also Hispanic, for charging nights on the town to his city hall–issued credit card.

Those prosecutions only fueled rising racial tensions as critics claimed that Miller, like many of San Diego's establishment whites, was having trouble dealing with the browning of the community. There was no hiding that California's population explosion had brought with it an expansion in the minority community as every end of the social spectrum came to cash in on California dreams.

But like oil and water the races did little mixing in modern San Diego County. Whites ruled the halls of power and ultrarich suburbs like seaside La Jolla where Ed Miller lived and the newer inland bedroom communities like Rancho Bernardo, where all the homes had to be Spanish-style architecture and the garage doors closed by sunset.

The blacks and Latinos were left to fend for themselves in beat-up inner city neighborhoods splintered by freeways and lacking even the barest neighborhood staples like supermarkets. There are no postcards of the ghettos of America's finest city, of the junkyards and taco stands and storefront churches adjoining liquor stores, each dispensing its own brand of spirits. There, the major business opportunities seemed to be in crack and cocaine, delivered freely by the newest urban gift to San Diego, gangs, drugs' most energetic messengers. These black and Hispanic youths thought they saw the graffiti handwriting on the wall: drug peddling was the only way for them to get out of the ghetto and into the driver's seat of a big Cadillac. It never seemed to work out that way, but they kept trying.

The law enforcement community was having the toughest time of all coping with the restlessness wrought by the sudden urbanization of San Diego. Perhaps the biggest symbol of that struggle was Sagon Penn. In the year before Cara Knott died, a young black man named Sagon Penn became infamous for shooting two white cops during a fight in the ghetto. More than forty witnesses testified that police attacked the youth with nightsticks, and two separate juries found Penn innocent of murder. The second trial yielded only more charges of racism against the DA and the establishment, more charges that the white brotherhood of policemen stuck together to protect their own no matter what the cost. The few cops who dared to testify against their fellow police officers were ostracized. Even the trial judge publicly lashed out at the cops for using what he called "nightstick justice," and imposing an unspoken code of silence among officers about the conduct of their fellow cops. For many police critics, the traditional code of silence among cops never spoke louder.

All this controversy was a real about-face for the DA who had stampeded into elective office twenty years earlier as a law-and-order reformer bent on cleaning up San Diego. Edwin Louis Miller, Jr., the son of an insurance salesman from Los Angeles, had learned his lessons at Princeton, Northwestern, and Dartmouth, where he'd played football; then he saw action in the navy during World War II, and returned to UCLA for his law degree.

It was the mid sixties and San Diego was a carefree boom-or-bust navy town, with financiers and speculators unabashedly ruling the city and county, and no one seemed to stop them. All everyone else seemed to care about, like all those ex-military men, was soaking up sunshine and buying up suburban shorefront property at rock-bottom prices.

Behind the tranquil postcard scenes, though, San Diego was the wild west, beachfront division. Take downtown. Its economy wasn't pumped up by gleaming corporate high rises. There weren't any skyscrapers; the highest they went was twelve stories. No, it was shore-leave sleaze: massage parlors, tattoo joints, and strip bars with a police vice squad that seemed to spend most of its time looking the other way.

In San Diego, Miller saw the opportunity to carry out his dream of being a public servant and prosecutor. The town to him looked like an adolescent mess that had to be straightened out. The city to him looked like a Monopoly board for wheeler-dealers who seemed to think they could use every bank and every cop as their way to land on the free parking lot of corruption. But there was at least one very big obstacle. Here, the Republican GOP was treated as if it were G-O-D, and Miller was an FDR Democrat, certain he could cure society's social ills. Miller was talking about the plight of crime victims long before it became in vogue at cocktail parties. Being a Democrat was almost anathema in San Diego, if a man wanted to make it to the top.

Miller did make it to the top, though, to become San Diego's first US Attorney following his appointment by then-president Lyndon B. Johnson in 1966, and within five years took over the more prestigious and visible office of district attorney. In the years before the Peyer case, Miller was seen as one of the best district attorneys in the country. He was a prosecuting pioneer. He began antitrust, consumer fraud, and other crime-fighting units long before anyone else in the nation.

Miller took on one of San Diego's biggest fish, C. Arnoldt Smith, a powerful financier who was called Mr. San Diego. Smith owned just about everything in town, a taxicab firm, a tuna cannery, a luxury hotel modeled after the palace at Versailles, a shipbuilding yard, an airline, huge tracts of land, and a bank with one billion dollars in assets. In the end, Mr. San Diego was indicted for manipulating 170 million dollars of bank funds and channeling 27.5 million dollars to himself and cronies, and he eventually did time, six months in local jail.

Now twenty years later Miller had a big mistrial on his hands with the Peyer case, and the DA's critics had a field day—especially since the judge in the case was one of Miller's best friends, his former top assistant district attorney, Richard Huffman. If you can't win a case overseen by a judge who's your buddy, what can you win?

The Peyer loss also reminded Miller how difficult it was to convict a cop of such a heinous crime as murder. In 1982, California highway patrolman George Gwaltney had been charged with stopping an aspiring actress for drunk driving on a desert freeway in the remote town of Bishop in San Bernardino County, raping and then killing her—in the backseat of his patrol car. The highway patrol and the heavily Mormon town of Bishop stuck by Patrolman Gwaltney, who was a local leader in the Church of Jesus Christ of Latter-day Saints. The county prosecutors presented all sorts of evidence about Gwaltney's shady past, about how he had trysts with his mistress in his patrol car. Yet two juries refused to believe that this upstanding Mormon and highway patrolman could kill anyone.

When those state charges didn't stick, a determined US attorney in Los Angeles four years later filed federal charges against Gwaltney, charging that he violated the victim's civil rights by depriving her of her life. A federal jury convicted Gwaltney of those charges, and he is currently serving a ninety-nine year term in federal prison.

Miller wondered if he was facing the same problems with Peyer as the San Bernardino prosecutors had in the Gwaltney case. What if another jury failed to believe that Peyer, an upright cop for all his career, could ever kill anyone? All Peyer needed was another Victor Dingman, one of the five jurors who had reasonable doubt about the district attorney's circumstantial case.

Miller thought about all these things as he leaned in his high-backed leather chair in his high-rise office overlooking San Diego Bay. With a heavy heart, he made the decision to replace Joe Van Orshoven. His top deputies were pushing one of his newer prosecutors, Paul Pfingst, a young deputy from New York who had won fifty-three murder convictions there, more than anyone else in the local office had even tried.

Pfingst had an idea what was up when he was called to the DA's headquarters. He walked into Miller's office and found a frustrated, unhappy man. Transcripts from the Peyer trial covered his desk.

"I told Joe he's not going to try the second one," Miller told Pfingst. "We need a change. You should be the person to try it. I've known Joe a long time and I don't like to do this.''

Miller patted Pfingst on the back, and wished him good luck. But he was still not convinced that his chief deputy, Brian Michaels was right, that Paul Pfingst was the DA to put Craig Peyer in jail.

Van Orshoven, it was no secret, didn't like the idea of the Knotts in the courtroom all the time. Their presence stood out, he said, "like an open wound." But Michaels felt drawn to the family and believed their passionate involvement in the case could only help. Now that the first trial had ended in a hung jury, Michaels knew that Sam had trouble letting go, and that he wouldn't be satisfied with anybody else but Michaels or the DA himself trying the case.

"Come on, Paul, I'll take you over and introduce you to the Knotts; let's see if you pass inspection," Michaels said, half jokingly. They climbed into Pfingst's golden brown Datsun 280Z and headed east.

A half hour later, they were inside the Knotts' home being shown the library the family had compiled, of newspaper clippings and law books, devoted to their beloved Cara. Pfingst was stunned. Sam Knott showed the new prosecutor volume after volume of news clippings, while Joyce brought out photographs, letters, awards, report cards, every remaining piece of Cara's life. They were especially proud of the "Knotty Peanut" book Cara and her father had made before she had learned to write; she had drawn the pictures and told her father the story so he could fill in the pages with the words.

The family had had Cara's school picture enlarged and hung it in the living room. Pfingst felt it was as if the dead girl's spirit were watching his every move, watching if he had what it took to carry her mantle. He was a confident man, sometimes downright cocky, but this family's devotion to their slain daughter was unnerving him.

"Look here," Sam Knott said. He was pointing to pencil drawings that outlined distances between the off ramp and the bridge where Cara drove. Sam's drawings figured in time calculations down to the second and distances down to the hundredth of a mile. "I think this can help you," Sam said. "I did it myself."

It wasn't that Sam didn't trust the police or the district attorney's office. It was just that they never went far enough or dug deep enough for his taste. With this new guy, Sam wanted to make sure he went the extra mile.

"Thanks," Pfingst said, carefully tucking the papers into his briefcase. With that, the tension in the room eased. The new man had passed the Knotts' first test: he was going to accept their help. Van Orshoven had made it clear that he wanted to prosecute the case by himself; he didn't want the family to interfere. Sam had plenty of suggestions bubbling up inside him throughout the first trial, but Van Orshoven felt it was best that he remain at arm's length to the family. The Knotts obliged.

But now the family felt this was their last chance to let the district attorney's office know that they would not accept anything less than a conviction against the monster. Joyce Knott carefully put down her cup of coffee and looked straight at Pfingst. "We let Cara down. We thought there would be justice in the courtroom. Are you going to be able to get justice for Cara?"

Pfingst tried to sound sincere, but he had only had the case for two hours now. He promised to do his best. Cara's brother-in-law cut in.

"Paul, you're a young guy. We had an experienced guy who we were told was the best, and we got nothing," Bill Weick said with a chilly tone. "What did you do, and what can you do, to assure us that we can get a conviction on that bastard who killed Cara?"

Pfingst stared him down. "I've tried a lot of cases," the prosecutor said simply. "I always approach each one the same way. We are going to win. We are going to win because this man killed Cara and we are going to prove it. I think with the evidence we have, we are going to prove it."

He took a sip of his coffee and explained how he'd felt when he had first heard about Craig Peyer's arrest. "I didn't want to get involved in prosecuting a police officer for a murder like that," Pfingst said. "It was such a tragic circumstance. You could never walk away from that feeling. It's bad for the police department, for the public and the family.''

Pfingst recalled how he had followed the first trial only in the newspapers, and rarely joined in the courthouse speculation over the outcome of the case. Then one day he had walked into the courthouse and seen a group of defense lawyers abuzz over something.

''Hey, Paul, did you hear? Did you hear?'' they had said to him. ''The jury was hung on Peyer!'' Pfingst had been aghast. ''They all got excited and happy and I was repulsed,'' Pfingst recalled later.

Now the case was in Pfingst's hands and he sat in the Knotts' living room. Sam was pleased with the determination he saw in the prosecutor's eyes. This guy really wants to win, Sam thought. Pfingst assured the Knotts that he would work diligently, but he warned them they would never be satisfied no matter what the result because Cara would never return.

''We understand,'' Sam said gravely. But he told Paul that as a father he desperately needed to see Cara's killer convicted. ''We want to do this for Cara,'' Sam said, echoing what Joyce had told the prosecutor when he first walked in the door. Sam added his blessings, ''Good luck, Paul.''

Finally the inspection was over and Pfingst and Michaels were heading west back to San Diego. ''That was the toughest job interview I ever had,'' Pfingst joked. It had gone well and they both smiled with relief.

Pfingst turned serious. ''We have fences to mend,'' he said, and Michaels agreed.

Paul Pfingst grew up on Long Island in the land of yacht clubs, sailing, tennis, and summer houses. It was his father, an attorney, who introduced him to the law, by way of Babylon village night court. The little lad with a shock of red hair pranced around the courtroom, touched the oak desks, the thick leather-bound volumes, and watched the masses march in and out. Even then he knew he belonged in a courtroom.

It was the sixties and revolution was in the air, and Paul Pfingst was swept along the idealistic ride with the rest of America's youth. He wanted to right the wrongs of the world by going into law. He wanted to defend the underdog; to him, that was the great, good fight.

From private schools he went on to St. John's University in New York, then right into its law school. But first it was important to him to understand the system thoroughly so he figured he would start as a prosecutor for a few years and then switch to the other side. Six months out, intent on learning to become a defense lawyer, Pfingst joined the huge bureaucratic district attorney's office in Brooklyn run by a man he never saw.

Pfingst kept sailing on bucolic Long Island Sound on the weekends with his family. But he longed for the workweek. He loved strolling on the cracked sidewalks of Brooklyn streets past the old brick apartment houses. He thrived on the stale smell of the gray corridors of the courthouse. From inside those walls, Pfingst became acquainted with America's melting pot—a volatile mix of emotions, of pride and trouble. He tingled with excitement talking to thieves and murderers. He yearned to know what went on inside their crazy heads and learn about a world to which he would never otherwise be exposed.

Pfingst made his way around his new world of misdemeanors and felonies with all the excitement of his grandfather two generations before, who had fled World War I–torn Germany with sheet music in his hand, and barely anything else. He had landed in New York and played a piano for money, making enough to help put a son through law school.

Paul's first case was one typical in New York. He prosecuted a young guy who rubbed another man's face in the snow. His argument was that when it comes to rage in the city, even snow can be a potentially deadly weapon. The defendant, Billy Roantes, was quickly convicted of assault and got fifteen days in jail. To celebrate his first victory, Pfingst named one of his houseplants for Roantes.

Eventually, he prosecuted people accused of gruesome slayings. "That stuff never grossed me out; it's just fascinating," Pfingst said.

But something happened while he was making a name for himself on behalf of the People of the State of New York. Pfingst's grand plans changed. Experience was showing

Pfingst that prosecutors were the lawyers who made the difference in criminal trials, not defense attorneys. They were the ones who decided whether to charge the person. They were the ones who made the bargains. In real life the cases in Brooklyn criminal courts rarely turned out the way they did for Perry Mason, that remarkable defense lawyer on TV who always won for the cause of justice over a system that wronged his client.

After spending eight years prosecuting murderers and working the most exciting cases, something else was happening to Pfingst. He lost his fascination with New York. He began to feel cramped. In 1984, his family had moved to the West Coast while Pfingst stayed behind and slugged it out in the New York courtrooms. Finally, in 1985, he hit the sunny sunny shores of southern California with a job in the San Diego County district attorney's office.

District Attorney Ed Miller welcomed him on his staff, and warned him that things weren't nearly as hectic in San Diego as they were in New York. "There are a lot of murders out there," Miller said of the East Coast. Here too, Pfingst replied. The San Diego papers that morning were all about the massacre of eight people over in Palm Springs, sixty miles away, and more well known for the green of its country club than the red of its streets.

Just when Pfingst started to dream of his beach house, Miller's assistant Richard Neely told him he wasn't going to be assigned to a position in San Diego. He was going to the Vista branch courthouse.

"Where's Vista?" Pfingst asked Neely.

"Oh up in North County," Neely said. "Take Highway seventy-eight, and . . ." he fumbled. He asked a secretary to get a map, and Neely bowed his head searching for the little city in the northeastern part of the county forty miles from San Diego.

Oh, boy, Pfingst thought. The boss doesn't even know where this place is. This is going to be a lot of fun.

When Pfingst arrived at the plain stucco Vista courthouse his first impression was, Hey, there are no people. While Brooklyn was bustling with anonymity, everyone knew each other at the Vista courthouse. By the end of Pfingst's first week as a prosecutor, the guy at the candy counter knew the exact chocolate chips and potato crisps that Pfingst liked.

What a comedown for the veteran prosecutor of murderers. In his first California case, he prosecuted an avocado thief, still not exactly sure what an avocado was. "It's some sort of green fruit, right?" he would ask in letters to friends back east.

But Pfingst grew to love the cases he found in California. The criminal docket was full of characters. Many were U.S. Marines, whose drunken brawls had gotten a little too rough for some of the northern San Diego County towns, especially Oceanside that skirted Camp Pendleton, one of the country's largest marine bases. On the court calendar were also crimes of desperation committed by Mexican nationals who had crossed into San Diego's borders, trying to eke out a living one step ahead of the Border Patrol. Pfingst worked smoothly and effectively, one case to another. As a result, he was moving up fast in the little branch office. Within his first year, Pfingst was assigned to prosecute the first capital case in the county after California reinstated the death penalty.

Laura Troiani, a twenty-six-year-old mother of two children, arranged to pay some teenage marines five hundred dollars each to kill her marine sergeant husband, Carlo, to obtain his one hundred thousand dollar insurance policy. It took the marines four tries to carry out their grim task. On a warm August night, the marines arranged for Carlo to meet Laura on a desolate road outside Camp Pendleton where she pretended her car had broken down. As Carlo walked to his wife's car, they shot him, and the bloody victim stumbled to his wife's car. With his last breath, Carlo Troiani, called out to the woman he loved for help, "Laura, Laura."

Pfingst was repulsed by Laura Troiani and her associates, as he was by all killers. He put a lot of them in jail, including Ms. Troiani, and was just completing convictions of her fellow killers when he was handed the Peyer case. This time, he knew, there would be no winners. It would be a tragedy for everyone if this cop actually had murdered someone. That would mean he had betrayed his trust. He could not imagine rejoicing in victory if he successfully obtained a murder conviction against a cop.

In New York, Pfingst had prosecuted an off-duty New York cop who had strangled a woman. As in the Peyer case, he hadn't had much evidence. It had been purely circumstantial. It had been only a piece of pizza and a wallet on the edge of the Hudson River that Pfingst brought together to prove the ex-cop had strangled a young stockbroker in Brooklyn in 1982.

The cops had found her nude body with a cord wrapped around her neck. Her wallet and a tape recorder had been missing. It turned out the stockbroker had spent her off hours hitting sleazy bars and she'd met up with a cabbie named Arnie Kane. The investigation had stalled for weeks, until they'd discovered her phone book with the name Arnie Kaye, NYPD. There were no Arnie Kayes in the police department, but some detectives were steered to the likely guy: Arnie Kane, a heavy-handed cop who had just quit the force and taken up residence in the hack trade. When they'd looked for Arnie, they'd found his wife, who complained that he had a new tape recorder he played too loud.

Detectives had also checked the pizza the victim ate and by finding out when it was digested, they'd figured out when she had died. They'd matched that with Arnie's cab receipts that had placed him in the area; they recovered the tape recorder and a wallet that Arnie had flipped from the outbound lanes of the Verrazano Narrows Bridge intending it to vanish into the river. But it had only fallen over the bridge ledge.

Arnie had been pretty shaky on the witness stand, Pfingst told Michaels later. "Cops telescope their lies on the stand," Pfingst said. The new prosecutor believed that Grimes had gained a tie of sorts in the first trial. He wondered if he would put Craig Peyer on the stand the second go-around. Pfingst said he couldn't wait to cross-examine the patrolman and crush him like he had Arnie Kane.

The day after being handed the Peyer case, Pfingst called up Joe Van Orshoven and asked him to lunch. He was surprised that the senior deputy was so gracious, considering that his once-in-a-lifetime case had been given away to a younger man. They spent their lunch break walking around the colorful outdoor mall of Horton Plaza downtown, locked in serious conversation. Van Orshoven came right to the point. He thought he'd flunked jury selection. The other disasters in the trial, well, those were just bad luck. Pfingst swore right then he would weave his case so tightly, prepare his witnesses so carefully, that luck would have nothing to do with this trial. It would be a matter of justice.

17

Invisible Witnesses

IT seemed like an ordinary sunny day in April when Paul Pfingst picked up his messages in his new office at the downtown district attorney's main branch. The worst storms of the century that had pelted San Diego during Craig Peyer's first trial had blasted out of town and spring was in the air.

Pfingst shuffled the stack of message slips and one caught his eye: a tip from an ex-navy man that would blow the Peyer case wide open.

Pfingst sighed. He had already fielded calls from all sorts of people—some crazy, some cranky, a few helpful—but he didn't want to waste any more time on the telephone calls. Still, the prosecutor dutifully called the navy man back, because there was one thing he'd learned about the lawyer business: you never know everything.

"I'm glad you called," the tipster said excitedly. "I know where there may be video of that Knott girl getting killed," the navy man said.

Pfingst sat a little straighter.

"Yes, sir, all you need to do to get the footage," the navy man continued, "is call the CIA." It seemed the tipster believed the Central Intelligence Agency had spy satellites that could have filmed coordinates at the murder scene, and if the spy satellites can pick up from the sky the surgeon general's warning on a pack of cigarettes on earth, then they can see a murder too.

"You might want to call the Kremlin, too; they would more likely have their satellites in that area," he added helpfully.

"Yes, well, that is something to consider," Pfingst said politely. "Thank you for calling." He hung up and smiled a little as he filed this newest pink slip away in his dead-end file. After all his years in the Brooklyn DA's office handling what he thought was every weirdness possible, it had to be in southern California that he would get his first tip from outer space.

"You can't believe all the rumors and stories people are calling me with," Pfingst told Brian Michaels. "I'm going to start a file just for this Peyer folklore."

Dozens of people, even supposedly sharp lawyers, told Pfingst they were convinced that Peyer was the killer when they heard that detectives found Cara's driver's license sitting on the front seat of her car, as if she had pulled it out to show a cop. But that information was a fairy tale, since Cara's license had been tucked inside her white wallet as usual. Then there was the mystery of Cara's white leather jacket. People regularly called the DA's office with sightings of the missing jacket. These people are unbelievable, Pfingst told Brian Michaels. One guy had even reported seeing Karen Peyer walking around in a white leather jacket.

"Well," Michaels smiled. "The jacket has to be some-where."

It was true that Cara's brand-new white leather jacket had disappeared the night she died. And of course, if the Peyers had Cara's coat, that would provide the damning link between the lawman and the victim. Since the prosecution obviously had trouble convincing a jury that six microscopic fibers also linked them, the jacket would practically clinch the case. But how likely was it that Peyer would risk so much by stealing something so trivial from a victim? Or that his wife, Karen, would fall for such a sudden gift? Or that a four-hour search of his house had never uncovered any white leather jackets? Not to mention the obvious question of how Mrs. Peyer, mother of two children and a size sixteen, could even fit into anything owned by Cara Knott, a young athlete and size six.

One night, soon after the hung jury and after Pfingst's picture appeared in the paper with the announcement that he was taking over the Peyer case, Pfingst went out for dinner at the Fish House West, in the posh beach town of Del Mar near his condominium.

Here he was practically a newlywed, trying to have a relaxing dinner with his wife, a defense attorney named Constance Shaner. Then a man appeared at their table saying he was a psychologist and launched into an involved tale of his work in serial-killer behavior. The doctor announced that his expertise could help Pfingst crack the Peyer case wide open.

The ever-bemused assistant DA nibbled the bait, maybe because his mother had brought him up to be polite, or perhaps because he knew that his office needed to win this case so badly they would take any suggestion short of voodoo dolls.

"All right, doctor," Pfingst countered, "how would you proceed?"

All the shrink needed, it seems, was Craig Peyer's complete cooperation. "Four hours of interviews should probably do it, with some testing of course," the doctor answered, smiling helpfully.

Pfingst sat there with his smoked chicken chilling as fast as his patience, and explained to the learned doctor that Peyer was on trial for his life. "For the last sixteen months, Craig Peyer has refused to talk to anyone, except his wife and his mother and maybe God. So, doctor, it's unlikely that Peyer would turn his mind over to our side," Pfingst pointed out.

Those were dark days that followed the indecision of that first jury, while the beleaguered district attorney's office cranked up for the second Peyer murder trial.

The guys up in the northern hinterlands branch courthouse where Pfingst had been laboring mostly anonymously these past three years, had always joked with Pfingst whenever he'd started to get too full of himself, whenever they'd felt he was turning into just another smug attorney.

"Hey, Pfingst, when those Hollywood guys make this into a movie, who they gonna get to play you?" Detective Augie de la Rosa would ask.

Pfingst would swell out his slender chest and suggest William Hurt, Kevin Costner? Maybe Redford, although he was a little old for the part.

"Nah," the detectives would say. "It's gotta be Pee-wee Herman." They'd all have a laugh over that one, even Pfingst.

Detectives knew if you wanted to zing a guy like Pfingst, you do it outside the courtroom. Because once inside the inner sanctum, Pfingst's sense of humor evaporated and he turned as intense as a marathon runner only halfway home.

Six weeks after being handed one of the most important murder trials in county history, Pfingst felt he was gaining control of the case the way he wanted it. His approach was careful. No surprises. Organized. Trial was set to start in only twenty-one days.

And then the letter arrived.

The letter came in with the morning flood for District Attorney Ed Miller, mixed in with all the cranks confessing to every crime since Eve bit the apple. But this letter stopped Ed Miller cold. The DA looked at the blue printing covering that small single sheet of paper no bigger than his hand, and sat back in his brown-leather swivel chair. Could this letter be for real? It was written by somebody not totally familiar with English, somebody who had a point and got right to it:

If you want 3 eye-witness [sic] to Knott's murder—look for 3 Mexicans who were under bridge and saw it happen . . . they saw a policeman kill a lady . . .

The DA handed the letter to Michaels and said, "You'd better pass this on to Paul. Have him look into it."

Paul Pfingst was an outsider who still hadn't developed that peculiar southern California ability to blithely ignore the plight of the Mexican and Latin American refugees he watched from behind his car window, on his television screen, and in the newspapers.

In his three years in San Diego, Pfingst had seen how the illegal aliens operated in a world all their own, an underground world, literally. They actually lived under bridges, bushes, cardboard shacks, even holes they dug in the ground. The idea was to find any cheap shelter away from the elements and *La Migra,* the Immigration Service's policing border patrolmen whose job is to play an international game of cat and mouse with the illegal aliens.

As one local farmer once summed up the problem on the *San Diego Union*'s front page, "We treat our dogs better than we treat these people."

Most of the refugees, both economic and political, come from rural villages where graduating fourth grade is rare and electricity is downright magic. But they understand international arithmetic: when thirty thousand Mexican pesos equals one American dollar, that means the same day of fieldwork that earns them two dollars below the border is worth more than twenty dollars in *El Norte,* the Mexican name for "the north." Thus, legions of fugitive Latinos come to pick California's fruit.

No one knows how many illegals hide out in the fields of San Diego County, but no doubt thousands more were assembling that very moment along the border to slip across, not twenty miles from the downtown courthouse where Pfingst now sat.

How in the world would the prosecutor find three mystery men in that huge sea of refugees?

Pfingst stared at the letter as if it were a law school test question. Maybe if he stared at it long enough, the answer would come to him. He thought about what a perfect hideout the bridge at the remote Mercy Road dead end was for illegal workers. The cops found those half-empty beer cans right by the body the day after the murder, that indicated somebody might have been there to see her fall. Surely Mexican farm workers would never leave behind something so costly as a beer—unless they'd left in a hurry because they'd seen something that scared them off.

The prosecutor sat back looking at the bare walls in his new temporary office and let his daydream run like a kite: if he found those witnesses, and all his troubles were over, there would be no more long debates over microscopic fibers, no more biology lessons on the genetics of blood drops to confuse the jury, no more headaches over what had happened to Cara's liver temperature record. No more would people doubt that an officer of the law could betray their trust, because he would have living witnesses. Pfingst would be a hero.

If illegals had been under the bridge the night of the murder, that could also solve the mystery of Cara's white leather jacket. She had it at her boyfriend's house. It was a very cold night. Was she wearing it? Did her killer throw it after her? Did illegal workers see her fall and steal her jacket off her body when they discovered she was dead?

Pfingst knew there was only one man to call for help finding those answers: Augie de la Rosa.

De la Rosa was the only investigator Pfingst knew with the reputation of being able to make dead men talk. That skill would come in handy, Pfingst noted ruefully, because he needed de la Rosa to raise an almost-dead lead, to find three guys who obviously didn't want to be found in an underground population of tens of thousands of people who hate talking to lawmen for fear they will be turned over to *La Migra*.

And on top of all that, none of these people had addresses; they lived under bushes, for God's sake.

Augustine "Augie" de la Rosa had grown up wanting to be a cop, an odd wish for a young hotshot in the tough East Los Angeles gang-breeding town of El Monte. The U.S. army had taken him away from all that to Hawaii, where he'd served with the MPs and then in intelligence. "I was the only guy who could type, and that was a prized skill in the army," de la Rosa liked to say.

But neither the military police nor college were where he learned his greatest skills for police work. No, his best training had come from The Thunderbird, a biker bar where he'd earned his way through school working as a bartender. "I was taking sociology and psychology courses at the time and sometimes I'd just have to interrupt the college professors, because they didn't know what they were talking about when it came to people."

De la Rosa had gone on to lead a charmed life in law enforcement, working every kind of exciting beat, from riding herd over the Hell's Angels, to narcotics, to cracking into the Mexican mafia, to homicide investigations. On a cop's salary, he'd managed to put his only son, Steven, through the University of Southern California, home of the mighty Trojan football team, and pampered kids light-years away from the barrio where Augie grew up.

De la Rosa loved being a cop and was proud of his investigating skill. It bugged him when the district attorney's office got cases full of gaping holes left by the cops who had supposedly investigated the crime in the first place. If de la Rosa had been there at Mercy Road doing scene work on Cara Knott's murder, he said he would have seen those beer cans left under the bridge where she fell and immediately started combing the illegal world for possible witnesses. "You can bet on it. It makes me so mad. There's a whole world out there of information in the illegal population and nobody pays them any attention."

Now Pfingst was handing de la Rosa the chance to prove how important the underground world of illegals was. And Augie was a man who loved challenges, and this lead was so old it could apply for Social Security.

He was told to investigate discreetly, so the press and public wouldn't find out and whip up a storm that ended up blaming the DA for playing tricks and sitting on evidence and trying to taint the jury pool and whatever other perfidies came to mind. De la Rosa had to interview people about the hottest case of the decade and trust them to keep quiet about it. He would have to go everywhere and spread the word, but not let anyone know. No problem, just as easy as playing tennis with yourself. You can do it if you're really, really quick.

And, oh yes, Pfingst told him, you only have six days. Pfingst needed time to prepare and he didn't want any loose ends flapping with the trial less than three weeks away.

It helped that de la Rosa believed he was not chasing ghosts. To him the letter made sense. "Figure you're an illegal, you paid your coyote to cross, you're making good money picking strawberries and it's Saturday night. You just got paid, tomorrow is your day off so you have some beers. Then you see this dead body bounce right in front of you and you see what you think is a policeman do it. Who can you tell? You don't go to the cops. They've probably seen that kind of thing in their own country or back in Central America. No, the only one they can trust is one of their own.''

De la Rosa memorized the letter like a prayer. He mulled it over and over, knowing full well he was the only one he could tell about this, and analyzed every word for clues.

> . . . *look for 3 Mexicans who were under bridge and saw it happen. They came to fast food place near there and ask [sic] for ride north. They were scared and said they had to get out of this place as they saw a policeman kill a lady. They spoke fair English and worked in a packing plant in Escondido.*

''See, I figured it was a bilingual person writing the letter who was told in Spanish and was translating it as he or she heard it. The trouble is, the word for 'packing house' is *impaque,* but that colloquialism could mean any number of things. It could mean warehouse too, and how many more of those are there in North County? Dozens and dozens.''

De la Rosa went to five packing houses where fruit from area growers was brought together to be boxed and shipped out nationwide. He felt he could only ask the heads of the companies, not their Latino workers, and he found nothing. He went to the only three nearby fast-food joints and asked to check their work schedules for a year before, as if any of those burger servers were still around. Again, nothing.

That was as far as de la Rosa could go on that dime. He hated that phone call he had to make downtown. ''Paul, I'm sorry, I came up empty,'' he told the prosecutor. ''But I know they're out there. I can find them. Let me go into the fields and put it out on the Mexican radio and I'll get them. I swear.''

Pfingst wanted to give de la Rosa everything he needed, even an airplane to skywrite the message in Spanish if he wanted it. But the prosecutor had to proceed cautiously.

''Let me talk to the DA and see what I can do,'' he told the detective.

Pfingst took the long walk from his office in the courthouse across Broadway to the district attorney's headquarters in the

Wells Fargo Bank Building, complete with a stagecoach in the foyer. He rode up to the fourteenth floor and knocked on the big man's door. "Mr. Miller, we've got a problem. . . ."

Pfingst sat in a precarious position. Here he had taken over the most sensational criminal case in local history from a senior lawyer who had failed, a native San Diegan from an important local family. Being cocky would make Pfingst look cruel and likely turn everybody from the judge to the public and the press against him. Pfingst surely had to do some dazzling stuff to pull off one of the most difficult cases he'd ever tried, a circumstantial mass of tiny bits of evidence. He knew he could pull it off. He didn't need to risk his butt on some anonymous letter.

Considering all that, what he did next was most unusual.

Pfingst walked into Judge Huffman's chambers 8:30 A.M. April 14, acting as if this would be an ordinary pretrial conference.

"I was scared. I knew Judge Huffman doesn't like surprises, and this was a doozy," Pfingst said.

Judge Huffman, Pfingst, and defense attorney Robert Grimes started discussing motions concerning whether the prosecution would be able to put as many of the women on the stand as allowed in the first trial to tell how Peyer had scared them and flirted with them at Mercy Road. Like his predecessor, Pfingst won.

Then Pfingst moved the meeting to more quibbling over what kind of experts could be called to testify about the genetic markers found in the blood on Cara's white boot. The prosecutor moved as deftly as a chess hustler. Never dive for the prize king first, maneuver the knights a little, but feign innocence all along.

"And next, your honor, in advance of the last trial the defense made a motion to change the venue in this case."

Pfingst began moving his knights by talking about how Peyer's lawyers wanted to move the trial out of San Diego County because the sensational publicity may have prejudiced the community and thus potentially the jurors.

"We have yet to hear whether that motion is being renewed and if there are any new grounds for that motion or any new arguments," the prosecutor pointed out, innocently enough.

Grimes equivocated, "Well, your honor, the prosecution has basically asked us to take a position that we are withdrawing our motion for change of venue. And we are satisfied that there's no problem with getting a fair trial in San Diego County."

As far as Pfingst was concerned, Grimes was off the fence and finally saying what the prosecutor wanted to hear: the defense wanted to stay in the San Diego courts.

With the change of venue discussion, the prosecutor had moved his queen to put his opponent's king in check. All set, he took a big breath and launched his gambit. "Finally, your honor, there's been a substantial development in the case, which Mr. Grimes is aware of and the court is not."

Here he tried to deflect some of the heat from himself to Grimes. They both had kept the same secret from the judge.

"It has to do with information that has been received by my office and information that has been received and given to Mr. Grimes through another channel." The two men watched the prosecutor warily, but said nothing.

Pfingst continued. "The information that our office received came in two ways: one was through an anonymous letter to the district attorney himself, Mr. Miller, and the other was the identical letter being sent to a friend of the defendant, Craig Peyer.

"I'm going to ask the court to read the letter because it is about . . . it's about something that worries the people a great deal."

Pfingst was talking fast to get the whole speech out. "The district attorney has conducted an investigation in hopes of finding the person who wrote the letter, and we have conducted discreet inquiries in the hope of locating not only the writer but those three people mentioned," the prosecutor said. "We have been very, very careful in our inquiries to try and shield as much of the detail in that letter from the people we've talked to because we've been very sensitive to the possibility that if the contents of that letter were to come into the public domain it would or could severely taint the jury panel and that the people's motives with respect to our investigation could be questioned. . . ."

After this 71-word sentence the judge and Grimes knew

better than to jump in front of a train about to wreck. "And
we could be accused of intentionally attempting to taint the
jury pool. . . . We have had, frankly, our fingers crossed and
our toes crossed over the course of the last week hoping that
our investigative efforts would not be discovered by the press
because of the potential hue and cry it would create with
respect . . ."

Pfingst kept talking. He brought up how he had discussed
the letter with the DA, the chief assistant DA, the chief deputy DA. He tried pulling in a little weight here. After all, Ed
Miller had been the judge's boss too at one time. "It is the
district attorney's suggestion that the court grant the defendant's venue motion."

There, he said it: I want the trial out of San Diego County.

If the prosecutor had accused Peyer of breaking into Sea
World and molesting Shamu the killer whale, the principals
couldn't have been more surprised.

"This is absolutely contrary to everything his office has
done in this case, everything he himself has said or implied,"
Grimes sputtered angrily.

Moving trials is something defense teams want, never
district attorneys. Familiarity and publicity on a case usually is on the DA's side. Besides, DAs are supposed to be
working for the people, the taxpayers, and moving trials
out of county is a very expensive gamble to take with the
people's wallet.

Only two doors away from where they now sat in Judge
Huffman's chambers was a very painful example of the
public's money being literally flushed away, two million
dollars worth. The millions were wasted trying to get a
second set of convictions on the Trailside Killer, the infamous nickname for wimpy and balding David Carpen-
ter, a stuttering psychopath, who killed and raped young
women along some of California's most scenic hiking
trails. After more than three dozen people spent a solid
year trying the Trailside Killer, a mistrial was declared
and his second conviction thrown out.

Yet, two weeks before Craig Peyer's retrial, here stood Paul
Pfingst in his gray suit, angering the judge and upsetting everything that he had taken great pains to get under control.

Still, Pfingst was not sorry. First of all, he thought the letter was real. Second, what if he won the case and the appeals court decided the authorities hadn't tried hard enough to find these witnesses and threw the case out on that technicality?

And third, he'd forced a showdown with defense attorney Grimes, a nice little in-your-face psych-out maneuver as the two men approached final battle in open court. Pfingst was gambling that Grimes didn't really want to move the trial out of the county.

By keeping the trial local, Grimes himself was gambling that he had some momentum going his way, that after almost half the initial jury was left unconvinced, an even bigger question would have been left in the mind of the public and hopefully the next jury.

The judge cut in on Pfingst's windy speech. "I feel a little bit handled at this point in time. I've watched the process of trying to box Mr. Grimes into fishing or cutting bait; I think that's your business. To then have you do that, then spring this on me is not a practice that I appreciate." From another judge this kind of rebuke would sound like he was annoyed, like someone parked in his parking space. But in a controlled guy like Richard Huffman, Pfingst knew, the judge was boiling with anger.

Judge Huffman told Pfingst, "You have no right to a change of venue motion. The right rests with the defense." He ordered Grimes to get Peyer down here fast so they could ask him whether he wanted his trial moved.

Judge Huffman then ordered Pfingst to stop the investigation on the letter immediately.

Grimes decided the best strategy was to let his opponent self-destruct, but he couldn't resist one question: "If you found nothing, why do you think there's something of substance to be found?"

The nervous Pfingst was delighted at this chance to keep talking and explain his reasoning, that the half-drunk beers found near where Cara's body fell indicated farm workers might have been camping out down there. "And that was just idle questioning at that point as to whether somebody just got scared to death when they saw a body plop down off a bridge in front of them, Cara Knott's body, and just decided to take off. And that was just idle speculation at that time with many other idle thoughts. And then when this letter came in . . .''

Judge Huffman summed it all up with his usual style, short and deadly accurate. "You are searching for a needle under an entire field of haystacks."

Finally, Pfingst could stop talking because Peyer had arrived in the judge's chambers.

Grimes moved to take the upper hand. "I have discussed with Mr. Peyer the conversation we had and at this time, we withdraw our request for change of venue."

Judge Huffman turned to Peyer and explained. "You know the law. You have an absolute right to have this case tried in this jurisdiction. You also have the right to have a fair and impartial trial and to have the remedy of change of venue if you wish to do so. You've had a chance to discuss this with your attorney?"

Peyer, the military-trained ex-cop, was respectful as always to authority and never said more than necessary. "Yes, your honor," he said.

"Have you had a chance to discuss the reason for and against the decision to withdraw the motion?" Judge Huffman asked.

"Yes, your honor," Peyer replied.

"All right," Huffman said. "Is it your personal desire at this time to withdraw your motion for change of venue?"

"Yes, it is," Peyer said.

And that was all he or anyone got to say on the anonymous letter. The matter was closed. The invisible witnesses would remain forever invisible.

Much later, Grimes would get a disgusted tone into his ever-pleasant voice when he spoke about the possibility of phantom witnesses. "That was a bunch of smoke," he maintained.

For his part, Pfingst merely shrugged the episode off as a might have been, a mystery unsolved but nothing to lose sleep over.

But to Detective Augie de la Rosa, much was lost. His big

grab, his chance to change the way law enforcement investigated crime. He had spent thirty-two years in law enforcement, he was fifty-three years old, and he doubted very much that another case like Peyer's would ever come his way again.

18

Round Two

A neatly sealed large brown envelope was sitting on Jim Okerblom's desk when he got back to the *San Diego Union* newsroom that afternoon from the county courthouse, where he had been covering jury selection for the second Peyer murder trial. The envelope was plain and bore no return address. Okerblom ripped it open, shuffled through the pages inside, and stared at them in amazement.

"Peyer took a lie detector test, and flunked!" Okerblom said, half out loud. "This is a great story."

Okerblom, running his hands through his light brown hair, got up and ran across the newsroom to the desk of assistant city editor Sandi Dolbee. "I've got something hot," Okerblom told Dolbee, and before he could say more, she grabbed her reporter by the arm and rushed him into an empty office. Dolbee closed the door, and Okerblom filled her in on the lie detector test papers.

"Jim, this is dynamite stuff," she said excitedly, leaning back in her chair. "We've got to contact our lawyers and the attorneys on the case. We can't run this unless we verify it's for real."

Okerblom hustled to his desk and impatiently dialed the district attorney's office. The phone kept ringing. "Come on!" he nearly shouted at the receiver. Finally, he heard Paul Pfingst's voice on the other end of the line.

"Hi, Paul, it's Jim over at the *Union*," Okerblom said. "I

was wondering if you could confirm something for us. I received what is purported to be a polygraph examination of Peyer.''

The prosecutor was dumbstruck. He pulled the receiver away from his ear and whispered to his assistant, deputy district attorney Joan Stein, who was sitting in his small cubicle. ''Do we have that polygraph?'' Pfingst asked Stein.

Peyer had indeed taken one, but neither Pfingst nor Stein had thought much about it, since they couldn't use it in court. The accuracy of lie detector tests has been widely debated, and they are banned for use as evidence in California courts. As Pfingst held the phone with Okerblom, Stein started rifling through boxes on the floor to find their copy, to check and see if Okerblom had the real thing. There, in a black folder, she found the district attorney's original copy, a relief to both prosecutors that at least Okerblom didn't have theirs.

Pfingst, thumbing through the folders, asked Okerblom to spell out again what he had. The reporter obliged. ''I've got these documents, it looks like the results of a lie detector test that Peyer flunked,'' Okerblom said.

Pfingst's eyes narrowed as Stein sat in her chair, bewildered at the conversation taking place. ''I'm not going to confirm or deny anything like that ever took place,'' Pfingst said in his most lawyerly fashion.

''Well, are you denying that Mr. Peyer took a polygraph test?'' Okerblom asked.

''Jim, I'm not confirming or denying anything,'' Pfingst said. ''I hope you're not going to run a story. Remember, Jim, we're in the middle of selecting a jury, and if word gets out about this to them, this could affect the entire trial.'' The prosecutor decided to play hardball. He told Okerblom in his best closing statement manner, ''Grimes will be asking for a mistrial, and it will be the newspaper's fault.''

''Look, Paul, it's out of my hands,'' Okerblom said. The reporter's eyes moved to the glass-enclosed offices across the newsroom, where he saw his bosses discussing what to do with the astounding information in his hands.

''I'm not even sure we have a story,'' he added. ''We haven't found anybody to say whether the polygraphs were authentic or not.''

"Well, good luck, Jim," Pfingst said, not meaning it.

Okerblom started calling everyone whose name appeared on the documents. It was getting close to four o'clock, two hours from deadline. He called the company that had given the polygraph and asked for the examiner who had administered the test. "Yeah, that's ours," the examiner told him. "Where'd you get that?"

Okerblom called Pfingst back. He had his confirmation, but he wanted to make doubly sure.

"I found somebody who can authenticate it," the reporter said hurriedly. "Are you going to now confirm or deny it?"

"No, we're not going to confirm or deny that any polygraph or anything took place," Pfingst said sternly. "We're not going to discuss it."

"It looks like we've got a story," Okerblom said.

"I wish you wouldn't run it—think of the ramifications," Pfingst said.

Pfingst hung up with Okerblom and called Grimes, who listened to the prosecutor in silence. Stunned, the lead defense lawyer called his assistant Diane Campbell.

"We've got to call the judge," Campbell said. "Maybe he can block publication."

Campbell got Huffman on the phone. "Your honor, someone—nobody is saying who—gave the press a copy of the polygraph examination. It looks like they're running a story in the *Union* tomorrow. We request that you stop publication, your honor. We contend it will seriously damage our client's constitutional right to a fair trial."

"I didn't even know there was a polygraph examination," Huffman said. "But I don't think I can issue a prior restraint order against the press. It would be irresponsible if they ran with a story, but my hands are tied."

Pfingst called Grimes, and the two adversaries tried to figure out what to do.

"If we started talking about a judge stepping in, that might tip the scales against what we were trying to accomplish, that is not having a story run," Pfingst said. "There's a better chance of not having it published if we didn't have judicial machinery."

Huffman agreed that it wouldn't be a good idea for a judge to interfere with a story. He felt he didn't have much of a legal precedent behind him. The Supreme Court routinely ruled against prior restraint of the press where the national security wasn't at stake. The judge decided not to call Okerblom.

As for the reporter, Okerblom slept fitfully that night, unsure he had done the right thing. He could just imagine the lawyers and the judge cursing him over their breakfasts when they read the *Union*'s front page on Wednesday, April 27: DECEPTION IN PEYER TESTS CITED.

In his article, Okerblom had written that six days before Highway Patrolman Craig Peyer was arrested on suspicion of killing Cara Knott, a police department report showed that Peyer had voluntarily taken lie detector tests, and four examiners who reviewed the results agreed that he was "attempting deception" when he denied knowing anything about how Knott died.

He quoted a two-page report dated January 8 and January 9, 1987, in which a police polygraphist wrote that he had administered a series of six tests to Peyer and had then reviewed the results, as well as two other polygraph examiners from the police department, along with an examiner who operates a lie detector school in San Diego.

"It is the opinion of the examiner, based on careful evaluation of all the subject's polygraph charts, that the subject was attempting deception when he answered 'No' to the above relevant questions," the examiner had written in the report.

The relevant questions were:

Are you responsible for the death of Cara Knott?
Regarding the death of Cara Knott, did you strangle her and throw her body off that bridge?

To both questions, Peyer had responded, "No."

The examiner was quoted as saying additional questions were asked of Peyer in two exams known as "peak of tension tests":

If you are the one who strangled Cara Knott, did you stran-gle her with
A) a shoestring
B) a piece of wire
C) a necktie
D) a piece of rope, a belt, a seat belt, a coat, a rag?

"It appears that the subject is attempting deception when he denies he strangled Cara Knott with a piece of rope," the examiner had concluded. "An extensive interview was con-ducted with the subject at the conclusion of the polygraph examination; however, the subject maintained his denial of knowledge of involvement in the death of Cara Knott."

Peyer had volunteered to take the lie detector tests, Oker-blom noted in the story. He had been advised of his rights and had signed a waiver stating that he was voluntarily sub-mitting to a polygraph examination.

Huffman was steaming by the time he got to the court-house. Grimes and Pfingst, both nervous, were waiting for him.

"Well, it's on TV and radio, all over the place, fellas," Huffman said. "And here we are, trying to pick a jury."

Grimes was ready to take advantage of the overwhelming negative publicity that had fallen in his lap. "Obviously this could have, will have, catastrophic effects on this case and on Mr. Peyer's ability to have this case based on the evi-dence," Grimes charged. "Both the whole jury pool of this county and perhaps this state has been contaminated."

The defense lawyer insinuated that someone in the DA's office had to know what was going on, or at least the police department. "Somebody who's out to get Mr. Peyer did this—there's no doubt about that," Grimes said.

Pfingst bristled. "This is just plain wrong. Whoever did this for whatever reason, has seen fit to enter a domain they had no right to enter. To have somebody, some interloper, mail an anonymous thing to the *San Diego Union* makes me livid."

"I'm ordering this report sealed. No one else should be

able to get a copy of it,'' Huffman said. ''And I want an investigation by the DA's office—now!''

There had already been one trial in this case, and Huffman didn't want to spend any more money on a third trial if he could help it. He made sure he ran a tight courtroom, and now it could all be turned upside down because of something totally out of his control—the press.

''I'm going to have to order all these jurors who were screened before to be reinterviewed,'' Huffman said. ''I wish the media thought about the taxpayers before they start running a story.''

Huffman went out into the courtroom and informed the seventy-eight prospective jurors sitting there that they had to be interviewed again to see whether they had been tainted by the publicity surrounding these latest revelations. The judge was careful not to mention the lie detector test, or precisely what the brouhaha was all about. He just wanted to make sure the pool of jurors was staying away from media accounts of the case.

The judge took the occasion to lambaste the press, saying, ''It's a shame that we lose your services because of the need to get a few more inches of ink and the blast on the radio.''

Sam and Joyce Knott were on edge. They worried that the newspaper's disclosures about the lie detector test would ruin any chance to convict Peyer in the second trial. Months earlier, they heard that the highway patrolman had flunked a lie detector test, but they didn't think much about it because it wasn't going to be used for the trial.

''Now what?'' Joyce asked. ''Is this going to wreck everything?''

''I don't think you have to worry about it,'' Sam said. ''I talked to Paul, and they are going to go forward with picking a jury. We must be strong and have resolve to see this through—for Cara.''

Paul Pfingst rocketed into the spotlight, and his name was everywhere. People were saying such great things about him, and it made him nervous.

''The harder they build you up, the harder you fall,''

Pfingst would say, trying to get all the cheerleaders to stop lavishing the praise. But he was riding high, and happy about the buildup, nevertheless. A guy like him can't go so far in the trial lawyer business without a healthy ego.

But those words were said in dark days that followed the indecision of the first jury, as the beleaguered district attorney's office cranked up for the second Peyer murder trial.

Pfingst liked to joke and laugh. It was a good release valve from the pressure building up inside him. He knew he would have to work the Knott case like a homicide gumshoe, re-shaping the second trial almost from the beginning, even though he had only a few weeks until round two.

He moved to San Diego from Vista and piled stacks of Joe Van Orshoven's huge files in Brian Michaels's office, while the chief deputy was in neighboring Orange County prosecuting a cop killer.

Then, he called Deputy District Attorney Joan Stein and told her to drop everything, she was on the Peyer case with him.

"Are you sure?" she asked.

"Yes. I'm the Peyer czar now," Pfingst said.

Pfingst had sized up the enemy, the defense team, and he wanted the prosecution to gain the same emotional footing as the other side. Bob Grimes's co-counsel was the beautiful Diane Campbell, her eyes like dark pools and her long brown hair worn like a prom queen's. Throughout the first trial, Campbell clung near Peyer. The implied message to the jury was clear: I'm not afraid of this man, and I'm definitely a woman.

Pfingst decided he wanted a woman by his side as well. "I felt Joan would make a nice presentation of Cara—a female presence, serene and also very competent," Pfingst said later.

Of all the worries Paul Pfingst carried with him those weeks before the trial, his biggest fear was that Grimes would bring up the serial killer. For months, a secret task force had been investigating the possibility that dozens of murders of local women, most of them prostitutes, had been committed by the same killer who had been slaying women in Green River, Washington, 1,500 miles up the coast. When Cara was killed, there were some who believed it was the work of the mysterious Green River Killer, for some of the local victims did not always fit the prostitute–drug user mold. Pfingst feared that once Grimes mentioned the possibility of a serial killer, he would unleash a range of possible suspects that would be a mirage for the jury. "This would be the proverbial red herring," he kept telling Joan Stein. It could even hurt the ultrasecret serial killing investigations.

But the prosecutor felt he couldn't dwell on what Grimes's plan of attack might be. He had his own formidable tasks ahead. Pfingst wanted to move quickly and set the tone early for the prosecution in the retrial, something he believed Van Orshoven had failed to do in the first showdown. So Pfingst came out swinging with dozens of pretrial motions aimed to cut in on the defense's punches, and he was winning most of the decisions.

Grimes had made legal overtures to bar testimony from the women who had been pulled over by Peyer at Mercy Road. Pfingst stopped that move—and added salt to the wound by finding even more women to testify about being brought to Mercy.

Pfingst's biggest blow to the defense was blocking Grimes from presenting witnesses who saw the weird hitchhiker on the road Cara had driven the night of the murder. His argument was that the hitchhiker was irrelevent because he was never a suspect, had never been interviewed by police, and had been nowhere near the murder scene. Thus the defense was left with no other potential suspect besides Peyer.

Perhaps equally as crushing to the defense was what Pfingst did about Peyer's scratched-up face. The prosecutor won his maneuver to bar Grimes from letting witnesses talk about how Peyer said he got those scratches. At least six witnesses in the first trial had parroted Peyer's excuse that he'd scratched himself falling on the chain link fence while gassing up his cruiser. But, Pfingst argued successfully to the judge, "It's hearsay for them to repeat that excuse. If Mr. Peyer wants to say that his face got scratched up on a chain link fence, then let Mr. Peyer get on the witness stand and say so himself."

Pfingst's analysis of the first case was that the prosecution had lost because their case had been unorganized. For one, Van Orshoven's young assistant, Jim Atkins, had done much of the courtroom presentation, especially questioning witnesses about the fibers and other key evidence. Even DA Miller hadn't been very happy about that, but Joe Van Orshoven had explained that Atkins knew the nitty-gritty of scientific evidence.

That didn't wash with Pfingst. He also didn't like the idea that Atkins had walked around the courtroom in cowboy boots. Pfingst may have adapted to southern California style casual, but the city boy in him detested cowboy boots.

Pfingst and Stein worked constantly. He drew up chronologies for the jurors tracing everything from when Cara Knott left her house to the time she was killed. And every speech he planned to make before the jurors, he wanted to lace with Cara's name. The idea was to make her real—just like the defendant, who had the advantage of living and breathing and sitting in the courtroom.

San Diego Police Detective Bill Nulton just couldn't believe it when he found out that the first trial had ended in a hung jury. When Pfingst was named prosecutor for the retrial, Nulton pleaded with his boss, Homicide Lieutenant Phil Jarvis, to keep him on the Peyer case so he could help out the new prosecutor. Nulton was determined to put his fellow lawman away if it was the last thing he did. Jarvis agreed.

Nulton helped Stein and Pfingst interview jurors from the first trial, several of who admitted that they had been confused about many aspects in the trial. Then the trio plotted out their case to make sure they didn't make the same mistake. Logic was the key to everything Pfingst wanted to present in round two.

The prosecution team reinterviewed the women Peyer had pulled down Mercy Road and found more there than was reflected in the transcripts of the first trial. "There is a side of these women that the jurors in the first trial didn't have a chance to see before," Pfingst said. "They were in absolute fear."

"We've got to get that across," Stein said. "Let's do it."

They reinvestigated the thousands of traffic stops Peyer had made in the months leading up to the murder, looking for more women pulled on to Mercy Road. And sure enough, they found more, although on the paperwork the stops would fudge the location saying "stopped near Penasquitos" or near one of the other exits beside Mercy.

Pfingst went to see the highway patrol headquarters for himself to see where Peyer gassed up and supposedly fell against the fence, and see where he came into the office that night past all his colleagues with a scratched face. The prosecutor met with Captain Lee Denno there and asked about the CHP's investigation that had led to Peyer's firing. Denno showed Pfingst the CHP records that backed up the final report declaring their own patrolman guilty. The CHP had exactly what the new prosecutor was looking for—a time line of events from the numerous stops Peyer made to the last scratched-out ticket. "Did Van Orshoven see this stuff?" Pfingst asked Denno.

"No," he was told. "He didn't ask."

Pfingst reinterviewed witnesses who had testified the first time, and meticulously went over their testimony. Two of his crucial witnesses were the Gulli brothers, who had had their ticket altered, and the teenagers had been so burned by their first experience, they didn't want to go through it again.

Pfingst had them come downtown to talk to him. "You have to testify," he told the twins. Because they had received the last ticket of the night from Craig Peyer, he felt their testimony was crucial.

Jean-Pierre Gulli tried to be polite. But his frown was all over his face like a giant billboard. "But my words were all twisted, I didn't get a chance to say anything that really happened, because of that defense attorney," the teenager said.

Pfingst laughed. "All right, let's pretend I'm the defense attorney. Let's see how you do." The prosecutor rehearsed with the Gulli brothers what he thought Grimes might say the second time around. It took hours, and the young men gradually figured out how to stick to their statements under constant challenging from Pfingst.

The deputy DA was meeting with the Knott family on Monday nights to keep them up with the progress of the case and listen to their suggestions. The first meetings were a little tense when the family repeatedly tried to make Pfingst push for the death penalty for Peyer. "If it were the other way around, if someone kidnapped a highway patrolman and then strangled him, they would get the death penalty," Sam kept insisting.

Sam had been arguing with the district attorney's office for months about the issue, and he had done extensive research himself in the county legal library. "The monster deserves the death penalty," Sam said. "I reviewed the laws, and the crime fits. Someone who kidnaps someone and then murders that person should be put to death. Especially a cop who violates his sacred trust. He kidnapped my daughter, brought her to that bridge, and threw her off a bridge. He staked my daughter out."

"We just can't do it, Sam. There's not enough there," Pfingst would tell him.

"Is it because he's a cop, is that why?" Sam asked, growing angry with the prosecutors.

"No, it's not. We've got to work on one thing at a time. We've got to get a conviction first, Sam. So far, we haven't even been able to do that."

"Are we going to see one?" Sam asked testily.

"Yes, we'll keep trying this case until Craig Peyer is convicted of murder," Pfingst promised. He held his ground, and gradually the family trusted that he would fight hard for Cara, but in his own way.

As the trial grew closer, the Monday night meetings ended with Pfingst explaining the theory of jury selection to the family. "I don't want loners on the jury. I don't want showy types, people with big egos." Those people would have their own mind and be less inclined to vote as a group, or be swayed by emotions, Pfingst explained.

Being a baseball fan, Sam Knott understood what Pfingst was saying. "It's the same on the diamond," Sam explained to his unsports-minded daughters. "In baseball, the pitcher is eighty percent of the game, just like the jury is in the legal game."

And then it was show time—auditions for the jury for the second trial. But this time the lawyers did not sail through the selection process as before. Pfingst was taking his time, carefully analyzing the two hundred people identified in the potential pool. Sam Knott was impressed with the psychological profile Pfingst prepared for each prospective juror being questioned. While sitting in the near-empty courtroom during the tedious voir dire process, Sam couldn't help but smile when he heard many jurors explain that they just knew Peyer was guilty and that they were outraged.

Sam and his family kept their own notes of telltale signs that the prosecutors might miss—which jurors wore flashy jewelry, what they did when they thought nobody was looking.

"It's hard to convict a police officer of murder. Everyone will be looking for a way out," Sam said. "But we've got to keep fighting."

Pfingst was under the gun. He had gotten his case organized in what must have been record time, but he was feeling the pressure. And then, with opening testimony due to start in a few days, Pfingst received a call from Detective Nulton. A surprise witness had come forward. It was a young woman who said she had seen something off Interstate 15 the night Cara Knott had been killed.

The prosecutor felt a stab of worry as he remembered what a disaster Van Orshoven's surprise witnesses had been in round one. Pfingst was cautious when he called the woman, a Traci Koenig.

"Mr. Pfingst, we have some information for you, we think we can help your case," Koenig said in a sweet, nervous voice. "We were down there—at Mercy Road—that night."

Pfingst was ready to hang up. Fifteen months after Cara Knott was killed, this kid says she and her boyfriend saw something suspicious the night of the murder. Come on, Pfingst thought cynically.

But he beat back his instincts and told her, "Okay. Let's talk."

He and Stein drove to the woodsy affluent Scripps Ranch suburb northeast of San Diego, where her parents lived. "We'll hear this kid out. Go in, say hi, thank you, and goodbye. Right?" Pfingst whispered to Stein as they stood at the door.

But once inside, Pfingst found himself impressed by the house and the book-lined shelves, something he didn't see enough of in southern California. Koenig's husband, Scott, was there, and her mother and father, a retired naval officer, greeted the prosecutors warmly.

Over cups of coffee, Koenig's father, Richard Reichner, made it clear they were not interested in publicity. "We're not these type of people who want to make headlines. In fact, we told Traci we'd be better off if she wasn't involved. I'm afraid for my daughter."

Pfingst was skeptical and told the family so. "You realize that this hurts your credibility to wait more than a year to come forward."

Mrs. Reichner spoke up, "You know, they were in the midst of wedding plans right after that happened. We were worried that any involvement in a trial would just wreck those plans."

"And besides," Scott Koenig shot back, "we thought it was a slam-dunk case for the prosecution."

Inwardly, Pfingst winced. "Okay," he said. "What happened?"

Traci and Scott told their story: Between eight and nine o'clock the night of December 27, they had been driving south on I-15 when they'd spotted what they thought was a CHP cruiser pull over a light colored VW beetle, and then disappear down Mercy Road.

"I remember telling Scott, 'She's going to be busted,' " Koenig said, turning to her husband. "I just knew it was a girl in the car."

Koenig had told her parents about the stop when she'd returned home that night, and had mentioned it again after she saw TV news reports about Peyer's arrest. The Reichners insisted that she shouldn't get involved at the time, and besides, they didn't think her story would be that important to the case.

"After what happened with the first trial, though," Koenig said, "one of my friends told me I should tell police what I had seen. Maybe there was a killer loose."

Those words clung to Traci Koenig's conscience, and now she told Pfingst: "I can be a witness. Use me."

But there was a problem—a problem she had had with the law.

She had been arrested more than a year earlier for giving

away to friends and relatives three thousand dollars worth of merchandise while she worked as a clerk at a Mervyn's discount department store. Koenig had pleaded no contest to misdemeanor charges and repaid the store.

"I know this was a mistake," she said apologetically.

"I don't think you have to worry about that," Pfingst told her. He knew the defense would try to bring up the criminal record to discredit Traci, but he also knew that misdemeanor offenses were inadmissible as evidence to impeach a witness.

Pfingst found Traci Koenig articulate and intelligent. It wasn't only her potentially damaging testimony he found attractive. At twenty, she had those all-American good looks that Cara Knott had had. Pfingst wanted the jury to latch onto that image.

Traci and Scott left the room to get more coffee, and the prosecutor turned to Traci's father, who was still hoping she would bow out. "Well," Pfingst said, "she's making up her own mind. She's a woman now."

In mid-May 1988, six men and six women were sworn in as the jury for the second murder trial of Craig Alan Peyer after intensive screening that had stretched out nearly a month.

The jurors included a bartender, a utility company lineman, a retired marine biologist, a secretary, a hairdresser, and a housewife. They ranged in age from twenty-two to sixty-six, and lived from the northern city of Escondido to the Mexican border.

Pfingst didn't sleep all weekend as he thought about his opening argument coming up. He didn't eat, either, and hadn't been since he took the case and although it seemed impossible to his friends, the thin man got thinner. He holed up in his study in his Del Mar condominium, poring over his yellow legal pads, putting together a simple narrative to leave jurors with one overwhelming feeling: that Craig Peyer was no regular, nice-guy cop.

On May 17, testimony in the trial officially began.

Pfingst entered the courtroom looking every inch the preppy prosecutor with his close-clipped red hair and tortoiseshell glasses. He moved through the courtroom with a style that was understated but confident. He wanted to make his message clear.

"The dozens of times Craig Peyer ordered those women down that dark and lonely ramp," Pfingst said in his opening argument, "were preludes to murder, the one he would eventually commit against Cara Knott."

"He would segregate, he would look for females," Pfingst said. "Men need not apply to go down Mercy Road."

Pfingst spent forty-five minutes laying out testimony of the witnesses to come, pacing the room, moving his arms and hands to punctuate his words. His voice rose in anger, and often took on an edge of sadness.

"Cara Knott said good-bye to her boyfriend and got into her car. That [was] the last time her boyfriend saw Cara alive. Cara Knott was never seen alive again. You will hear [that] a CHP officer disappeared for a period of time. He also fell off the face of the earth at that time.

"Although she was killed on December twenty-seven of nineteen-eighty-six," Pfingst said, "it's going to come as a point of interest to you the testimony in the case starts much more before December twenty-seven. The case begins in May of the same year. Something unusual began happening in the Mercy Road off ramp, there was a CHP official—when he made stops, he took a certain select part of the people he stopped down Mercy Road. The people that he drove down there were generally young women and only young women. If he directed anyone else down there it was an accident."

Defense attorney Robert Grimes tried to pick up where he had left off in the first trial. He hammered away at the prosecution's lack of specific evidence that would link his client "without a reasonable doubt" to the slaying.

"The evidence isn't going to show when she died on December twenty-seven; it's going to be inadequate to show even what day she died," Grimes said. As for Craig Peyer, it was just another night on duty. "He went home for dinner like he normally does. He didn't drop off the face of the earth or anything of the sort. He was out giving tickets."

Grimes looked at the jurors, folded his hands, and then turned toward the defense table, looking warmly at Craig Peyer. A connection. "No patrolman can say where they are every minute. He went home and had dinner with his family. He had a normal dinner; he didn't drink alcohol; he didn't do anything startling. He went back on his beat.''

Grimes said that Peyer talked longer to women than he did with men after making the stop. Grimes conceded that most of the men received tickets on the freeway. The women were willing to chat with this highway patrolman, who was a talker himself, just a nice fellow, Grimes said.

''He talked about his family in those conversations; you'll find in many cases the conversations were two-sided,'' the defense attorney said, his delivery slow and deliberate, his movements more restrained than his opponent's. Grimes conceded that many of the women would testify that they were nervous being alone with the officer on the desolate roadway.

''There was a law enforcement presence in the area—some of the young women had no way of knowing that,'' the defense lawyer said. Cops often used the off ramp area to write reports and tickets. Patrol cars frequently came and went off the Mercy Road exit from Interstate 15.

Grimes turned again to Peyer. ''He never asked for a phone number; he made absolutely no advances toward any of them; he did not touch them.''

Grimes described Craig Peyer as the ultimate California highway patrolman, a reliable officer ready to assist anybody.

''If you had a Lion's Club or other group, if you needed someone, Officer Peyer was there to tell you about those things; he would give a ticket, he talked about his family.''

Grimes predicted that the prosecution would try to take advantage of perceptions among witnesses who said Peyer seemed upset whenever someone mentioned the Knott case. There was a reason for that, the defense attorney explained, ''The death of a woman on his beat was something that he didn't consider funny and was perhaps somewhat upsetting to him.''

Grimes leaned into the podium, his face earnest, ''There is no evidence that he ever saw Cara Knott.''

Pfingst wanted the jury to feel the eeriness of Mercy Road from the beginning. He wanted them to remember the isolation whenever anyone testified about the murder scene. So instead of waiting until the end to make a lasting impression as the first prosecutor had done, Paul brought the jury down to the scene soon after the trial began.

The Knotts had been upset that they weren't allowed to attend the jury tour the first time. This time they insisted, and Judge Huffman allowed them to go along. They watched as Craig Peyer pulled up in his wife's station wagon. The jurors looked on as Peyer got out of the car, which had emblazoned on it a large sticker telling the world that Peyer belonged to a group of Christian patrolmen.

The jurors toured Mercy Road both before and after dark, so they could actually see the scene and so they could feel its desolation. They spent six and a half hours walking the dead end and looking over the old freeway bridge from which Cara had been thrown.

Sam Knott felt anguish as he visited the scene of his daughter's killing. His eyes scanned the area he had last visited after spending a sleepless night searching for her car. He looked for the barricades, the symbol of Peyer's guilt in Sam's mind, because he knew as sure as the sun came up in the morning that only the power of the law would lure Cara beyond the barricades.

Sam grew angrier as he scanned the scene. It looked different than on that awful day he had stood here and watched police find his daughter's body. The barricades weren't there. Things had been rearranged. There was a construction trailer there now, when there hadn't been before. The jurors weren't viewing an honest picture, he thought, it was almost as if evidence had been tampered with and nobody was allowed to tell them.

He took Pfingst aside, but the prosecutor told him, "There's nothing we can do about it." Pfingst knew that while Mercy Road did not look as it had on the night of the murder, its creepiness was getting to the jurors anyway; he saw two of the women, total strangers, holding hands for comfort.

Back in courtroom 22, the early trip to Mercy Road was paying off. So were the weeks Pfingst and Stein had spent interviewing dozens of women who had been stopped by Peyer.

A young dark-haired Patrice Diaz took the witness stand first. Peyer had stopped her on June 5 at 9 P.M. as she was driving her Datsun B210.

"Were you nervous?" Pfingst asked her.

"Totally. I thought I was fearing for my life," Diaz responded.

"What were you scared of?"

"I knew that there was no light down there; it was an off road type of place that, you know, I know of a lot of people that go off-roading down there and I couldn't understand why I was pulled over, if I was speeding, why was I pulled down there."

Diaz continued, "I remember pulling over and the officer ordered me down the ramp. I was shaking, totally. I was fearing for my life. I knew there were no lights down there. I knew it was an awful place."

At first she had refused to roll down her window, the witness testified.

"Why was that?" Pfingst asked.

She had been worried that the guy wasn't a cop, so she'd asked him to read her her rights.

"I didn't believe he was working for the law," Diaz testified. "He said, 'I can't read your rights because you haven't done anything for me to arrest you. You only do that when you're being told you're under arrest.' "

Peyer started writing her a fix-it ticket and then warned her to be careful, Diaz said. "He said, 'Well, you know in these days a lot of men—mechanics—take advantage of women and you can't always trust them,' " she recalled. "Then he went into my car and started pulling the emergency brake up and down and said, 'This is how you can test whether or not it works.'

"That's when I got out of my car and was standing outside of it; he came out and said there's something wrong with my headlights. I said that couldn't possibly be because my brother just bought a new headlight for me."

Diaz said she then got in her car and scolded the highway patrolman for his conduct during the forty-five minutes she was alone with him.

"I told him that was unprofessional of him to get in my

car to figure out whether the brake was wrong or not," Diaz said. "I was so scared and shaking all over. At that point, what was going to happen was going to happen."

"Thank you," Pfingst said. He turned to the jurors to see if she had gotten across his message: total fear. He went to the table, and looked at Peyer. The defendant sat stone faced at the defense table, looking straight ahead.

Next Karen Hollenberry took the stand and related how she was stopped by Peyer in her Chevy Luv truck around 7:45 P.M. on November 10.

"I was scared because it was the middle of nowhere and I had not been in control," said Hollenberry, who had long red hair. "I am a very controlling person as far as where I like to be, and I knew that down there in the middle of nowhere I was at risk."

Peyer gave her a ticket for a broken headlight.

By now Grimes had seen what was coming and he didn't like it. It was not the Miss Poway pageant anymore. It was much more sinister. There would be a parade of women, pretty young things, who would instill a mindset in the jury.

"We object, your honor," the defense lawyer said. "This line of questioning would be cumulative. We have heard every question about these witnesses; the vast majority of these people who received tickets are doing their best to recount what occurred on these tickets. Whatever point the prosecution is going to make has been made."

Pfingst jumped from his chair. "The testimony establishes a pattern and that distinguishes a pattern," the prosecutor argued.

The judge allowed the testimony to continue.

Susan Termine, a young woman with long dark curly hair, took the witness stand and said she was ordered to drive down the ramp the evening of May 22. For fifty minutes, she said, she talked to Peyer about interest rates, VA loans, real estate appraisals, the flow of traffic, his personal life.

"It felt like I was sitting there talking to a friend—somebody I knew for a while or somebody that I knew from school. It didn't seem like somebody I had just met half an hour ago," said Termine.

At first the witness was echoing what the defense had been

saying all along, that Craig Peyer was merely a friendly guy. But the friendly witness shifted gears. A disabled car creeped down to where they were parked in the dark of Mercy Road, and Peyer didn't pay attention to it. "When I realized that other people were down there, I felt it was unsafe and decided it was time to leave," she said.

"Did you feel you might hear from the officer?" Pfingst asked.

"I thought it was quite an unusual circumstance to be ticketed. I just remember thinking, this is really weird. Am I going to hear from this person? It appeared to be a come-on situation."

Grimes was on his feet in a flash trying to push the witness back to the friendly direction she had been going. He established, as he had for all the women, that Peyer never touched her, never said anything suggestive, never took her phone number.

Next up was Ramonita Sanchez who had been in a hurry to get home to Poway on May 25 to see her favorite television show *Dynasty* when Peyer had stopped her Datsun. Peyer had ordered her to drive down the ramp off Mercy Road. After she'd stopped, the highway patrolman had approached her and told her that the car headlight was improperly aligned. "I was nervous to start with, just being in that environment was really bad," she said. "I was extremely nervous."

"What were you thinking about at that time?" Pfingst asked.

"Just getting out of the area."

"What impact did that have on you the rest of the evening?"

"By the time I got home, I was just in no shape to watch any movie. Just really by the time I got home, I was just shaking."

Lisa Tumbiolo told jurors Peyer stopped her November 10, slightly more than a month before Cara Knott was killed. Pfingst wanted the jury to make a connection between her and the victim, as he asked her about the courses she was taking at San Diego State University, the same school the victim had attended.

She and Peyer had quite a talk down on Mercy Road, she

testified. They had talked about State, which had been having a problem with rapes at the time. Peyer had told her, she testified, "You really have to be careful around campus."

Judge Huffman tried to keep his jurors away from the madding crowd, but he wasn't always successful. They were forced to take their breaks in the hallway with the rest of the public, since the overcrowded courthouse had no lounges for the jury. One afternoon a scary-looking young man wearing a skinhead tattoo across his forehead, the mark of the neo-Nazi movement, approached some of the Peyer jurors during a recess and asked them for directions inside the courthouse. A juror wearing the little white badge denoting him as such pointed the youth in the right direction. The skinhead walked off, saying, "Whoever's got the Peyer case, I hope he fries."

Jurors dutifully reported the incident to the judge, who took the attorneys aside and informed them of the incident.

"What a glowing endorsement from a lovely source, just what we need," Pfingst remarked. Nothing further developed from the little exchange.

Pfingst and Stein were calling more people ticketed by Peyer to the stand than Van Orshoven had done in the first trial. But first they had to get the new witnesses in court, which the defense was fighting every step of the way. Pfingst explained why he wanted to bring men in to testify. "It looks like the men that Peyer pulled over," Pfingst said, "he had no interest in their love lives or even guy talk."

"You can't allow that testimony, your honor," codefense attorney Diane Campbell protested. "The government is trying to suggest that some sinister operation was going on here."

"But that's what it was, judge," Pfingst said.

Judge Huffman sided with Pfingst and soon a parade of men testified that the highway patrolman just wasn't that chatty with them. A long-haired man, John Jones, had been stopped December 15 by Peyer and ordered down the ramp at Mercy Road. Jones testified that when he finally stopped his Honda Prelude, Peyer walked over to the driver's door and shined a flashlight into his eyes. "He gave me a surprised

blank stare.'' The patrolman briefly asked why he was speeding, the witness testified, and then told him to leave.

Another long-haired man, David Smith, was driving from
Poway south to San Diego on December 19 when Peyer
stopped his yellow Volkswagen and ordered it down Mercy
Road.

After Peyer had shone a flashlight in the young man's eyes,
he too was told to leave.

"Did the officer ask about your personal life?" Pfingst
asked, almost gleefully.

"No."

"Did you have any discussion about your personal life?"
"No."

Finally the parade ended, twenty-four men and women who
had been pulled over to Mercy Road, all of them with long
hair but treated entirely differently depending on their sex.
Pfingst was pleased with that portion of the trial, feeling he
had put a dent into the code of honor that the former member
of law and order hid behind.

But the next hurdle had been the downfall of his predecessor: the autopsy and the elusive liver temperature record. The
prosecutor knew better than to be unprepared for the distracted professor Dr. Bockhacker. In his private interviews
with the pathologist, Pfingst told him to give simple explanations to the jury, that he didn't have to be a man with all
the answers. Pfingst instructed Bockhacker, "Just answer the
questions directly."

And so when it was his turn to testify in the second trial,
Dr. Bockhacker came across calmer, more in control of his
information, and made the autopsy seem much more routine,
not the bungled mess he had presented in the first trial.

As before, Grimes tried to bore in on the missing liver
temperature record and the lack of a precise time of death.
But Bockhacker couldn't be confused. He simply gave yes
and no answers, and escaped from the witness stand basically
unscathed.

On May 26 came the biggest gamble for Pfingst: the
Koenigs would testify. But not before Grimes fought behind
closed doors to be able to attack Traci's credibility in open
court. He wanted the judge to dismiss her as a witness be-

cause of the criminal conviction. Pfingst argued that her conviction was for a misdemeanor and not a crime of violence.

But Grimes countered that she was basically a liar, someone who could not be believed on the witness stand. "What she has confessed to," Grimes argued, "was a conspiracy over a long period of time." Now, Grimes said, the young couple were again carrying out a conspiracy, this time to say damaging things against Craig Peyer.

In the end, Pfingst won again. Traci and Scott Koenig took the stand and related their story just as they had to Pfingst and Stein at their first meeting.

The court took its fifteen-minute recess after the Koenigs testified, and Sam Knott headed to the men's room. It was the basic too-small tiled affair and as he swung open the wooden door, he walked smack into Craig Peyer.

It was the first time Sam had ever gotten close to the man accused of killing his daughter. No hi's, no excuse me's were exchanged. As he washed his hands, Peyer's eyes focused on the sink and faucet. Sam's eyes were all over Peyer. He wanted to scream and kick him and punch him. There he was, just inches away, *inches,* the monster!

He walked right up to the accused killer's face and stood before him, towering a good few inches above, and locked onto Peyer's eyes as if he were trying to bore into his brain. That head held the eyes his daughter had stared at, in horror and terror and fear, for the last time. Cara's eyes blinked at Peyer's, and never moved again, Sam thought. "I wanted that guy to feel my presence," Sam said later. "I wanted him to remember me for the rest of his life."

But inside the little room, neither man said a word.

Pfingst rested his case after thirteen days of testimony during which he had called 120 witnesses to the stand—thirteen more than Van Orshoven presented in the first trial in two fewer days. It was time for the defense.

Grimes tried to attack one of the key elements of the prosecution's case—the scratches on Peyer's face.

"Did you take any type of injury report for officer Craig Peyer related to the injuries he suffered on December twenty-seven, nineteen-eighty-six?'' Grimes asked Peyer's supervisor at the CHP, Gary Symonds.

''Yes, sir,'' Symonds answered. But Grimes couldn't ask him where those injuries came from, all he could do was try to show the jury that Peyer was not trying to hide the fact that he had scratched his face up that night. Forced to curtail this line of defense, Grimes had to concentrate on raising doubts about the state's evidence. But here again, Pfingst had left him virtually nothing to work with.

The preternaturally cool defense lawyer, the Gary Cooper of the courtroom, was visibly off his mark this time around. His smooth calm manner was being taken over by frustration and his objections were sounding shrill instead of the reasonable-guy approach he usually wielded.

Grimes couldn't raise the spectre of someone else like the wild hitchhiker who might have had the opportunity to kill Cara Knott because Pfingst had barred it in earlier motions. As for Peyer's explanation of the scratches, Pfingst had also blocked him from letting witnesses testify that Peyer had said he had fallen into the chain link fence. That left Grimes with only one man who could testify about them—Peyer himself.

Grimes went around and around on whether to let Peyer take the stand. On the one hand he knew jurors generally wanted to hear the explanations coming from the man himself rather than his paid attorney. On the other hand, Grimes knew if Peyer's fellow officers doubted his story, what kind of holes could an aggressive attorney like Paul Pfingst punch into Craig Peyer's account of what happened?

Grimes thought seriously about what Peyer should do. The word was out in San Diego's gossipy legal community that the defense lawyer had rehearsed cross-examination with his client. Finally, the decision was made that Peyer should not testify. ''It is a decision that will haunt me the rest of my life,'' Grimes said later.

As the trial unfolded, however, Grimes played his cards close to the vest and kept Pfingst hanging, wondering if Peyer would testify. Pfingst was eager for Peyer to take the stand. He kept thinking back to his days in New York when he had the chance to cross-examine Arnie Kane, the ex-city cop who had strangled a woman. Arnie had been pathetic on the witness stand. Pfingst held fast to his theory: a cop can't lie about a thing like murder on a witness stand. They aren't subtle; their noses seem to grow like Pinocchio's.

Pfingst didn't have long to fantasize about cross-examining Peyer. One of his legions of tipsters called to tell him he had overheard Karen Peyer mention to a friend in a movie theater that her husband wouldn't be testifying in his second murder trial. The prosecutor grinned, thinking how mad Grimes would be if his strategy had been blown at the cinema.

In the meantime the defense followed much the same lines as it had in the first trial. Grimes again hammered away at flaws in the investigation, particularly the one that had worked so well for him in round one: the elusive time of Cara Knott's death.

Grimes called a former county pathologist, Dr. Hormez Guard, to the stand to say that the coroner's office botched its chance to find the time of death by mishandling the procedure to determine the liver temperature of Cara's body. Taking the liver temperature is one of the most important elements of a homicide investigation, Guard testified. The defense witness suggested that if investigators blew this, imagine how they had handled the little things.

Under Pfingst's cross-examination, however, Guard acknowledged that liver temperatures weren't always the perfect math equation to time of death. They can be affected by many factors, making time of death harder to pinpoint, such as if it had been a cold night, if it had been windy, if the humidity had been high, the length of time it had taken to find the body, all those were variables to figure into the time equation.

Pfingst went one step further than casting doubt on the defense witness. He matched Grimes's expert with one of his own, another pathologist who testified that liver temperatures are highly unreliable means of determining time of death.

The second trial was a more subtle contest between the two attorneys than the first time out, Sam Knott noticed. The difference was that Pfingst had control of his game and the prosecutor wasn't giving the defense any kind of slack to take advantage of. But as much as he liked the way Paul Pfingst handled himself, Sam tried not to let himself expect too much.

Grimes slipped in a surprise witness of his own.

He brought up a young pretty woman named Susan Lambert to testify about how she was driving south on Interstate 15 on the night of the murder when a white VW beetle sped past her.

In the first trial, the defense had a nurse who had seen a white VW bug stopped further south down the freeway much later in the night, and had seen a blonde woman with white shoes fighting a man on the side of the road. But this new witness had seen a VW bug near the scene of the murder at the same time all the prosecution witnesses had seen the bug. And she had seen what could have been the victim in the car with other people, potential murderers who were definitely not Craig Peyer.

"In the front seat was a man about thirty, thirty-five years old, beard, mustache, kind of scruffy looking. He had a female passenger in the front seat. There was a male and female in the back," Lambert testified. "They were wrestling around a little bit."

The car had gone down the Mercy Road off ramp as Lambert had continued on along the freeway, heading home from her friend's house, which she distinctly recalled leaving at 9:20. She and her friend were Buddhists and had attended a chorus that night so she knew what time she had left based on what time the concert ended, she explained.

"How do you recall you left around 9:20?" Grimes asked.

"I don't know. I just know. I think we were watching TV," Lambert answered.

"What did you do when you heard about the girl?" Grimes asked her, meaning the news about Cara's death.

"I was very upset because it made me realize, well, I remember the car, but you know it made me remember it more. That stuck in my mind that evening, and when I heard about it the next day I felt really sad," the witness testified. She had called police a few days afterward.

The couple in the front seat had been smiling a lot, messing around and having fun, Lambert said. "But the man in the backseat was teasing a really pretty blonde woman, who looked upset—blonde, real pretty blonde.''

''Did you tell anyone what you had seen?'' Grimes asked.

''Yes,'' Lambert said, ''my mother.''

It was Pfingst's turn.

He wanted to know how she was so sure she had seen all this going on in the car she'd passed on the freeway, and how she knew what night it had happened.

''I believe when I came home at ten P.M. *LA Law* had come on, but I also remember that was—it wasn't scheduled at its normal time, that it was like a fill-in show or something, but it wasn't on its normal evening.''

''There is no question, in your mind, that *LA Law* was on?'' Pfingst asked

''Yes, it was,'' the defense witness answered. ''I remember it being—I thought it was unusual because normally it's on a Thursday night.''

She had checked the television schedules later in the week to see when the legal drama was on, Lambert testified, ''Because I was afraid I would end up right here where I am right now.''

''If *LA Law* was not playing on that Saturday night, that would mean that you saw it on Thursday?'' Pfingst asked.

''Yes,'' she answered.

Her mother followed her up to the witness stand and Pfingst asked her what TV show they were watching that December night. Lambert's mom also remembered distinctly that it was *LA Law*. Pfingst gave a little smile.

The attorney had checked with the television network. *LA Law* had only played on Thursday nights. Cara Knott had died on a Saturday.

And so it went, through the fiber experts, the blood experts, testimony about the footprints, the tire tracks, the fingerprints, the pile of bits of physical evidence presented and argued over during round two of the *State of California* v. *Craig Alan Peyer*.

On June 10, the defense rested its case, its last witness again being Karen Peyer, who lovingly described life with Craig as she had in the first trial.

Then it was time for the climax, the closing arguments.

Pfingst saved most of his dramatics for his closing. He talked about the predatory habits of highway patrolman Craig Peyer, about all the women he had pulled over and held at his mercy for hours at a time.

"It was an appetite to which he appeared to be addicted," Pfingst said. "Unfortunately for Cara Knott, she didn't know she fit the profile. Her parents didn't know she fit the profile. The CHP didn't know she fit the profile. Because the profile was a secret."

The prosecutor's passion even got to the defense attorney. Grimes attempted to halt Pfingst's remarks four times during his two hours of closing arguments, to no avail.

"If you had watched this, and if you were aware of it, each and every one of you would have said to yourself, 'This is just a time bomb that's ticking and waiting to go off,' " Pfingst said. "The clock had its last tick—the situation exploded."

"On December twenty-six, this officer did it not once and did it not twice, but did it on three separate occasions. And that two of these women came from Via Rancho Parkway the night before Cara Knott was killed." It was the same road Cara would take the very next night to get on the freeway home.

"It was certainly a tragedy that what was waiting to happen had ultimately happened. In the aftermath a young innocent woman was strangled to death in a deserted and desolate location in this county by a police officer. No one knew about the pattern of behavior, so it was left to family members to try to find out what happened to their daughter, their sister, it was up to citizens of the county to provide the information that. You have eyewitnesses, you have circumstantial evidence, you have a pattern of behavior.

"Cara Knott was on her way home. There was only one way that Cara was going to stop on that off ramp. There was only one way that Cara Knott was going to go down into the dark and the desolate location. The only way would have been at the request of a police officer.

"This woman was very apprehensive about her personal security and she acted differently than the other women who had been stopped by the defendant. As a result of that behavior she was killed.

"The defendant gave us a clue when he spoke to Officer Jill Oglivie. He said, 'It got out of hand,' simply got out of hand there and what happened? We don't know, because Cara Knott is dead and can't tell us. We do know that she struck out at the person who killed her because the person who killed her had claw marks on his face later. Cara Knott left you a clue as to her killer, and that is the claw marks.

"And then the defendant realized he was in deep trouble. Everything he had was at risk. His job was at risk. His Ships at Sea program was at risk. His TV programs were at risk. The house that said Welcome to the Peyers was at risk. Everything he cared for was at risk because it had gone too far.

"A police officer was calm, cool, and professional at 8:10. He's a man self-assured, good at his job, and there's nothing to be afraid about; but don't you know that right after Cara Knott was killed, that man exists no more. That man is totally changed. Craig Peyer killed Cara Knott to save his own butt. It's that simple. He created an intolerable situation that got out of hand."

Pfingst sat down, every jurors' eyes on him.

Grimes took over.

In his final statement, Grimes evoked the American flag, the U.S. Constitution, and the principles of law that separate us from totalitarian countries.

Again and again, Grimes leaned on the barrier that separated the jury and reminded them that guilt must be proven beyond a reasonable doubt. Each juror should make an individual decision, he said. "Each of you is just as alone as Craig Peyer, who is alone facing the power and the might of the state attacking him."

Grimes turned to the evidence, and the lack of it. "Let's talk about common sense. Is he going to be going around exposing his scratches to people?"

If Craig Peyer committed the murder, Grimes asked, why would he stop to aid a motorist at ten o'clock, a disabled motorist not even on his beat, someone could explore his face and see if he had been scratched. The scratches themselves were not claw marks, he told the jury, pointing out witnesses who had described them as welts.

Why, Grimes pointed out, was no skin or blood found on the rope if it was the murder weapon? And if the rope had been used to strangle Cara Knott, why didn't Peyer simply throw it out?

"This prosecution has dropped the ball in certain respects. There's certain glaring errors in the burden of proof. Mr. Pfingst doesn't miss a thing. You notice that. He doesn't miss a thing, he can get any mileage out of anything. He's very talented."

Pfingst interrupted. "I appreciate the compliment, but this is not related to any evidence in the case." A little zing, just to pay back the defense attorney, to let him know what it felt like to have *his* rhythm thrown off by trivial objections.

Grimes highlighted the unanswered questions of the investigation. When did Cara die? What wounds were inflicted by her killer, what ones by her fall? "We don't know if the ligature was applied before or after her death," Grimes said. "There's the unexplained baffle in the backseat of the car . . ." How did the baffle get out of the tail pipe, after her brother-in-law spent hours trying to pry it loose only days before? Why didn't police try to find out where the six fingerprints in her car had come from? They didn't come from Craig Peyer. They weren't Cara's. They didn't belong to anyone in her family, or to her boyfriend or his family.

"And stopping other women at Mercy Road does not provide any motive because motive is the motive to kill. You will find no such motive in just talking to women.

"Somehow, he's going to get in trouble for stopping Cara Knott, the highway patrol would be mad at him. We do know that when the patrol officials found out he stopped motorists off the freeway on Mercy Road, their reaction in front of Peyer was in the form of a commendation."

There wasn't a single piece of evidence, he pointed out, that ever showed that Craig Peyer came in contact with Cara Knott.

Pfingst stood for his rebuttal. "As I was sitting, listening to Mr. Grimes, I kept waiting for Mr. Grimes to address the defendant's behavior prior to the killing of Cara Knott.

"I kept waiting for Mr. Grimes to address the months of stopping young women at the bottom of Mercy Road. I kept waiting and listening for an explanation as to why it would be that Cara Knott disappeared and the defendant was not seen for hours. Has it occurred to you yet to wonder what the defendant was doing [during] this period of time?

"Where was the defendant while Cara Knott was being killed? Up until that time, you can follow the defendant up and down his beat, up to eight-forty, eight-forty-five.

"You are waiting to find some . . . evidence that could tell you where the defendant was when Cara Knott was being killed? Of course, there is no explanation and the reason there is no explanation is because he was killing Cara Knott."

And then, the lawyers stopped talking. The decision now rested with the jury alone.

The first day of deliberations passed quietly. The Peyers waited in their house twenty minutes from the courthouse. The Knotts waited in the courthouse hallway. Paul Pfingst and Joan Stein walked the boardwalk along San Diego Bay and played skee-ball. They ate popcorn and acted silly and just generally didn't think much at all.

On the second day of deliberations, the jury requested testimony from Scott and Traci Koenig and her parents be read to them. Cara's friend Joni Gonzales stopped by the fifth floor of the courthouse to show the Knott family her infant daughter, whom she had named Cara.

On the third day of deliberations, the jurors went home early.

On the fourth day, the jury requested testimony from four prosecution witnesses be read to them. Joyce Knott cried. "When they want to hear testimony, that means they don't believe them," she said to Cheryl as she wiped tears from her eyes.

Cheryl remembered the first jury kept asking for testimony to be read over, too, but never four in one day. Maybe that was a good sign. Detective Nulton tried to cheer the Knotts up at lunchtime. They talked about the case, they talked about Cara, they talked about the weather, they talked about everything except what they would do if Craig Peyer was not convicted.

While biding time in the hallway, Joyce wore Cara's Mickey Mouse watch for good luck. When the fifth day without a verdict passed, she said as cheerfully as she could, "Looks like Mickey didn't do us much good today."

Then on the sixth day of deliberations, the phone rang on Paul Pfingst's desk in the district attorney's office. It was Judge Huffman's clerk summoning him down. "Come on, Martha, what is it? You can tell me," Pfingst joked, he begged, but the famous charm couldn't budge her. Pfingst and Stein ran down the steps, into courtroom 22 and took their seats. Meanwhile, the press started arriving and jamming the courtroom. Spectators started piling in as well.

Finally, the entire cast was assembled. Pfingst sat at the prosecution table, still waiting. The judge came in, and they all stood until he was seated. The jury filed in. The judge asked the jurors if they had reached their verdict. The jury foreman stood and said yes. The foreman handed the piece of paper to the bailiff. The bailiff walked over to the judge and handed him the note. The judge unfolded the note and looked at it.

Pfingst felt like he was going to explode if somebody didn't start moving faster. The bailiff was walking in slow motion back to the judge, every step seemed like an hour. Now the judge had handed the bailiff back the note. The bailiff was walking back to his post and opening his mouth. From the audience, Nulton noticed that a juror who had occasionally looked at the Knotts now stared openly at the family. This was it!

On June 23, 1988, in San Diego County Superior Court, Craig Alan Peyer was found guilty of murder in the first degree for strangling Cara Knott.

Peyer had made history as the first California Highway Patrol officer ever to be convicted of murder. Pfingst smiled. Peyer showed no emotion whatsoever.

Armed guards whisked the former lawman out the back door of the courtroom. He was taken across the street to the county jail, where sheriff's deputies booked him, dressed him in a jail-issue orange jumpsuit, and put him on the suicide watch.

"Our trust is in the Lord Jesus Christ, as it has always been from the beginning," Karen Peyer said quietly to the glare of television lights and clamoring reporters outside the courtroom. "I love my husband and stand by him. I always will. I always believed in my husband's innocence."

The Knotts knew of a secret way out of the courthouse, an escape route they knew they could only use once. This day they took it, slipping away from the crush of reporters and cameras. There would be plenty of time for a statement.

Sam wanted to talk to the press, he felt so close to many of them now, having spent all those hours and days together. But his emotions were so raw now that he didn't trust himself, he didn't know what anger would seep out and what might come out wrong and upset all that they had accomplished to put the monster away and change the system that had taken his daughter from him.

Instead, the Knotts quietly climbed into Sam's car and took the long drive east to the cemetery where Cara was buried. They stood at her grave and prayed.

The Knotts were in a somber mood when they finally pulled into the driveway of their home in El Cajon. People were everywhere, in and outside the house, waiting for them. All the counselors who had helped them through the pain, the neighbors and well-wishers who had cooked them casseroles to ease the burden of the trial, all the families who had held their hands, all the new friends they had made in the legal system, all the reporters who had spent so much time with them that they felt like family. There were jurors from the first trial, there were police officers, there were detectives, there were lawyers. It was overwhelming.

Joyce Knott looked at the crowd of people in her house and listened to their laughter. It had been a long time since she had heard so much joy. This should be a great celebration, she thought, and she stood in the kitchen and waited for all the tension and pain to evaporate magically. But instead the realization hit her like a shot to her heart. Her Cara was really gone.

19

Final Tears

I awaken every morning, often against my will. Whether I like it or not, my life goes on. I would give anything to trade places with Cara. I think every mother would give her own life to save her child. Without a moment's hesitation, I would give my life to bring Cara back. I only wish I could have the chance.

Cara's murder by a law enforcement officer, one she had been taught to respect and turn to in time of need, is beyond anything my mind and heart can accept. My days are filled with thoughts of Cara, missing her, wanting to hold her in my arms and take away the pain and fear I know she suffered.

My nights are long and agonizing as I am haunted by Cara's terror, her pain, her dying.

There can be no true justice because Cara cannot be returned to life. The only semblance of justice we have available is to assure that her murderer is imprisoned for the rest of his life. It isn't enough. It isn't just. It's all we can do.

—Joyce Knott, statement to the court

Ben Killingsworth didn't have to wait until the last act. He just wanted the verdict. As commander of the San Diego sector of the California Highway Patrol, Killingsworth had crawled out on a thin limb when he'd fired Peyer, coming right out and saying that the patrolman killed Cara Knott six months before the first jury was even picked.

"I don't think we have to apologize for cleaning our own house," Killingsworth had said at the time of the firing. He weathered the full brunt of the storm of controversy and then two months after sacking Peyer, Killingsworth quietly left his command. He moved one hundred miles up the coast to Orange County, to fight the toughest of his life—a battle with cancer.

Killingsworth had given his life to the California Highway Patrol. Thirty-three years he spent climbing to the top command of one of the biggest and most populated sectors in the whole patrol. He was respected. A lifetime of public service Killingsworth gave, and what will he be remembered for? That one patrolman murdered somebody on Killingsworth's watch.

Killingsworth figured he didn't have much time left to see this mess finished. And then the legal battles dragged on, eight months, a year, two years. But, finally, Killingsworth was proved right by this jury. Peyer was guilty. Killingsworth felt good for the first time in a long, long time.

The ex-commander couldn't resist a final I told you so, as he told reporters after the verdict. "We believed Craig Peyer was guilty all along, otherwise we would not have fired him."

Even as the final verdict released Killingsworth, it also gave telephone repairman Lawrence Kamber back his own life. Kamber was a man possessed by the Knott slaying ever since he sat through the first murder trial, day after day looking at that picture of sweet golden-haired Cara Knott, looking at the brave Knott family struggling through the most grisly testimony, and then looking at the accused killer and never seeing a flicker of emotion in him.

Kamber felt like a failure for not being able to give the Knott family a murder conviction when he had served on the first jury. He was only an alternate juror in the first trial, a courtroom benchwarmer who never got to deliberate on the decision. But Kamber made it up to the Knotts and himself by sort of adopting them. He took his three kids over to their home for visits. He took off work from Pacific Bell Telephone

Company so he could be near the Knotts during the second trial. "I could feel their hurt, and their hurt became my hurt," Kamber said.

Sometimes during the retrial, Kamber would sidle into the seat behind Peyer, the seat right in front of Peyer's gray-haired mother, and he'd whisper to him, "Monster! You're a monster."

Peyer must have heard him. But the ex-lawman never even blinked an eye, which enraged Kamber even further. "How could he not react? Only a monster could do what he did to that girl and then sit there with a straight face."

Kamber had become addicted to the Cara Knott case and was even given to public scenes. When he'd overhear shoppers in the grocery store talking about how Peyer was being framed, he said, "I'd start shouting about the evidence and by the time I left, everyone in that store knew he was guilty."

But with this final verdict, Kamber needed to convert nobody. For the guilty decision hit town like an evangelical earthquake and shook almost all those nay sayers and fence sitters into the camp of the true believers, like Kamber, who were now convinced that Cara Knott and society had both been betrayed by the man wearing badge 8611.

No longer was the raging public debate over did he or didn't he. The guilty verdict settled that argument, but failed to satisfy the people's hunger for answers. Who was to blame?

Was Peyer alone to blame? Nobody got much argument with that theory around Dobson's, the downtown pub of the rich and powerful, nor in most other quarters. The *San Diego Union*'s opinion pages brimmed over with vitriolic letters demanding Peyer suck up cyanide in the gas chamber to pay for his awful crime.

"After all," one letter writer pointed out, "a law was just passed stating that anyone who kills a police officer gets the death penalty. What about police officers who kill in cold blood? I think it should be mandatory death penalty also! We teach our children to trust the police but how can they? When police do kill, they don't receive the same penalties as a common citizen does? . . . 'To serve and protect'—that has become a joke."

Dozens more people wrote letters to the judge demanding the same ultimate punishment for Peyer.

Some of the more philosophical townspeople blamed Cara's death on the California Highway Patrol organization. After all, the Chippies were the ones who allowed Peyer to be loose. They were the good old boys so bent on protecting their own, so the theory went, that they ignored warnings from women who tried to complain about Peyer's dangerous games at Mercy Road. There was even a faction of folks who blamed what happened to Cara Knott on the dozens of other women Peyer pulled over at Mercy Road, for not complaining loud enough.

Everybody seemed to be playing the blame game, trying to find the answers that would make them feel better. They wanted an explanation for why one of the good guys went homicidal. They wanted reasons why they should believe that line about law and order, or was that just a fairy tale?

Just as the keepers at San Diego Zoo hauled out the daily ration of raw meat for the lions, the news media stayed filled with a daily fix of Peyer-related tidbits to feed the hungry public. Local politicians made speeches about justice being served. No highway patrol officers were allowed to talk publicly about the case. But one top official stated the obvious to the local newspaper. ''The highway patrol will be a long time living this down.'' Everyone else down to dive bartenders and deejays on rock radio stations had something to say publicly about the whole criminal affair—none of it nice.

Hollywood announced a television show on the trials of Craig Peyer.

District Attorney Ed Miller celebrated the end of his losing streak. He took his winning prosecutors Paul Pfingst and Joan Stein to lunch at a popular local out-of-the-way Italian restaurant, the Old Trieste.

Up north in the state capital, the politicians couldn't resist the chance to put in their two cents' worth. A state legislature committee approved a bill that would give motorists who were being stopped by the police the freedom to pull over wherever they felt safe. Supporters felt such a law would have stopped Knott from driving down the Mercy Road off ramp to ath, and the bill was even nicknamed the Cara Knott

Bill. The point became moot months later when the law-enforcement lobby forced the bill into a legislative U-turn. The law eventually enacted wound up actually giving police officers like Peyer more power by stiffening the penalty for motorists who *didn't* pull over exactly where officers demanded.

County officials dropped yet another bombshell that aggravated public sentiment against Craig Peyer. They estimated that taxpayers had paid $262,000 to put the ex-lawman away in prison. The outrage over the costs prompted another Peyer-inspired law to speed through the full California legislature. From now on, accused criminals in the Golden State cannot get free defense attorneys—as Peyer had—if they own property, as Peyer did.

The convicted man still refused to leave the protective fortress of his family circle. But his wife, Karen Peyer, gave long interviews that focused on her absolute faith in God and Craig. "A killer is loose on the streets," his blustery father, Hal Peyer, declared solemnly to the television cameras, "because my son killed no one."

The Peyers were finally jumping into the media game, but far too late to even get wet in the ocean of sympathy that belonged solely to the Knott family. The tide of public opinion had turned so for Cara and venomously against Craig that whenever Karen Peyer plaintively spoke of what a rough future lay ahead for her and her three young children, the community responded with angry letters to the editor, saying, in effect, Tough luck.

San Diegans remained riveted on the most watched criminal case in their local history that begged the question: could cops be trusted?

Within hours of the guilty verdict, Peyer's defense attorney Diane Campbell locked herself in her office with her law books and began the tedious hunt for legal reasons why the ex-lawman deserved a retrial. Craig Peyer had one last chance. There were only seconds left in the legal game, and the last play was up to attorney Diane Campbell. Legal motions and appeals briefs were Campbell's bailiwick. While Grimes handled the courtroom dramatics, she did the digging for legal precedents and the dozens of motions declaring the judge unfair, the prosecution unfair, the press unfair.

For her final play in the Peyer case, Campbell seized upon the biggest offensive score of the match: the unauthorized leak of Peyer's lie detector test. While his second murder trial publicly wore on, authorities quietly investigated how this damning document could have been leaked. Two days after Independence Day, a little more than two weeks after the guilty verdict, the results of the internal investigation were in. The results were not good news for Peyer: at least two hundred people from at least four different departments of local law enforcement and government had had the access to and thus the opportunity to leak his lie detector test to the press.

On July 6, top officials from San Diego Police and the district attorney's office met in Judge Huffman's courtroom 22 with prosecutor Pfingst and defense attorney Grimes to announce the dismal results of their internal probes.

"We have abandoned the investigation," a police official told the judge. Bob Grimes struggled to keep his preternatural cool. An abandoned investigation was not what he wanted to hear. The instant Grimes saw that lie detector test story on the *Union*'s front page back in April, he must have seen his whole case sliding down the bluff, and way back then he marched into Judge Huffman's chambers and demanded—not something the amiable attorney did—that the court get to the bottom of the leak.

Back then, Grimes insisted they call in the state's top cops from the California Attorney General's office. The investigation was too important to leave up to local law enforcement, who after all might very well be investigating themselves. But Grimes never got the independent investigation he asked for three months before, and he was furious at the court for giving up so easily. Grimes knew it was too late for him and that now it would be up to the appeals attorney to try and win Peyer a whole new ball game.

Campbell filed a hefty document asking for a retrial, claiming in part that Judge Huffman made mistakes in preventing the defense witnesses from testifying about the hitchhiker and from letting witnesses explain what Peyer had told them about how he had gotten his scratches from falling against the fence. Campbell knew better than to bet her Nordstrom's department store charge card on that. Besides, she felt she had one last ace up her sleeve: the lie detector test. If the court found that the prosecution did the leaking, well, not only would they be in big trouble, but also Peyer might get a new trial.

Obviously, it was someone who wanted to see Peyer behind bars, someone who saw the prosecution's case as too weak to handle the job alone. It was someone akin to a Lone Ranger leaker, leaving the lie detector test as his silver bullet.

Was the prosecution team to blame, as the defense attorneys would so love to prove? The polygraph tests were so secret even the judge didn't know about them. Was it a cop? Most of San Diego's finest must have known about Peyer's polygraphs, since the police community was so tight they know when one of their own so much as breaks a fingernail.

Then again, anybody who knew anything about law enforcement knew the cops love lie detector tests and use them routinely. Anyone can learn that by watching *Colombo* and *Hill Street Blues* and any three dozen cop-show reruns.

The identity of the Lone Ranger leaker was an interesting mystery, yet another one piling up in the case. On top of who leaked the lie test there were the others. Where was Cara's white leather jacket? What happened to the weird hitchhiker? Where were the phantom witnesses? What time did Cara die?

Despite all these questions, the polygraph leak was the only mystery that the court was taking seriously at this point.

Judge Huffman asked the *San Diego Union* and reporter Jim Okerblom to waive their First Amendment right to protect sources and help the court find the leaker. ''In my humble opinion as a judge, this is not the kind of thing that should be left stinking on the table while we debate the parameters of the shield law.''

The newspaper stood firm: no way would they snitch on a source. Reporters were protected from doing so by the state shield law. The *San Diego Union* was the oldest business in town and flagship of a powerful conservative newspaper empire, the Copley Press, owned by one of the richest women in the nation, Helen Kinney Copley. The Copley Press was not easily pushed around. As one company lawyer told Judge

Huffman, "We will move mountains not to have Mr. Oker-blom testify."

Peyer's attorneys argued that the lawman's right to a fair trial was more important than a reporter's right to protect sources. So the ever-unpredictable Peyer murder trial was now turning into a constitutional showdown: the newspaper's First Amendment rights versus the defendant's Sixth Amendment rights. But despite the might of the Copley Press and the state shield law, Richard Huffman was wearing the robes here. On Friday, July 15, the judge ordered Jim Okerblom to get up on the witness stand the following Monday morning, and talk.

Okerblom spent the weekend biting his fingernails up in his suburban Escondido home. He knew the judge might send him to jail for refusing to testify about who might have leaked him the polygraph. "I didn't think he would do it, but in the back of my mind I wasn't sure," he said. Up in northern San Diego County, Okerblom knew, another judge actually ordered jail time for an investigative reporter named Bob McPhail, an aggressive journalist whose name even rhymes with jail. McPhail had refused to squeal on his source and just missed being sent to jail by a few hours when an appeals court gave him a reprieve.

Now Okerblom, after fifteen years of sitting in courtrooms taking shorthand on what other folks said in the witness box, was about to get his turn in the hot seat. On Monday, July 18, Okerblom was sworn in inside courtroom 22. "Do you swear to tell the truth?" the bailiff asked. Okerblom promised yes even though he knew he couldn't tell the whole truth.

His pregnant wife, Sue Scott, took the day off from work to be there. She sat in the audience with ramrod-straight posture and flashed him a little private smile of encouragement.

"Mr. Okerblom, when did you receive the documents?" Campbell started him with an easy question.

Okerblom answered, "After careful consideration, I would have to refuse to answer that question on the grounds of the First Amendment of the U.S. Constitution and the California constitution."

"Mr. Okerblom," the judge said, "you are ordered to answer that question." Emphasis on the ordered. Huffman sounded like a stern father not used to being disobeyed. But Okerblom did defy the man in black, "I would refuse to answer that question."

Campbell tried again: "Mr. Okerblom, please describe the envelope."

"I would refuse to answer that question," Okerblom repeated.

Again the judge chimed in on cue, "You are ordered to answer that question."

"I would refuse to answer that question," Okerblom repeated.

Campbell was not giving up easily. "Mr. Okerblom, what markings were on the document?"

No response, the judge ordered the reporter to answer, and he refused again.

"Mr. Okerblom, what did the handwriting look like? . . . Who else saw the polygraph? . . . What was the postmark? . . . Where is the document now?"

The trio kept up the Samuel Beckett dialogue, none of them backing down and all of them steadily getting nowhere. Finally, after twelve questions in forty minutes, Campbell gave up and sat down, disgusted, at the defense table. For once, prosecutor Paul Pfingst had nothing to say.

Campbell wanted Okerblom held in contempt of court, in jail. She argued that the source of the polygraph was anonymous and therefore not protected under the state shield law.

"There was no promise made by the newsman and thus no expectation on the part of the person sending him the information that he would remain confidential," Campbell argued.

Clearly Judge Huffman was frustrated that his careful work on this trial over the last two years was in jeopardy. He knew all too well what the social consequences would be to the town and the state if the verdict was overturned all because of one sensational news story.

However, the judge didn't buy the defense argument, and he also knew the chance of getting even close to the leaker, even with the documents, was pretty slim. "I am satisfied that the information that I could receive is not such that it's likely to materially change the question of the rights of the defendant,'' Huffman declared.

Judge Huffman looked down at the nervous Okerblom and said, ''I must say, I have not enjoyed the exercise of calling a witness and having the witness politely raise a certain digit in the court's direction.'' The judge had just accused the reporter of flashing his middle finger in a figurative show of contempt of court—except Okerblom wasn't going to be sent to jail for figuratively giving the court the finger.

The courtroom was dark most of the week while Judge Huffman pondered the previous case law that defense attorney Campbell had cited to support her argument that several of his decisions were wrong during the Peyer trial.

On July 20, Huffman gathered his black robes about himself, adjusted his square-shaped glasses, and took his seat overlooking the now-full courtroom. From there he summarily rejected all quibbles with his legal reasoning. There would be no retrial. No surprise there.

But then the judge did an uncharacteristic thing. The eternally calm Judge Huffman could hold his tongue no more. There in court, in front of little Michelle Peyer sitting wide-eyed with a big blue bow in her black hair, the judge came out of the closet of judicial restraint and called Craig Peyer a cold-blooded murderer to his face.

''There is not a question in my mind—I am absolutely convinced to a moral certainty that Mr. Peyer killed Cara Knott,'' Huffman declared and related his theory of how the murder happened. ''He went and got a rope . . . and he wrapped it around that youngster's neck. . . .''

Peyer's defense attorneys sat at the defense table speechless. Obviously they knew better than to ask again for a retrial. After that speech it was pretty clear Richard Huffman wouldn't even give Peyer change for a telephone call.

While the court awaited word on what the state appeals court would say about forcing Okerblom to testify about the leaked lie detector tests, the media broke one last rule of court tradition. Another classified legal document was leaked to the *San Diego Union*'s sister newspaper, the *Tribune*.

The story hit the streets on the afternoon of July 19 and told more about Peyer than both trials and lie detector tests put together. If the guilty verdict was the legal equivalent of an earthquake, this was the resulting tidal wave. It featured a calm Peyer absolving himself of all blame, saying to a jailhouse interviewer that, "God must want me in here for a reason."

As soon as the *Trib* story hit, a very weary Judge Huffman decided to give up playing by the rules, because he was obviously playing alone. He gave copies of the report to the media so at least they would have no reason not to get their facts straight.

The facts were presented in a fascinating document by San Diego County probation officer Marjorie Huntington, a twenty-year veteran of this strange science of combination psychology and criminology. Probation reports give judges guidelines to follow in punishing newly convicted criminals, a summation of the cases, the possibility of their recommitting, what their state of mind was, what they had to say for themselves in their own defense.

Huntington has seen them all—killers, con men, and losers—and she knew her stuff. "For the most part, people are not a mystery," was Huntington's view. "To me, Craig Peyer is not a mystery. He was bored. Bored with his job, bored with his marriage, bored with his life. He was playing. It was a thing he did."

She spent two hours interviewing Peyer in the county jail, and she got the distinct impression that he thought he was charming her, which to her showed how deep his confidence in his own abilities went, because Huntington was one tough cookie underneath that tailored suit and strand of cultured pearls.

"Even his body posture was relaxed, leaning back, legs crossed. He smiled a lot," Huntington said. "He didn't talk about the crime at all except to deny it." An elegantly tall woman, she carried herself with a very professional manner that almost certainly unnerved men who had insecurities about dealing with women.

"Craig Peyer loves people," Huntington wrote in her probation report to the court. "He will strike up a conversation with anyone. He agrees that this propensity to talk to people has contributed to his present difficulty. He does not think it unusual that he would talk to some of the people he ticketed for extended periods, although he did think some of the witnesses exaggerated the time they were detained. 'When you're stopping someone, they are upset and it is necessary to calm them down . . . you don't want them upset and back out on the highway.'

"He viewed these extended contacts as public relations work," she wrote dryly. "It never occurred to him that a person detained might be scared. His view was 'nothing will happen to you' because he was a member of law enforcement. He laughed at the prospect that such extended conversations might be wasteful. He merely thought he was doing his job."

Huntington didn't lose sleep over the Peyer case. To her, the whole drama was clear-cut. "What was he building up to? We don't know. It was over the minute he saw her. Their fates became intermeshed. From that point, all sorts of things could have stopped it. If the limousine had broken down five minutes earlier, if that couple was was down there necking had been there another time.

"All these elements closed in on Craig Peyer to expose him. It was fate. Fate gave us the answers to who did it. Unfortunately, fate didn't save Cara Knott."

Huntington not only sized up Peyer faster than a politician talks, she also instantly cut through the fog of pain shrouding the Knott family. "They came in personally to talk to me. They didn't have to," Huntington said. When the Knotts began telling her the now-familiar theme about the police refusing to help them find Cara on that fateful night, Huntington didn't sympathize with them as so many others had.

Instead, Huntington told the surprised Sam Knott to drop his anger and get on with his life. "Don't you get it? She was dead before you even knew she was dead," Huntington told them bluntly. "If you got every member of law enforcement in this county out, you still wouldn't have saved her. Let it go, for God's sake."

But Sam wasn't fazed. He was used to people squarely inside the system not understanding why it needed to be reformed. He was getting ready to slap a multimillion-dollar lawsuit on the highway patrol to make them listen and change their ways.

While Huntington saw the case as black-and-white, Peyer's behavior fascinated forensic psychologist Reid Meloy, chief of the county forensic mental health services.

Figuring out what makes criminals tick and how to set them straight mentally was what he did for a living, but Meloy found himself drawn to the worst of all offenders, the serial killers, the pathological, the homicidal, all of those covered in his respected book on the subject, *The Psychopathic Mind*.

Meloy watched the Peyer case unfold from the sidelines. Neither he nor any psychological experts were called in to testify. But he and other students of the criminal mind tried to crack the patrolman's armor of silence and figure out what happened.

To Meloy, Peyer's behavior brought up a lot of parallels to the worst offenders. In his work Meloy said he finds people who are searching for sex or violence for its own sake and then in the heat of the moment something sets them off into murder. "In the brain the proximity of sex and violence are so close they are divided by a line as thin as a lint speck."

Meloy found another parallel in Peyer. "Another aspect of the psychopathic mind is that they are liars by nature," he said. Both ex-wives told the probation officer that Craig Peyer was a liar. One of the exes said he gave her a necklace and told her it was really expensive, meanwhile he told all his buddies at the highway patrol that it was a zirconia fake diamond. Another time he put tires on his wife's car and told her they were brand-new, the probation report noted, but again he bragged to everyone else he got them for next to nothing at a salvage yard.

Although nobody ever accused Peyer of being a serial killer, behavior like his had all the markings of a predator, in Meloy's view. "Predatory behavior is the emotionless violence of planning and preparing. . . . The predator literally goes out and stalks [his] victim," the forensic psychologist said. "They have a stereotypical victim. The predator rehearses. It's rehearsal fantasy. One serial killer dreamed of killing women by having them fall down and he would mount them when they were dead. Except in reality he was strangling them and [they] wouldn't just fall down like in his fantasy, because strangling takes a long time and the death does not come easy. So the killer switched to killing his victims with a gun and they started falling down, just like he fantasized.''

Craig Peyer had pulled the women over down to Mercy Road for tiny infractions of the law, for having bouncing headlights, crooked headlights, burned-out license plate bulbs. Always at night. Always alone. Always pretty. Always chatted up. Longer and longer periods of time. Sometimes even getting in their car or commanding them to get into his.

''Each time, the predator will go a step further. The fantasy lets him. And then when reality lets him, that's when there is trouble,'' Meloy said.

The day of reckoning arrived, August 3, a sunny lovely day when fifty thousand people spent their day watching Shamu the killer whale perform at Sea World or viewing the animals at San Diego Zoo. More than one hundred thousand kicked back on the county's famous beaches.

Only seventy-five people spent their morning at dark crowded courtroom 22 on the top floor of the San Diego County Courthouse.

The Knott family arrived outside the courtroom looking especially attractive in their expensive simple clothes, Joyce Knott in the same navy blue dress she wore for Cara's memorial. Sam Knott wore a gray suit with a red striped tie, while Cheryl wore a suit and Cynthia a plain blue dress. Their faces were pale and full of pain that did not ease up even as people lined up to hug them like survivors of a long shipwreck about to be rescued.

The Peyers sat apart from the buzzing crowd like wallflowers at the USO. No one hugged them. Karen Peyer's sad sweet round face took it all in. Craig's mother, Eileen, allowed a softened vulnerable expression to take over her tough tanned outdoorsy look. With father and sisters in tow, the only women who loved Craig Peyer silently trooped to their usual seats on the left side of the courtroom.

The Knotts took the right side.

The electricity of expectance was so strong in the courtroom it could have replaced the light bulbs. This was odd, because this last court procedure is technically a mere formality. Peyer was to be sentenced to twenty-five years to life in state prison. It was the only choice.

The judge had no leeway at this end, not even getting to pick which prison. How long the defendant would stay in prison was entirely up to the state probation board at the other end of the sentence. The board members are the ones keeping Charles Manson inside prison and Sirhan Sirhan, the assassin of Robert Kennedy.

But this crowd awaiting the sentencing refused to accept that anything was routine in this case. "Before I impose sentence," Judge Huffman began, "is there anything the family would like to say?"

They did. Four years before, when Cara Knott was just getting her driver's license, California passed sweeping laws giving crime victims greater rights and a stronger voice in the court system, and the final presentencing statement is one of those forums. Each member of the Knott family had prepared a statement for the judge.

Cara's little brother, John Knott, gave up his college life to become part of his family's campaign. "The trial is finally over now, but my grief will never end," was John's statement to the judge. "I know now that wounds this deep never heal. My only hope is that Cara's murderer will never be freed. For someone to have invested in him the ultimate trust in our society, and then to betray that trust and commit a crime of such barbarity is still inconceivable to me. . . ."

Sam Knott rose and walked to the front of the courtroom. As his family huddled around him he read his statement to the judge. "It is our fervent hope that this predator will never walk the streets again. He kidnapped and brutally murdered our sweet Cara, hiding behind his badge and breaking his sacred trust to society. . . . The punishment must be the maximum the law will allow."

It was now Karen Peyer's turn to speak. She stood up in court in her shapeless cotton blazer, a dark shirt with white piping setting off her simple gold necklace and tiny gem earrings. Unlike the Knotts' neatly typed statements bearing Cara's picture up in the right-hand corner, Karen Peyer's was written in childish hand printing, full of crossed-out words and occasional grammatical lapses.

But her words conveyed all the hurt in her soul. In a clear, strong voice she read them.

"This world is not kind. It does not promise you that if you are good to it, it will be good to you. . . ." Karen talked about her faith that God would take them into heaven even if mankind slings them through the mud. She turned to the right side of the courtroom and looked at the Knotts. Only Joyce Knott would look back at her.

"Cara Knott was a gorgeous, vivacious, well-loved young lady. During the trial, I felt the pain her family has had to endure and I am deeply sorry that she was killed. But my husband was a friendly, vibrant and well-loved person too, and in my heart I know you have the wrong man."

Karen had written "my husband *is*" but had scratched out the present tense and changed it to "my husband was."

"I love you, Craig, and I am glad to be your wife—I wouldn't change a thing. I will always be committed to you and I will always believe in you. God bless you!"

With that, Peyer's face cracked and he began openly weeping. This was the first emotion he had shown in public in two years.

By now, there were tears all over the courtroom, tears in the eyes of the Knott family, the Peyer family, the reporters, the photographers, even the armed guards, and most surprising of all, Judge Richard Huffman.

It was now the judge's turn to do the deed and finish this case once and for all. "I can't fix anything," Huffman began in a voice thick with emotion. "I can't order restitution to repair any damage. A young woman was brutally murdered on the very threshold of life."

He looked at the Knott family, so devastated still, and then turned his head to take in the Peyers across the aisle. "One family has almost been destroyed. And the sentence I am about to impose will almost likely destroy another.''

Prosecutor Paul Pfingst sat stoically, looking straight ahead. All four attorneys were one self-controlled bunch. Huffman turned to face Peyer and said, "I hereby sentence you to state prison to the term no less than twenty-five years to life.''

Judge Huffman was a brilliant man who had turned to law to make sense of the world, much in the way Karen Peyer had turned to religion. And as she found her comfort in the larger picture, so too did Dick Huffman. In the world of law, there was always a victim and a guilty party. So Huffman attempted to right the emotional chaos before him. His view was that they were all just players here; society was the victim and the system was the culprit.

Huffman was angry that the CHP had brushed off complaints about Peyer like so many mosquitoes, and then had gone so far as to reinforce Peyer's behavior by telling him what a good idea it was pulling people off the freeway for their own safety. Had the CHP supervisors conducted a simple investigation, Huffman said, they would have turned up Peyer's whole macho game before it turned deadly.

"They led inexorably to this tragedy . . . as sure as the sun came up this morning,'' Judge Huffman proclaimed. And with that, he stood and left the courtroom.

The Superior Court of the State of California, San Diego County, was finally, completely, absolutely, officially finished with Craig Alan Peyer.

Reporters rushed out the outer courtroom doors to telephones. Photographers raced to set up their cameras around the courthouse exits in order to catch one final word from the main characters. Seven armed bailiffs with grim faces handcuffed Peyer's wrists behind his back and led him through the inner courthouse door, through the tunnel to his solitary jail cell where he would have to pack and ready himself for state prison for perhaps the rest of his life.

The Knott family members slowly made their way out of the courtroom, and the crowd of well-wishers and reporters in the hallway mobbed them. Joyce and Sam Knott both knew they should feel happy and elated, but they found it impossible, somehow, to even smile. Where was the relief that should be easing their pain now that it was all over? They didn't know then that it would take years in coming.

Only Karen Peyer had nowhere to rush to. She remained in her seat long after the crowds departed. The courtroom was quiet, dark, and empty when she finally stood to leave.

Epilogue

CRAIG Peyer remains imprisoned in the California Men's Colony in San Luis Obispo, where he started as a janitor and earned his way into a class on television repair. He is considered a model prisoner. His case is on appeal. He will be eligible for parole in the year 2004.

Karen Peyer recently moved with her children to San Luis Obispo to be closer to her husband.

Putting Craig Peyer in jail was the last public service done by Paul Pfingst. He left the district attorney's office for a partnership in the prestigious San Diego law firm of Higgs, Fletcher, and Mack. His twenty-fourth floor office is ten floors higher than District Attorney Ed Miller's and has a view of San Diego Bay. He has now crossed over the aisle to the defense side, defending doctors accused of malpractice. He has been mentioned as a candidate for district attorney. Mostly, he enjoys the good life in the small elite beach town of Del Mar with his wife, who is also a lawyer, and their newborn daughter.

Judge Richard Huffman, after only three years on the Superior Court bench, was promoted by Republican Governor George Deukmejian to the fourth District Court of Appeal. He spends his spare time teaching law at the local Catholic college, University of San Diego, where his son, Richard, attended. In his spare time, he sails.

Sam and Joyce Knott live quietly in the country. Joyce

continues running the nutrition department at the prestigious University of California at San Diego. They spend all their spare time crusading for victims' rights, and Sam is working on a computer program for law enforcement that will allow headquarters to track all patrol vehicles at all times. The Knotts filed a nine million dollar civil suit against the CHP, saying it should have known a killer was in its ranks.

Cara's oldest sister, Cynthia, decided to skip graduate school in San Francisco and instead became a nutritionist like her mother. She and her husband, Bill Weick, have settled in San Diego, near the family.

John Knott, Cara's baby brother, attends the University of California at San Diego studying computer science.

Cheryl Knott left the anthropology department of the San Diego Museum of Man in the internationally renowned Balboa Park, and is pursuing her doctorate in archaeology at Harvard University.

Cara Knott's body lies in a grave on a grassy hill, near an oak tree and the grave of her grandfather.

The Best in Biographies from Avon Books

IT'S ALWAYS SOMETHING
by Gilda Radner   71072-2/$5.95 US/$6.95 Can

JACK NICHOLSON: THE UNAUTHORIZED BIOGRAPHY *by Barbara and Scott Siegel*
                                     76341-9/$4.50 US/$5.50 Can

ICE BY ICE
by Vanilla Ice   76594-2/$3.95 US/$4.95 Can

CARY GRANT: THE LONELY HEART
by Charles Higham and Roy Moseley
                                     71099-9/$5.99 US/$6.99 Can

I, TINA
by Tina Turner with Kurt Loder
                                     70097-2/$4.95 US/$5.95 Can

ONE MORE TIME
by Carol Burnett   70449-8/$4.95 US/$5.95 Can

PATTY HEARST: HER OWN STORY
by Patricia Campbell Hearst with Alvin Moscow
                                     70651-2/$4.50 US/$5.95 Can

PICASSO: CREATOR AND DESTROYER
by Arianna Stassinopoulos Huffington
                                     70755-1/$4.95 US/$5.95 Can

---

Compelling True Crime Thrillers
From Avon Books

BADGE OF BETRAYAL
by Joe Cantlupe and Lisa Petrillo

76009-6/$4.99 US/$5.99 Can

THE BLUEGRASS CONSPIRACY
by Sally Denton   71441-8/$4.95 US/$5.95 Can

A KILLING IN THE FAMILY:
A TRUE STORY OF
LOVE, LIES AND MURDER
by Stephen Singular with Tim and Danielle Hill

76413-X/$4.95 US/$5.95 Can

LOSS OF INNOCENCE:
A TRUE STORY OF JUVENILE MURDER
by Eric J. Adams   75987-X/$4.95 US/$5.95 Can

RUBOUTS: MOB MURDERS IN AMERICA
by Richard Monaco and Lionel Bascom

75938-1/$4.50 US/$5.50 Can